W9-AVS-301

CRITICAL INSIGHTS

Oscar Wilde

CRITICAL
INSIGHTS

Oscar Wilde

Editor
Dr. Fredrick S. Roden
University of Connecticut

SALEM PRESS
A Division of EBSCO Information Services, Inc.
Ipswich, Massachusetts

GREY HOUSE PUBLISHING

Publisher's Cataloging-In-Publication Data
(Prepared by The Donohue Group, Inc.)

Names: Roden, Frederick S., 1970- editor.
Title: Oscar Wilde / editor, Frederick S. Roden, University of Connecticut.
Other Titles: Critical insights.
Description: [First edition]. | Ipswich, Massachusetts : Salem Press, a division
        of EBSCO Information Services, Inc. ; Amenia, NY : Grey
        House Publishing, [2019] | Includes bibliographical references
        and index.
Identifiers: ISBN 9781642653090 (hardcover)
Subjects: LCSH: Wilde, Oscar, 1854-1900--Criticism and interpretation. |
        English literature--19th century--History and criticism. | Social
        perception in literature. | Ethics in literature.
Classification: LCC PR5824 .O827 2019 | DDC 828.809--dc23

First Printing

Contents

Critical Contexts

Critical Readings

Resources

Dedication

In memoriam Arlene Roden—astute businesswoman, sensitive curator of the beautiful, and sweet soul—who disproved Oscar Wilde's epigram that no men become their mothers.

About This Volume

Frederick S. Roden

Critical Insights: Oscar Wilde aims to serve as a primary (and complementary) resource for expanding your understanding of a major author among the world literary canon. In the interest of understanding the nature and structure of this book, we will take a moment to review a history of his works' reception.

Oscar Wilde (1854–1900) established himself as one of the first modern "celebrities," cultivating his relationship with media and popular culture. Scholars have regularly struggled with the significance of his literary production versus Wilde's fascinating biography and indeed role in shaping the cultural history of his time, as well as identities for the modern world. With this in mind, *Critical Insights* balances studies of Wilde's particular texts— sometimes those least known or read by a general audience—with his important place in the western civilization of his time and the century (and more) following. Oscar Wilde hit his stride as a public figure before his literary works made their mark on the canon of texts we read. He used these compositions to constantly negotiate between social controversies of his moment and the intellectual and artistic traditions that preceded him.

Thus *Critical Insights* aims to help in the spirit of Wilde's pioneering life and authorship, balancing between his places as public figure, artistic thinker, and literary producer. Our strategy looks to familiar works in sometimes-unfamiliar ways for the general reader, even as we introduce riches to be found in some of Wilde's lesser-known pieces. Following the editor's introduction (a personal reflection on the ethics of Wilde's message for today), the biography included here is one written by a newer major scholar of Wilde, Kimberly Stern, who has published in 2019 a book-length biography of the author. Our aim here is to reconsider Wilde for and at our moment. Stern also compiled the volume's chronology of Wilde's life, highlighting some often-neglected aspects of his experience.

The Critical Contexts section of this book exemplifies the approach that is our goal. Art historian Anne Anderson's essay with its many illustrations provides insight into the Victorian world of art and its public culture that Oscar Wilde engaged. That was in dialogue with (and parody of) him, and it served as the most significant audience/backdrop for his literary production. Without an understanding of this nineteenth-century scene, it is impossible to truly comprehend the dynamic and radical nature of Wilde's genius. He is so close to our culture and ourselves in the twenty-first century, with its many forms of social media that connect us and create platforms for comment and conversation. In contrast, Colin Cavendish-Jones's chapter on Wilde as a dramatist compared with his contemporary George Bernard Shaw grounds us in these figures' roles as writers in a particularly literary form. Cavendish-Jones chooses the other major playwright of the late nineteenth century in Britain and places the two authors in context and dialogue with one another. This contribution is valuable because of Wilde's significance in literary history, rather than solely biography or popular culture. Focusing on plays—even as Wilde's and Shaw's are so different from one another—also bridges the approaches to our author. Like Wilde's visible role in the society of his time, these works were crafted for public performance and they shaped cultural pronouncements they delivered to their audience.

In his study of what he calls the afterlife of Wilde, Ben Hudson's chapter on Wilde's critical reception begins with an analysis of Wilde's own critical theory. Advanced students usually encounter these works; discerning their meaning is a key to our understanding of the author's view of life and art in the abstract. Hudson proceeds to review the broad range of strategies critics and historians have employed about Wilde: from gender and sexuality studies, to considerations of his Irishness, to interrogations of material culture as well as the "immaterial," such as Wilde on/and religion. Next, Nikolai Endres takes a particular critical strategy and theme, exploring gay and queer approaches to Wilde. Because

Wilde was tried and imprisoned for crimes of "gross indecency"—for having sex with men at a time when it was punishable by the law—this "afterlife" of the writer is especially significant. Wilde's public identity as a husband and father was challenged by his private life as a lover of men. There are few major authors in the canon who are convicted criminals, who died in shame and disgrace, and whose reputations were ruined and works censored or expelled from view. Over the past fifty years, following the development of the late twentieth-century gay rights movement, Oscar Wilde became a hero, a rebel with a cause. Endres studies the homoerotic themes in his texts while he also examines popular cultural representations (in a range of genres) of the homosexual Wilde. This aspect of the author, as demonstrated in many of the essays included here, is inextricable from his theories of art. Wilde's sexuality is significant enough to warrant a singular focus given the impact of his biography and thought on social change in the century after his death.

Following this cluster of contextual studies that set the stage for the volume, thirteen essays follow to provide closer focus on aspects of Wilde's literary and cultural experiences and legacies. Most readers of Wilde are familiar with *The Picture of Dorian Gray* and perhaps *The Importance of Being Earnest*. Because so much scholarship, as well as study guides and resources, have devoted themselves to these works, this volume offers opportunities to more deeply understand Wilde through lesser-known texts, to integrate the better-known into larger arguments, or to take newer strategies for coming to well-worn familiarities. *Critical Insights* is not exhaustive in its coverage of Wilde's compositions. Rather, the volume integrates a wide range of genres and forms in order to provide the greatest understanding of the artist's impact. For example, the critics here study Wilde's journalism and public lectures in the context of his role as a social commentator and intellectual. Similarly, most of Wilde's poetry shows aspects of the author's style found elsewhere in his biography and literary production. Our goal has been to offer a balanced, unexpected, intellectually challenging yet accessible guide to Wilde studies for both the new and experienced reader of this diverse and innovative author.

The Critical Readings section begins with Annette Magid's essay on Wilde's American tour. Magid sketches a broad overview of all things Wilde while charting his unique experience in America lecturing on "aesthetics," art for art's sake. Magid's style opens this part of our book by inviting the reader to share the perspectives of both the author and his audience. Continuing this theme of the public Wilde, Eleanor Fitzsimons's chapter focuses on the topic of women in a manner that is biographical, social, and textual. She discusses his famous mother "Speranza"—a poet and activist in her own right—as well as Wilde's role in editing a periodical addressed to a female audience; the essay also considers the author's marriage. In the process, both Magid and Fitzsimons also give us glimpses of Wilde as the public intellectual and journalist.

Melissa Knox-Raab's essay transitions the reader from these social essays to Wilde's best-known works—his plays—yet she considers one of the least known among them. Knox-Raab introduces the Victorian culture's views of sexuality, suggesting the period was a break from the past: one in which indirect rather than direct speech was the rule. She suggests how to decode meanings through this lens, using the play "Lady Windermere's Fan" and its themes of infidelity, parentage, and deception. Anne Varty's subsequent chapter is a complement to Knox-Raab's approach. By focusing on plays concerning issues of gender, Varty models a formalist analysis of how Wilde dealt with the theme in relation to contemporary expectations for and understandings of a proper play's structure. Finally, Ruth Robbins takes Wilde's best-known "comedy," *The Importance of Being Earnest*, and provides the reader with a strategy for analysis through theories of language and performance. Engaging linguistics and performance theory, Robbins develops a roadmap on how to follow Wilde's experimentation with language's ability to both reveal and conceal meaning.

Opening the next cluster, Julie-Ann Robson gives a guide to Wilde's own critical theory. She situates it with respect to intellectuals of the time, including Walter Pater and John Ruskin, while studying both Wilde's journalism and his philosophical essays. This chapter sets the stage for the two that follow, both of which concern Wilde as writer, a lesser-known prose work, and the author's theories of authorship. First Sharon Bickle and Marie Heneghan take *The Portrait of Mr W. H.*, a writer's mystery of sorts concerning the identity of the dedicatee for Shakespeare's sonnets, and deploy it to explore Wilde's own thoughts about literary composition and authority. Then Chris Foss examines *Pen, Pencil and Poison* for literary history, murder and mayhem, and symbolic themes in Wilde's creative fiction. Neither of these essays (nearly novellas) by Wilde has received the general readership attention it deserves, and these chapters invite their study by a broader audience.

Rebecca Nesvet's reading of Sherlock Holmes in relation to Wilde and his legacy serves to follow up these two chapters on literature. Nesvet demonstrates in Doyle's stories the aesthetic, potentially queer qualities of his classic sleuth in the style of Wilde's literary explorations found in *Mr W. H.* and *Pen, Pencil and Poison*. She does the work of literary history on afterlives like Wilde imagined by tracing the Holmesian legacy into its twentieth-century struggles with the specters of both the aesthetic and the queer. Oswaldo Gallo-Serratos's chapter on Wilde, Newman, and *De Profundis* strikingly brings us full circle here. Gallo-Serratos's concern with Wilde's own reading and the legacy of figures such as John Henry Newman (an "anxiety of influence," if you will) resonates with Nesvet's approach to the Wildean Holmes. Themes of the pleasure of the text, such as a detective story in Doyle (or Wilde) stop short with very different kinds of books and their concerns: namely scripture and "truth" as *religious* faith. Even so, in both of these chapters homophobia, as well as same-sex desire (often policed and in the shadows), frame how we think about Wilde.

These themes are most poignant in the next pair of essays. Legal scholar and literature professor Todd Barry turns to the seminal trials of Oscar Wilde—first that of libel (Wilde's response to his lover's father's accusations of "posing as a 'somdomite'[*sic*]," then prosecution for vice. The trials' dialogue is part of the Wilde literary canon. They have become so in the past half-century of study as texts, part of the recovery of the author and his significance. It was not simply homosexual acts, but rather theories of art and life that were put on trial. Barry analyzes Moisés Kaufman's play *Gross Indecency, The Three Trials of Oscar Wilde* written and produced a century later, in a sexually decriminalized and less homophobic time. That work includes transcripts from the Wilde trials and yet Kaufman shows (as does Barry) that this is no historical question. Kaufman would later gain fame for his play *The Laramie Project* about the 1998 hate-crime murder of gay college student Matthew Shepard—often depicted as a crucified Christ figure, like the sacrificed Wilde. Margaret Stetz's study of Wilde's fairy tale "The Happy Prince" and its many recent retellings and visual depictions likewise reminds us of a Wildean literary form worth academic analysis, along with the art of adaptation and its assumptions. Here we find that Wilde's multiple genres lend themselves not only to multiple forms of consumption—a fairy tale can be subject to critical reading—but also that Wilde, the consummate actor and adaptor, will always provide source material for his afterlife.

For an artist who continually returned to a concern about the peril of not distinguishing between art and life—whose biography bore the scars of blurring those boundaries—it is appropriate that our volume closes with Amanda Farage's piece on "captivated" reading and twenty-first century media consumption. Wilde is a writer for our age, and the issues of selfhood, authorship, the pleasures of the text and the desires to lose one's self, are pervasive in his works. Even if our era may not ruminate on the danger of fiction taking us out of our worlds, we are cognizant of the boundaries of realities that new media, the digital and artificial, challenge us to transgress. And here we turn and return to Wilde's classic voice encouraging us to always embrace the mutually exclusive: to explore unlimited self-discovery *and* never lose who we are.

While these essays may be read individually, reading this book sequentially as I describe will also provide the narrative I've charted. Following the chapters, Rebecca Nesvet (with James Duffy) has provided resources on Wilde's texts and subsequent secondary works, with Kim Stern's chronology. We wish you a "Wilde" journey in your reading and studies.

On Oscar Wilde: Introduction

Frederick S. Roden

When approached to edit this guide to Oscar Wilde studies, I had to pause for a moment. Fifteen years earlier I published a collection of scholarly essays written by major Wildeans on various themes in the author's works and life.[1] What is new or different now? How would this volume be distinct from that one? Perhaps most importantly, in the intervening time, although I continued teaching courses in a literature department, my own academic interests as well as my extracurricular commitments had considerably strayed, and not for the first time. After an undergraduate career in the sciences, expecting a profession that would literally unravel the mysteries of life as a molecular biologist studying human DNA, I had abruptly transitioned to the study of the humanities. Perhaps the single most important reason I did so was the story of Oscar Wilde, an explanation for which I will flesh out later in this introduction.

To return for now to my justification for editing this book, even as I have worked on other topics in recent years, I have a few points to share with the reader. First, it had always been my goal and intention to write a book on "how Oscar Wilde can save your life"—in part because he saved mine. Second, after a quarter of a century of university teaching, it has become clear to me that the most important work that we do, the most impactful aspect of our careers as college professors, is not our conversation among ourselves about an author's life or works; nor is it even the pure content that we deliver in the courses that we teach. Rather, the most significant part of our contribution as liberal arts academics is inviting our students to look inward: to determine for themselves who (and what) they are; and to pay attention to that answer regarding what they're passionate about, what moves them, what they may be drawn to—however inexplicable it might be to them at the moment.

One of my heroes, the late Dr. Viktor Frankl—psychiatrist, Holocaust survivor, and author of the classic *Man's Search for*

Meaning—believed that the meaning and purpose of his life was to help others to discern the meaning and purpose of theirs. I have taken this wisdom as the means, the gospel (if you will), by which I will live as an educator (and human being). For the purpose of this volume, I want to explain here why Oscar Wilde is a writer, thinker, guru even, in this same tradition. When I accepted the invitation to edit this volume, I decided its contributors were going to have to answer an important question to justify their chapter's place here. That question is practical, given the audience for which this book is intended, but it also contains an element of the ethical, with which this introductory essay is concerned. The issue is somewhat counter-intuitive, since Wilde's theories of art claim to be apart from ethics, insofar as the good is that which is beautiful, rather than the beautiful being that which is good. Wilde rebelled against a Victorian morality seeking an ethics for artistic production; yet I've never ceased asserting the ethical Wilde.

I asked contributors what they would wish the next generation of readers of Wilde to know. There must be meaning and purpose in our continued reading of writers from other times and places. We need to justify doing so not to satisfy university administrators' standards or expectations but for ourselves as ethical human beings dedicated to the study on which this profession is based. Some of our chapter editors answered that question as master teachers; some as scholars or public intellectuals; and some with a keen sense of the ethical imperative of what we are passing to future generations—especially at this time when the humanities are changing greatly. The experience of reading is different in this digital, technological, virtual-reality age. The ways by which we communicate with one another have morphed. Our colleges and universities have altered dramatically over a short period of time. And yet (thankfully) certain messages, teachings, and values remain the same—even as they may need to be translated into a new language, as it were, even as they may have different resonance than they had for previous generations. Just so, their worth remains one constant to cleave to as these waves strike (read the Victorian Matthew Arnold to learn the disconnection of a society in flux[2]).

As I sit here in my study writing this essay, a representation of "The Happy Prince," the title character of Wilde's fairy tale that Margaret Stetz discusses in her chapter, is staring at me. An undergraduate student—not an English major, but rather one who studied Digital Media and Design, who took a seminar I taught on Wilde—painted this canvas and gave it to me. That story concerns giving: of one's deepest self for the benefit of others. He presented this painting to me (after the course had concluded and grades had been submitted, certainly) because he believed that I live this Wildean tale by giving of myself through my vocation. To be sure, I am deeply honored by this former student's gesture. As an alumnus, he would later attend my mother's funeral, a poignant testament to the power of the human bond that transcends the teacher-student relationship. I share this anecdote in order to demonstrate the breadth of Oscar Wilde's message and the range of ways it can touch people's lives. When in the early 1990s I began studying and writing on Wilde's religion and theology, it seemed absurd to people who associated the author with a gospel of pleasure and self-indulgence, materialism, and sensual excess. Similarly, some years later as I began to focus more on Wilde's ethical message, that seemed out of sync to those preoccupied with the author's emphasis upon ideal of form and devotion to the beautiful (Arnoldian Hellenic rather than Hebraic[3]). Just as in the Victorian age, when debates about religion and homosexuality were presuming the two to be mutually exclusive, likewise in our own historical moments, we struggle to develop an inclusive, universal ethic that welcomes the stranger, that denounces elites, despots, and oligarchs, and that still cultivates the beautiful. Judaism teaches the concept of *hiddur mitzvah*: to take the obligatory and make of it the beautiful. So, too, did Wilde, and herein we find his ethics, which are always social even as they depend on individual self-awareness. For another *Critical Insights* volume, on good and evil, I wrote on Wilde's *Dorian Gray*.[4] For our purposes here, I won't be dealing with such themes so abstractly, but rather by telling my own story and parsing Wilde's life and art for the most general of meanings: the humanistic that is the core of humane letters, the humanities, and indeed humanity.

As a university student of the sciences, I was digesting the large volume of information one is obliged to learn in preparation for advanced study. But inside, in a place where that knowledge wasn't simply shelved, I felt desperately empty. I had data, but not wisdom. I could conceptualize human biology, but not humanistic life experience. So, I had what used to be called a "nervous breakdown": really an existential challenge similar to what Victorian writer John Stuart Mill chronicled in his *Autobiography*. If all he hoped to learn and accomplish in the world came to pass, would it give him the contentment and satisfaction he craved? The answer for Mill was "no," as it was for me some century and a half later. Mill's response—his therapy, as it were—was to turn to the poetry of Wordsworth: to begin to feel, instead of just to think. In my case, I came of age as a closeted gay teenager in the last decades of the twentieth century, when the epidemic of AIDS was cutting down young men just a few years older than myself. In order to be and become who I was, in a loving family who encouraged my intellectual and personal growth, I needed a teacher whose philosophy of life meant self-realization in the present and hope for the future. That was Oscar Wilde.

So I abandoned my Honors thesis research on raptor genetics, during senior year met all the necessary requirements to complete an English degree, and applied to graduate school in literature prepared to study Wilde, and homosexuality—what was by then "gay studies" and the emergent "queer theory." What I wasn't prepared for or expecting was that I was also becoming a scholar of religion. Certainly, the two didn't seem to fit together—Wilde studies, religious studies? I had grown up in a reasonably religious family, and I didn't *think* that my homosexual identity forced me on some spiritual journey let alone theological inquiry. Rather, the ethical questions, the nuances of identity, and the matters of tolerance and mutual understanding of individualism would dominate my explorations. So I began to study Wilde's religious thought, a subject Oswaldo Gallo-Serratos discusses in his chapter in this volume. My analysis in this essay will be expressed through the lens of the Christian culture that produced Wilde, and whose language he deployed in speaking of those broad humanistic (and spiritual) questions. On a much larger level, as I have indicated, Wilde's ideas invite readers to ponder the mystery of being and becoming: the search for an authentic self that allows for the similar growth and development of the other in society. That is why (and how) I became a "Wildean."

A few of our contributors briefly mention Wilde's 1891 essay "The Soul of Man Under Socialism," but I'd like to take more extended space here to discuss that work. In the tradition of the Victorian "socialism" of William Morris and others, Wilde's thought really concerns "individualism." Whether prophetically or in the tradition of utopianism, Wilde imagines a world where machines will be used for the good of humanity, rather than to our detriment. Our culture struggles with the inability to "unplug" and to what degree technology is a blessing or a curse. We use social media to "stay connected," yet our "friends" or "followers" always seem so far away. Artificial Intelligence, Virtual Reality, and every possible innovation allow us to go on journeys, but do we really travel more deeply into the *self*? For the Victorians, technology brought similar challenges. The faster pace of life made possible through nineteenth-century technologies left heads spinning, and mass-production and material prosperity pressured the growing leisured classes to keep up with their neighbors. Even with the abolition of slavery in the British Empire during the 1830s, many Victorians saw manual labor as a form of bondage, particularly in the dehumanizing factories, the subject of many social justice works of literature and political activism of the time. Morris and others created nostalgia— theory and praxis—to model an idealized pre-modern world where individual laborers might gain the satisfaction of handiwork through creativity rather than being debased by mindless assembly-line style experiences.

Wilde took this notion and expanded on it to focus more deeply on the notion of individualism, and particularly diversity. In the tradition of Jesuit poet Gerard Manley Hopkins's "Pied Beauty," Wilde's "Soul of Man Under Socialism" is a celebration of the (Darwinian) diversity found in *human* nature. He aims to "reconstruct society . . . [so] that poverty will be impossible" (Wilde *Works* 1079). "Socialism will be of value simply because it will lead to Individualism" (Wilde *Works* 1080). In the best Wildean style, this celebrant of the beauty of life and material experience suggests that a utopian ideal would be the renunciation of private property, a marvelous paradox. Wilde demonstrates how ownership gets in the way of realization of the true self, individualism. While his essay has "Soul" in its title, Wilde speaks extensively of "personality" (*Works* 1084). Like Victorian women who wrote about religion as a means for claiming authority to speak on important social issues, Wilde uses Christianity as justification for the statements he proclaims. "'Know thyself!' was written over the portal of the antique world. Over the portal of the new world, 'Be thyself' shall be written. And the message of Christ to man was simply 'Be thyself.' That is the secret of Christ" (Wilde *Works* 1085).[5] These were revolutionary statements from a thinker who had rarely referenced Christianity before in public discourse.[6] Wilde merged his own thought with that of the faith of his time, like many nineteenth-century secular ("spiritual but not religious," if you will) intellectuals. He literally makes himself a "Christ-figure" here by turning artists into saviors.

Wilde writes that Christ teaches that every human being must develop the self. Personality isn't narcissism, vanity, or pride; rather, it is the spark of the Divine in each individual that allows one to uniquely contribute to the world. His "religion" teaches that one "reaches his perfection . . . entirely through what he is" (Wilde *Works* 1085). Wilde is a social radical insofar as he states that, "The world hates Individualism" (*Works* 1087). It is a struggle to be oneself, a notion to which many of us can surely relate. Wilde continues to preach tolerance and diversity in this essay. He refuses to accept the demands of conformity to society or the family, issues of particular importance to women who were duty-bound as daughters, sisters, mothers, and wives. Healthcare reformer Florence Nightingale had denounced this obligation of living for others in her essay *Cassandra,* and Wilde takes it further here. Wilde's Christ "would allow no claim whatsoever to be made on personality" (*Works* 1087). "And so he who would lead a Christlike life is he who is perfectly and absolutely himself. . . . It does not matter what he is, as long as he realises the perfection of the soul that is within him. . . . All imitation in morals and life is wrong" (Wilde *Works* 1087). Victorian women deployed religion to advocate for social change; here a male writer follows their example.

In keeping with his "aesthetic" theories, Wilde ties "individualism" to art. As he professes throughout his work, the general public should try to make itself more "artistic": to more definedly and refinedly pay attention to the sentiments of the self. Wilde maintains that this gospel of the individual will not lead to selfishness, but rather to generosity. To pay the fullest attention to one's own needs allows one to respect the needs of others. This is modern secular humanism and social ethics. Wilde's vision is one of mutual respect in a diverse society where everyone has the right to *be*, reminiscent of Mill's *On Liberty*. He states that, "what man has sought for is . . . simply Life . . . to live intensely, fully, perfectly. When he can do so without exercising restraint on others, or suffering it ever, and his activities are all pleasurable to him, he will be saner, healthier, more civilised, more himself" (Wilde *Works* 1103–04). This gospel of self-realization is not greedy manifest destiny. Rather, it follows the social-based Victorian reforms emphasizing the quality of life in *this* world, not the promises of eternity in heaven as rewards for obedience and self-abnegation.

In reading "The Soul of Man," it isn't difficult to see how Wilde's teachings can be generalized to society of any day, including our own. As a gay young adult in early 1990s America when homophobia was strong even in progressive spaces, Wilde's message spoke to me. I found Wilde's writing to be both personally affirming and vocationally inspiring. Reading Wilde's prose not only "saved my life," it made me want to do something good with it: to speak out against society's homophobia; to use Wilde's argument to counter religious anti-gay teachings from an ethical standpoint; and to develop myself into a scholar and educator who would broadcast that message far and wide. So, in 1993 I wrote my master's thesis on this subject, focusing on "The Soul of Man Under Socialism" and *De Profundis*, a text that I will also discuss here. Our second, almost third, decade of the twenty-first century is a different time. There are others invisible in our world in need of Wildean advocacy.

But that doesn't mean that his particular significance for gay/queer/ homosexual people has disappeared. The specifically homoerotic intentions and inflections of Wilde's writings and life have been more clearly revealed to us, for instance through Nicholas Frankel's 2011 "annotated, uncensored" *Picture of Dorian Gray* and his 2017 biography focusing on Wilde's post-prison life.

Even without newer works or the more accepting nature of twenty-first culture, Wilde's words speak for themselves. Perhaps the best example is found in his speech from the witness stand, while on trial (and later convicted) for crimes of homosexuality. In this famous soliloquy, responding to a question about a line in a poem written by his lover, Wilde makes same-sex love central to western civilization and art; he publicly speaks its truth.

> What is the "Love that dare not speak its name"?—"The love that dare not speak its name" in this century is such a great affection of an elder for a younger man as there was between David and Jonathan, such as Plato made the very basis of his philosophy, and such as you find in the sonnets of Michelangelo and Shakespeare. It is that deep, spiritual affection that is as pure as it is perfect. It dictates and pervades great works of art like those of Shakespeare and Michelangelo . . . It is in this century much misunderstood, so much misunderstood that it may be described as the "Love that dare not speak its name", and on account of it I am placed where I am now. It is beautiful, it is fine, it is the noblest form of affection. There is nothing unnatural about it. It is intellectual, and it repeatedly exists between an elder and a younger man, when the elder man has intellect, and the younger man has all the joy, hope, and glamour of life before him. The world mocks at it and sometimes puts one in the pillory for it. (Wilde *Trials* 236)

In this rousing monologue, Wilde's voice exorcises the shame from his culture's perception of same-sex love. Even so, it did not immediately change his own time or nation; Britain didn't decriminalize sexual acts between men until the last third of the twentieth century. Those homosexuals who could afford to leave became refugees in parts of continental Europe where the Napoleonic Code did not prosecute same-sex sexual acts.

There is another issue here, one that resonated in the 1990s when I was reading and writing about Wilde's radical voice. This point concerns the fact that Wilde's declaration relied on classical Greek models, and specifically Platonism: the older man, or *erastes*, loving the younger man, or *eromenos,* in a strictly spiritual union. Plato's philosophy transcended love of bodies to intellectual beauty. While today we might call this "body-negative," the paradigm itself, ancient though it may be, can make a contemporary reader suspicious of the link between homosexuality and pedophilia.[7] In the 1990s, the Roman Catholic Church sexual abuse scandals and crisis broke into the news, and there was a tremendous effort to scapegoat the gay person as a distraction from the abuses of power. As an example contemporary to Wilde, we may consider an excerpt from a scandalous story about the love between a priest and a teenaged altar boy. In John Francis Bloxam's "The Priest and the Acolyte"— written by a man who later became a beloved Anglican priest serving the London slums—included in an Oxford undergraduate magazine edited by Wilde's lover Bosie Douglas, we have a "defense" of difference in orientations. The quotation itself is liberationist: "Can you not see that people are different, totally different from one another? . . . Conscience should be that divine instinct which bids us seek after that our natural disposition needs" (Bloxam 42– 43). This work and others like it from the "uranian" school (those male writers from the turn of the century who praised young male, rather than female, beauty) are hard to reconcile with contemporary ethics and understandings of power and its deployment, especially in the #MeToo era.[8] But there were other members of Wilde's circle equally critical of such relationships—so much so that they have been criticized as being homophobic themselves. These include Marc-Andre Raffalovich, a gay Jewish convert to Catholicism, who famously rescued the poet John Gray when Wilde cast him off. Gray, later ordained a Roman Catholic priest, had famously signed letters to Wilde as "Dorian." Fascinated by their story, and their reconciliation of same-sex love within their religious friendship, I would continue writing about this couple and their literary works, later co-editing a translation of a huge book on "sexology," the "science" (or pseudo-science) of sex, that Raffalovich had published in 1896.[9]

The most significant discussion of Wildean social ethics, coming from his imprisonment for homosexual acts yet applicable far beyond it, is found in his famous letter *De Profundis*, written to his former lover Lord Alfred Douglas. Although a large portion of the work details elements of their shared life (in a scathingly harsh manner!), in this text Wilde puts forth a universal ethics through the character of Christ, to whom he compares himself as an enlightened artist following the "Soul of Man" tradition. Wilde's Christ is himself; as narcissistic as that may seem, as we have seen Wilde's Christ also advocates a revolutionized society. Wilde declares himself a "man who stood in symbolic relations to the art and culture" of his age (*Works* 912). He dismisses society's morality, religion, and reason as outside of his understanding as an artist—an individual. Wilde alludes to how he had written in "The Soul of Man Under Socialism" that "he who would lead a Christ-like life must be entirely and absolutely himself" (*Works* 923). Here he expands this point to state that whatever happens to another happens to oneself: true compassion in the form of artistic "sympathy," understanding. Wilde speaks of Christ belonging with the poets and his life as a beautiful poem. He asserts that when one "comes in contact with the soul it makes one simple as a child, as Christ said one should be . . . Christ was not merely the supreme Individualist, but he was the first in History" (Wilde *Works* 926). "To live for others as a definite self-conscious aim was not his creed. It was not the basis of his creed" (Wilde *Works* 926), noting that forgiving one's enemies is for one's own sake. Christ "pointed out that there was no difference at all between the lives of others and one's own life" (Wilde *Works* 926). This perspective leads to the expansion and retraction of humanity through the nineteenth-century notion of a universal unity and whole. It is the ethical imperative behind the age's compulsion to repair a broken world: the awareness that we are interconnected, a concept still proclaimed and celebrated (and so desperately needed) in the late twentieth and early twenty-first centuries.

Wilde domesticates Christ as the voice of an enlightened secular, humanistic teacher. But like other thinkers of his time, Wilde doesn't remove his exceptionalism or salvific role.

> With a width and wonder of imagination, that fills one almost with awe, he took the entire world of the inarticulate, the voiceless world of pain, as his kingdom, and made of himself its eternal mouthpiece. Those . . . who are dumb under oppression and "whose silence is heard only of God," he chose as his brothers. He sought to become eyes to the blind, ears to the deaf, and a cry on the lips of those whose tongue had been tied. His desire was to be to the myriads who had found no utterance a very trumpet through which they might call to Heaven. (Wilde *Works* 927)[10]

The gospel that Wilde proclaims makes the whole world kin. He gestures similarly in calling for sympathy (complete understanding or "fellow-feeling," literally) for prisoners in his poem "The Ballad of Reading Gaol." This is the ethical teaching of Oscar Wilde: The highest realization of humanity is the soul (or "personality") capable of one-ing itself with those who are most marginalized, thus allowing their voices to be heard so that oppression might be recognized and corrected.

Like many other progressive religious and secular thinkers, Wilde focuses on Christ's rejection of legalism, emphasizing the spirit rather than the letter of the law, its true meaning rather than shallow literalism. He values "sin" as society defines it since it can be transformative and "repentance" only because it leads to greater self-awareness. Even in prison, Wilde never loses his sense of humor or sharp wit, as found in his writings on Christianity. He unabashedly states that "There is something so unique about Christ," just as he felt there was about himself; just as Wilde saw in the discourse of his age that had made Christian teachings the basis of secular society rather than focusing upon their exclusively religious inflection (*Works* 933). He declares that, "there were Christians before Christ . . . The unfortunate thing is that there have been none since," with the exception of Francis of Assisi, the medieval saint who honored all of creation yet maintained attachment to no material things (Wilde *Works* 933). Wilde says that Christ "is just like a work of art himself. He doesn't really teach one anything, but by being brought into his presence one becomes something" (*Works* 934), underscoring the sacredness he finds in art. Wilde also observes that on the journey of life, "at least once . . . each man walks with Christ to Emmaus" (*Works* 934). We are challenged by epiphanies that lie before us as we have the potential to continually becoming more awake to the truth of our lives and others. Wilde wants us "woke," to use the jargon of our moment—for others, but first for our own sake: so that change can be possible.

In *De Profundis*, Wilde demonstrates the transformative potential of events that take shape outside the self, that come unbidden and yet change us—like going to prison and losing everything one has and everyone one loves. He also emphasizes the ways in which, as Viktor Frankl teaches, it is not the events themselves but rather how we respond to them that ultimately determines our experience (as the survivor of four Nazi concentration camps postulated).[11] Many years have passed—many courses taught, essays written, and lectures given on Oscar Wilde—and his life and works still continue to affect my life, as they did when I first read them as a university and postgraduate student. It is my hope that they will change yours, and perhaps that this volume might pave the way for you to explore Oscar Wilde further.

Notes

1. Frederick S. Roden, ed. *Palgrave Advances: Oscar Wilde Studies,* Basingstoke: Palgrave Macmillan, 2004.

2. See Matthew Arnold's "The Buried Life" or "Dover Beach."

3. See Chapter Four of Matthew Arnold, *Culture and Anarchy and Other Selected Prose*, edited by P.J. Keating, London: Penguin, 2015.

4. See Frederick S. Roden, "Decadence and Dorian Gray: Who's Afraid of Oscar Wilde?" *Critical Insights: Good and Evil,* edited by Margaret Breen, Ipswich (MA): EBSCO Publishing, 2012, pp. 79–94.

5. As was customary in Wilde's time, the author refers to "man" for "human[ity]" and deploys the masculine pronouns *he, him,* and *his* to signify people. This should not be read as sexism but rather common use of his day.

6. Wilde's early poetry speaks of Christianity largely because of the popularity of Roman Catholicism at Oxford University following what would be called the "Oxford Movement" and John Henry Newman's conversion. Gallo-Serratos discusses Newman's influence in this volume.

7. Compare David M. Halperin, *One Hundred Years of Homosexuality: And Other Essays on Greek Love,* New York: Routledge, 1989.

8. For more information on the "uranian," or same-sex loving writers of the turn of the century who idealized male beauty, see Timothy d'Arch-Smith, *Love in Earnest: Some Notes on the Lives and Writings of English "Uranian" Poets 1889–1930,* London: Routledge and Kegan Paul, 1970.

9. See, for instance, "Michael Field, John Gray, and Marc-Andre Raffalovich: Re-Inventing Romantic Friendship in Modernity," *Catholic Figures, Queer Narratives,* edited by Lowell Gallagher, Frederick S. Roden, and Patricia Juliana Smith, New York: Palgrave Macmillan, 2007 , pp. 57–68; "Marc-Andre Raffalovich: A Russian-French-Jewish-Catholic Homosexual in Oscar Wilde's London," *Jewish/Christian/Queer: Crossroads and Identities,* edited by Frederick S. Roden, Burlington, VT: L Ashgate, 2009), pp. 127–37; "Introduction," Marc-Andre Raffalovich, *Uranism and Unisexuality: A Study of Different Manifestations of the Sexual Instinct,* edited by Philip Healy and Frederick S. Roden, trans. Nancy Erber and William A. Peniston, Basingstoke: Palgrave Macmillan, 2016, pp. 1–21.

10. Here Wilde uses the word "dumb" in a period connotation to mean those who literally cannot speak. Again, this is not ableism but rather the common term at the time.

11. For more on my theological and religious reading of *De Profundis,* see my chapter on Wilde in *Same-Sex Desire in Victorian Religious Culture,* Basingstoke: Palgrave Macmillan, 2002.

Works Cited

Arnold, Matthew. *Culture and Anarchy and Other Selected Prose,* edited by P. J. Keating. London: Penguin, 2015.

Bloxam, John Francis (anon.). "The Priest and the Acolyte." *The Chameleon: A Facsimile Edition.* London: The Eighteen-Nineties Society, 1978, pp. 29–47.

d'Arch-Smith, Timothy. *Love in Earnest: Some Notes on the Lives and Writings of English "Uranian" Poets 1889–1930.* London: Routledge and Kegan Paul, 1970.

Darwin, Charles. *On the Origin of Species,* edited by William Bynum. New York: Penguin, 2009.

Frankel, Nicholas. *Oscar Wilde: The Unrepentant Years.* Cambridge: Harvard U P, 2017.

_____. *The Picture of Dorian Gray: An Annotated, Uncensored Edition.* Cambridge: Belknap P, 2011.

Frankl, Viktor. *Man's Search for Meaning.* Boston: Beacon P, 2006.

Halperin, David M. *One Hundred Years of Homosexuality: And Other Essays on Greek Love.* New York: Routledge, 1989.

Hopkins, Gerard Manley. *Gerard Manley Hopkins: The Major Works,* edited by Catherine Phillips. New York: Oxford World's Classics, 2009.

Mill, John Stuart. *Autobiography,* edited by John M. Robson. New York: Penguin, 1990.

_____. *On Liberty, Utilitarianism and Other Essays,* edited by Mark Philp and Frederick Rosen. New York: Oxford World's Classics, 2015.

Morris, William. *News from Nowhere and Other Writings,* edited by Clive Kilmer. New York: Penguin, 1994.

Nightingale, Florence. *Cassandra,* edited by Myra Stark and Cynthia Macdonald. New York: Feminist P, 1993.

Roden, Frederick S. "Decadence and Dorian Gray: Who's Afraid of Oscar Wilde?" *Critical Insights: Good and Evil,* edited by Margaret Breen. Ipswich (MA): EBSCO Publishing, 2012, pp. 79–94.

_____. "Introduction." Marc-Andre Raffalovich, *Uranism and Unisexuality: A Study of Different Manifestations of the Sexual Instinct*, edited by Philip Healy and Frederick S. Roden, trans. Nancy Erber and William A. Peniston. Basingstoke: Palgrave Macmillan, 2016, pp. 1–21.

_____. "Marc-Andre Raffalovich: A Russian-French-Jewish-Catholic Homosexual in Oscar Wilde's London." *Jewish/Christian/Queer: Crossroads and Identities*. Burlington (VT): Ashgate, 2009, pp. 127–37.

_____. "Michael Field, John Gray, and Marc-Andre Raffalovich: Re-Inventing Romantic Friendship in Modernity." *Catholic Figures, Queer Narratives,* edited by Lowell Gallagher, Frederick S. Roden, and Patricia Juliana Smith. New York: Palgrave Macmillan, 2007, pp. 57–68.

_____. *Same-Sex Desire in Victorian Religious Culture.* Basingstoke: Palgrave Macmillan, 2002.

_____, ed. *Palgrave Advances: Oscar Wilde Studies,* Basingstoke: Palgrave Macmillan, 2004.

Wilde, Oscar. *Complete Works of Oscar Wilde.* New York: HarperPerennial, 1989.

_____. *The Trials of Oscar Wilde*, edited by H. Montgomery Hyde. London: William Hodge and Company, 1948.

Oscar Wilde: A Biography_____

Kimberly J. Stern

Oscar Wilde was born on October 16, 1854, in Dublin, Ireland. This, at least, is an indisputable fact about an author whose life has always been open to dispute. To some extent, Wilde himself was responsible for muddying the waters. He repeatedly professed to be two years younger than he was in reality, a practice also followed by his mother. Wilde claimed moreover that he "went to no public school," though he attended Portora Royal School for seven years ("Oscar Wilde" 131). For Wilde, a catalogue of events was hardly the mark of a life well spent. Instead, he valued "the life that has for its aim not *doing* but *being*, and not *being* merely, but *becoming*" ("Critic as Artist" 178, emphasis in original). Elsewhere, I have remarked on the challenges of tracing a clear, linear account of Wilde's life.[1] Yet even readers who share Wilde's wariness of narrative biography cannot deny that he was the product of unique social and historical circumstances.

Wilde spent his early childhood at the family home at 1 Merrion Square, Dublin. His father, Sir William R. Wilde, was an acclaimed ophthalmologist, who was named the first Surgeon Oculist in Ordinary to the Queen in Ireland in 1853. In 1864, he was knighted for his work on the Irish census, a project he had undertaken in 1841 and would continue until his death in 1876. In addition to his accomplishments as a doctor and civil servant, William Wilde was also an amateur archaeologist, who was fascinated by ancient Irish artifacts, as illustrated in such works as *Irish Popular Superstitions* (1852), *Lough Corrib, Its Shores and Islands* (1867), and *Ancient Legends, Mystic Charms, and Superstitions of Ireland* (1887).

The last work was completed posthumously by Wilde's mother, Lady Jane Francesca Wilde. A noted writer of poetry, essays, and translations, Lady Wilde first entered the public eye in the 1840s when she began contributing to the *Nation*, a radical paper known for its support of Irish nationalism. Setting her apart from her avowedly

---

Unionist family, Lady Wilde's radical politics would persist throughout her life, and she would later become an advocate for the advancement of women. With these interesting and inquisitive parents at the helm, the family home at Merrion Square became an important site of Dublin intellectual life. Wilde and his brother Willie were reportedly permitted to attend his parents' gatherings, which over the years featured painter John Butler Yeats, activist Millicent Fawcett, writer Sheridan Le Fanu, and other noteworthies. This may explain Wilde's avowal that "the best of his education in boyhood was obtained from [. . .] association with his father and mother and their remarkable friends" ("Oscar Wilde" 131).

When Wilde was nine years old, he joined his brother at Portora Royal School, Enniskillen. Anecdotal accounts suggest that Wilde lacked academic discipline at this time, his older brother far outstripping him both intellectually and socially. It was only toward the end of his time at Portora that Wilde began to excel. He secured third prize for Scripture in 1869, captured the Carpenter Prize for Greek Testament in 1870, and the following year earned a Royal School scholarship to Trinity College, Dublin. At Trinity, Wilde continued to resist the prescribed academic program, reading widely but attending lectures selectively. He gained much, however, from his tutor John Pentland Mahaffy, the renowned classicist who had been a regular guest at Merrion Square. Inspired by Mahaffy, Wilde won the Berkeley Gold Medal for Greek at Trinity and in 1874 secured a scholarship to Magdalen College, Oxford.

Wilde's time as an undergraduate would prove to be transformative. Some have suggested that Wilde prized the academic pedigree itself, noting that he famously shed his Irish accent while at Oxford.[2] But Wilde's journals and letters also suggest that his undergraduate years were a fertile intellectual period. Wilde pursued a course in "Humane Letters," *Literae Humaniores* ("Greats"), thus extending the knowledge of Greek literature and culture he commenced at Trinity. At Oxford, these ideas collided with the work of German philosophers, as well as new approaches to scientific research and classification. Accordingly, Wilde's college notebooks overflow with references to Plato, Francis Bacon, Friedrich Hegel,

Immanuel Kant, Charles Darwin, Herbert Spencer and others. He also became enthralled by Catholicism, devouring the works of Cardinal John Henry Newman and speculating on the possibility of his own conversion. Although he would not formally convert at this time, Wilde's earnest reflections on theology suggest an effort to grapple with problems of vast spiritual and philosophical scope.

Wilde was successful in his pursuits at Oxford. In 1878, he won the Newdigate Prize for his poem "Ravenna," which was inspired by his trip to Italy with Mahaffy the preceding year. He also earned a rare "double-first" in Greats, hence solidifying his reputation as a man of intellectual promise. Immediately after graduation, Wilde's first instinct was to pursue a university career. Failing to capture one of the coveted college fellowships, he sought a post as Her Majesty's Inspector of Royal Schools. In the end, Wilde was not successful in attaining any of these positions, but he remained committed to intellectual work and in 1881 published his first volume, *Poems*. The book garnered mixed reviews, with several critics finding Wilde's poetry to be derivative and affected. *The Spectator* remarked that it was the "work of a clever man" who seemed to privilege "sensuous images" over true feeling ("Mr. Oscar Wilde's Poems" 1048). With some concern, the reviewer admits: "Perhaps he is right for the moment" ("Mr. Oscar Wilde's Poems" 1050).

Before long, Wilde would find himself before a much wider audience. In 1881, he was invited to America by Richard D'Oyly Carte, manager of W.S. Gilbert and Arthur Sullivan. The pair had just completed *Patience* (1881), an operetta in which the foppish Reginald Bunthorne plays a central role. It was hoped that Wilde's appearance would help to acquaint the American public with the cultural type suggested by Bunthorne—the British aesthete—thus garnering support for the production. Wilde toured America delivering lectures on art and aesthetics, while also cultivating his literary reputation through interviews and social engagements. The public response was, once again, mixed. While visual satires lampooned his attire, mannerisms, and esoteric views on art, the newspapers carefully tracked his public appearances and encounters with American celebrities like Walt Whitman and Henry James. By the time Wilde left America, he had become a noted, if controversial figure.

Wilde's lecture tour did not, however, catapult him into a position of popular acclaim. In 1883, Wilde's first play, *Vera; or, The Nihilists* (written in 1880, yet not staged in England), was produced in New York at the Union Square Theatre, but it closed after just one week. At this time, Wilde seems to have struggled to find a dramatic voice that would attract a popular audience. *The Duchess of Padua*, written the same year, would also fail when it was eventually produced in 1891.

Shortly after his return to London, Wilde proposed to Constance Lloyd, and the pair were married in 1884. Their first son, Cyril, was born the following year; a second son, Vyvyan followed in 1886. Initially, the couple seemed compatible. Wilde supported Constance's investment in dress reform and the advancement of women. Indeed, in 1887 he undertook the editorship of *Woman's World*, a post he maintained for two years. Under Wilde's leadership, the magazine became vastly more progressive, serving as a platform for serious discussion of literature, politics, education, and more. Both Wilde and Constance published children's stories during this time as well. Wilde's *The Happy Prince and Other Stories* appeared in 1888, the same year Constance published *There Was Once*, a collection of tales she claimed to have inherited from her grandmother. In 1891, Wilde produced a second book of children's stories, *A House of Pomegranates,* as well as *Intentions*, a collection of critical essays (including "The Critic as Artist," "The Decay of Lying," "Pen, Pencil and Poison," and "The Truth of Masks"). Published at a turning point in Wilde's personal and professional life, *Intentions* constitutes Wilde's most pointed articulation of the aesthetic principles that inform his creative work.

That year, Wilde also met and fell in love with Lord Alfred ("Bosie") Douglas, a twenty-one-year-old Oxford undergraduate. Although it was not his first relationship with a man, it is clear that Wilde's affair with Douglas was a transformative and in many ways defining one. Wilde claimed that his best work was produced during the period of his greatest intimacy with Douglas. To be sure,

Lady Windermere's Fan (1892), *A Woman of No Importance* (1893), *Salomé* (1893), *The Importance of Being Earnest* (1895), and *An Ideal Husband* (1895) all date from this period.[3]

It was, however, a troubled union. Douglas's father—John Douglas, the Marquess of Queensberry—objected to the relationship and confronted Wilde both at home and in public. When *The Importance of Being Earnest* premiered on February 14, 1895, Queensberry visited the St. James's Theater to present Wilde with a bouquet of rotting vegetables. He was denied admittance but only four days later left his calling card for Wilde at the Albemarle Club. It read: "Oscar Wilde, posing somdomite [sic]." Because the note constituted concrete and verbal evidence of Queensberry's harassment, Douglas claimed that it was libelous. He persuaded Wilde to bring a suit against his father. Commencing on April 3, the libel suit focused chiefly on establishing whether or not Queensberry's statement bore any traces of truth. In other words, the case hinged on the question of Wilde's sexuality.

Regrettably, the evidence brought to light during the libel suit seemed to justify Queensberry's suspicions about Wilde's sexuality. Douglas's father was acquitted, and the Crown charged Wilde with acts of "gross indecency" under the Labouchère Amendment (Section 11 of the Criminal Law Amendment Act of 1885).[4] Against the advice of his friend (and later literary executor) Robert Ross, Wilde elected to stand trial. The first trial was in many ways a public spectacle, and the courtroom transcripts often read like scenes from one of Wilde's stage comedies. Indeed, his literary output was a focus of the trial, with prosecutor Edward Carson taking special pains to present *The Picture of Dorian Gray* (1890–1891) as a "sodomitical novel" (Holland 97). Wilde's responses during cross-examination were extraordinary, and it is little surprise that the courtroom was filled with spectators applauding or denouncing Wilde's startling declamations on art, culture, and the "love that dare not speak its name." Indeed, Wilde's discussion of this term, excerpted from Douglas's poem "Two Loves," constituted one of the most powerful moments of his testimony. When Carson insisted that the poem described "unnatural love," Wilde replied by placing homosexual desire in a cultural lineage that included Plato, Shakespeare, and Michelangelo. In his startlingly frank and eloquent response, Wilde averred that "the love that dare not speak its name" was a "deep, spiritual affection that is as pure as it is perfect."[5]

Despite Wilde's sometimes dazzling utterances, the law was unyielding. The Crown extracted testimonies from several young "renters" (male prostitutes) who claimed to have either witnessed or participated in sexual acts with Wilde. The first trial ended in a hung jury, but a second trial resulted in his conviction. Wilde was sentenced to two years of hard labor.

A few days following his sentencing, Wilde was moved to Pentonville Prison. Two months later he was taken to Wandsworth Prison, and shortly thereafter he was transferred to Reading Gaol, where he would spend the majority of his prison term. The prison system at the time required that prisoners endure intense physical labor, such as "turning the crank" or walking the treadmill for extended periods. In accordance with the so-called "solitary system," they were also prohibited from interacting with other prisoners. For Wilde, who prized sociability, it was virtually unendurable. At Wandsworth, Wilde reportedly was approached by a fellow convict who whispered: "*I am sorry for you; it is harder for the likes of you than for the likes of us.*"[6] When Wilde expressed his gratitude, he was brought before the prison governor. Seeking to protect his fellow prisoner, Wilde insisted that he had commenced the exchange. He was placed in a dark cell for three days, subsisting only on bread and water.

While Wilde suffered alone in his prison cell, the world outside moved on. Wilde's mother died in 1896. Although Wilde was able to pay for a funeral, he could not afford to purchase a headstone. Wilde's idol and confidante—the woman who had loudly declaimed against English rule in Ireland—was interred in an unmarked grave. In addition to the physical and emotional strain of prison life, Wilde was deprived of the intellectual stimulation that had for years been his lifeblood. It was only at the behest of James O. Nelson, the prison warden who assumed management of Reading Gaol in 1896, that Wilde's requests for more edifying reading material and writing implements were finally approved. In the opening months of 1897, this concession made it possible for Wilde to compose that peculiar document, which Robert Ross would later publish under the title *De Profundis*. Commencing as a letter addressed to Douglas, the document comprises twenty folio sheets (amounting to approximately 80 pages of text), documenting Wilde's relationship with Douglas, experience of prison, and evolving views on art and life.

Although Wilde emerged from Reading Gaol in 1897 with little money and nowhere to live, he was hardly broken by his incarceration.[7] In his final years, Wilde not only produced his best-selling work of all time, "The Ballad of Reading Gaol," but also revised his earlier comedies (with new editions of *The Importance of Being Earnest* and *An Ideal Husband* appearing in 1899). He anticipated turning to more serious literary works, and one sees auguries of such a future in his letters on prison reform, where he describes in poignant and often graphic terms the abuses he witnessed during his imprisonment.[8]

Upon his release from prison on May 19, 1897, Wilde resided briefly with Anglican priest Stewart Headlam (who, despite not knowing him personally, posted half of his bail two years earlier), before heading to the Continent. In August of that year, Wilde reunited with Douglas in Naples, and it was during this time that he composed much of "The Ballad of Reading Gaol." The cost of seeing Douglas, however, was great. It forged a permanent rift between Wilde and Constance, who refused to let him see his children and threatened to rescind the allowance she had granted him as a condition of their separation. Douglas did not stay long in Naples, and in February 1898 Wilde himself removed to Paris. When Constance died later that year, Wilde lost his final tie to the children. He was, as his touching letters from this period reveal, heartbroken.

During the final year of his life, Wilde struggled financially, drank heavily, and reported feeling in poor health. With the financial assistance of Harold Mellor, he visited Italy once again in 1900, just a few months preceding his death. His letters from this period are lively, reflective, and overflow with references to the Catholic Church. Upon his return to Paris, however, Wilde again struggled in body and spirit. In October, he underwent a surgery to address an ear infection of which he had complained during his imprisonment. Wilde seems to have developed meningoencephalitis following the operation, and his health speedily declined. He died on November 30, under the attendance of Robert Ross and Reginald Turner. The day prior to his death, Ross fulfilled Wilde's request that a Catholic priest be brought to his bedside to administer final rites. Wilde was by this time weak and inarticulate; he was unable either to speak or to take the Eucharist.

Wilde was buried on December 3 in a humble grave at Bagneux (in the southern suburbs of Paris), and his remains were transported to Père Lachaise Cemetery in Paris nine years later. In 1914, Jacob Epstein's monument to Wilde was erected on the site, and in 1950 the ashes of Robert Ross were deposited into the tomb. Epstein's monument features the following inscription:

> And alien tears will fill for him,
> Pity's long-broken urn,
> For his mourners will be outcast men,
> And outcasts always mourn.[9]

The lines, excerpted from "The Ballad of Reading Gaol," testify to Wilde's status as a champion of cultural difference. Appropriately, the monument also features the body of a sphinx, that elusive, mythological figure that surfaces across Wilde's *oeuvre*. A famed guardian of the ancient world, the sphinx signifies paradox, hybridity, and the threshold between life and death. Given Wilde's reluctance to reduce any life to a finite timeline, it is fitting that the monument to his own life is not a final resting place so much as a site of speculation, transition, and possibility.

Notes

1. See Kimberly J. Stern, *Oscar Wilde: A Literary Life,* New York: Palgrave Macmillan, 2019.

2. See Joseph Pearce, *The Unmasking of Oscar Wilde,* San Francisco: Ignatius P, 2000, pp. 56–57; Michèle Mendelssohn, *Making Oscar Wilde,* Oxford: Oxford U P, 2018, p. 176.

3. Wilde was also at work on his play *La Sainte Courtesane* in 1894. He reportedly left the manuscript in a cab, and it would never be completed, though fragments of the play were published by Robert Ross in 1908.

4. The phrase "gross indecency" was deliberately ambiguous and facilitated the prosecution of individuals where sexual intercourse could not be proven. It would remain in effect until 1956, when it was slightly revised under the Sexual Offenses Act. It was not repealed until 1967.

5. See Oscar Wilde, *The Trial of Oscar Wilde: From the Shorthand Reports,* Paris: C. Carrington, 1906, pp. 58–59; see also H. Montgomery Hyde, *The Trials of Oscar Wilde,* Hodge: London, 1948, p. 190.

6. The complete anecdote is recorded by André Gide but repeated and verified in Wilde's own correspondence. See André Gide, *Oscar Wilde: A Study,* Oxford: Holywell P, 1905, pp. 66–67, emphasis in original; Oscar Wilde, *The Complete Letters*, Merlin Holland, New York: Fourth Estate, 2000, p. 762.

7. See Nicholas Frankel, *Oscar Wilde: The Unrepentant Years,* Harvard: Harvard U P, 2017.

8. See Oscar Wilde, *The Annotated Prison Writings of Oscar Wilde*, edited by Nicholas Frankel, Cambridge: Harvard U P, 2018.

9. Oscar Wilde, "The Ballad of Reading Gaol," in *Poetry and Poems in Prose*, edited by Bobby Fong and Karl Beckson, vol. 1, *The Complete Works,* Oxford: Oxford U P, 2000, pp.195–216, 212 [line 531–34].

Works Cited

Frankel, Nicholas. *Oscar Wilde: The Unrepentant Years*. Harvard: Harvard U P, 2017.

Gide, André. *Oscar Wilde: A Study*. Oxford: Holywell P, 1905.

Holland, Merlin. *The Real Trial of Oscar Wilde*. London: Harper Perennial, 2004.

Hyde, H. Montgomery. *The Trials of Oscar Wilde*. London: Hodge, 1948.

Mendelssohn, Michèle. *Making Oscar Wilde*. Oxford: Oxford U P, 2018.

"Mr. Oscar Wilde's Poem." *The Spectator,* 13 Aug. 1881, pp. 1048–50.

"Oscar Wilde." *The Biograph and Review,* 4, 1880, pp. 130–35.

Pearce, Joseph. *The Unmasking of Oscar Wilde.* San Francisco: Ignatius P, 2000.

Stern, Kimberly J. *Oscar Wilde: A Literary Life.* New York: Palgrave Macmillan, 2019.

The Trial of Oscar Wilde: From the Shorthand Reports. Paris: C. Carrington, 1906.

Wilde, Oscar. "The Ballad of Reading Gaol." In *Poetry and Poems in Prose,* edited by Bobby Fong and Karl Beckson, vol. 1, *The Complete Works.* Oxford: Oxford U P, 2000, pp. 195–216.

_____. *The Complete Letters,* edited by Merlin Holland. New York: Fourth Estate, 2000.

_____. "The Critic as Artist." In *Criticism,* edited by Josephine M. Guy, vol. 4, *The Complete Works of Oscar Wilde.* Oxford: Oxford U P, 2007, pp. 123–206.

_____. *The Annotated Prison Writings of Oscar Wilde,* edited by Nicholas Frankel. Cambridge: Harvard U P, 2018.

CRITICAL
CONTEXTS

Wilde's World

Anne Anderson

Aesthetic London

Wilde appeared on London's cultural scene at a propitious moment; with the opening of the Grosvenor Gallery in May 1877 the Aesthetes gained the public platform they had been denied. Sir Coutts Lindsay and his wife Blanche, who were behind this audacious enterprise, invited Edward Burne-Jones, George Frederick Watts, and James McNeill Whistler to participate in the first exhibition; all had suffered rejections from the Royal Academy.[1] The public were suddenly confronted with *the avant-garde*, Pre-Raphaelitism, Symbolism, and even French Naturalism. Wilde immediately recognized his opportunity, as few would understand "Art for Art's sake," that paintings no longer had to be didactic or moralizing. Rather, the function of art was to appeal to the senses, to focus on color, form, and composition. Moreover, the aesthetes blurred the distinction between the fine and decorative arts, transforming wallpapers and textiles into *objets d'art*. The goal was to surround oneself with beauty, to create a House Beautiful. Wilde hitched his star to Aestheticism while an undergraduate at Oxford; his rooms were noted for their beauty, the panelled walls thickly hung with old engravings and contemporary prints by Burne-Jones and filled with exquisite objects: Blue and White Oriental porcelain, Tanagra statuettes brought back from Greece, and Persian rugs. He was also aware of the controversy surrounding Aestheticism; debated in the *Oxford and Cambridge Undergraduate* in April and May 1877, the magazine at first praised the movement as a civilizing influence. It quickly recanted, as it sought "'*implicit* sanction'" for "'Pagan worship of bodily form and beauty'" and renounced morals in the name of liberty (Ellmann 85, emphasis in original).

As the "Professor of Aestheticism," Wilde launched his career as an art critic. He published a review of the opening exhibition at the Grosvenor in the *Dublin University Magazine* (Stokes and

Turner 2). He followed this with another review for the *Irish Daily News* in 1879 (Stokes and Turner 16). As an art critic, Wilde's success rested upon demonstrating that he had better taste and knowledge than his readers. Many doubted his abilities, especially Whistler who ranted "'What has Oscar in common with Art? . . . Oscar—with no more sense of a picture than the fit of a coat, has the courage of the opinions—of others!'" (Ellmann 257). The painter William Powell Frith also considered him an imposter, placing Wilde center stage in *The Private View at the Royal Academy 1881* (1883, Private Collection). Writing much later in his *Autobiography*, Frith maintained:

> Beyond the desire of recording for posterity the aesthetic craze as regards dress, I wished to hit the folly of listening to self-elected critics in matters of taste, whether in dress or art. I therefore planned a group, consisting of a well-known apostle of the beautiful, with a herd of eager worshippers surrounding him. (256–57)

An "exquisite," who lauded a correctly worn tie, Wilde's persona was apparently attractive to women. As Michèle Mendelssohn reminds us, "today Wilde's semi-seduction seems surprising because we think of him as a homosexual, and not—as the Victorians did—as a lover of women" (82). Frith implies Wilde is a phony art-flirter, the shadow rather than the substance, a ruse feigned to dupe gullible women. His real purpose was to get on in Society, to become rich and famous. In *A Woman of No Importance*, Lord Illingworth observes that to be outside Society was a tragedy. At the height of his notoriety, Wilde was welcomed into London's most fashionable drawing rooms. As the American writer Vincent O'Sullivan observed:

> In the upper reaches of English society, it was not the men, who mostly did not like him, who made his success, but the women. He was too far from the familiar type of the men. He did not shoot or hunt or play cards; he had wit and took the trouble to talk and be entertaining. (78)

Wilde satirized his own behavior.

As an alternative to the staid Royal Academy, the Grosvenor attracted an elite clientele, not just the moneyed but the cultured: "The glamour of fashion was over it, and the great help that Lady Lindsay was able to give by holding Sunday receptions there made it one of the most fashionable resorts of the London season" (Gere, 19). Wilde was able to rub shoulders with theatrical stars, Henry Irving, Ellen Terry and Mary Anderson, the so-called Professional Beauties, Lady Violet Lindsay and Mrs. Cornwallis West, who were famed for their "aristocratic loveliness," as well as the artistic establishment led by Frederic Leighton. This social mobility would enable Wilde, who graduated from Oxford in 1878, to move in rarefied circles. At this stage he was "the young dandy who sought to be somebody, rather than do something" (Ellmann 112). However, as winner of the Newdigate Prize (1878), Wilde aspired to be a poet; Edmund Yates, the editor of *The World*, initially supported Wilde, by publishing *Phèdre* and *Queen Henrietta Maria* (1879). His volume of *Poems* was published in June 1881.

Lodging with artist Frank Miles, first in Salisbury Street, off the Strand, and later at Keats House, Tite Street, Wilde hosted "beauty parties." In a letter to Harold Bolton, dated 1879, Wilde writes: "I was very sorry you did not come to tea as I could have introduced you to some very beautiful people Mrs Langtry and Lady Lonsdale and a lot of clever beings who were at tea with me" (Holland and Hart-Davis 86–87). Langtry's relationship with Wilde was reciprocal: both benefited from each other's notoriety. His antics attracted the *Punch* cartoonist George du Maurier's attention. This popular satirical magazine had already pilloried the Pre-Raphaelite artists; now it was the turn of the Aesthetes. Initially du Maurier set his sights on Oxford don Walter Pater (his "Conclusion" to *Studies in the History of the Renaissance* [1873] was taken as the aesthetic credo), the symbolist poet Algernon Charles Swinburne and the pugnacious Whistler. William Morris ushered in the fashion for tertiary colours, olive green, ochre and terracotta or russet, although even Lady Wilde admitted "'tints of decomposed asparagus and cucumber do not suit the long, pale English face'" (Mendelssohn, 55). Du Maurier's cartoon *Nincompoopiana–The Mutual*

Admiration Society (**Figure 1:** *Punch,* vol. 78, 14 Feb. 1880, p. 66), which introduced Maudle, a painter, and Jellaby Postlethwaite, a poet, who "puff" each other's work, appeared in February 1880. The *Nincompoopiana* series goes further than the earlier cartoons, openly suggesting dubious or even immoral behavior. They also seem more directly aimed at Wilde; Prigsby, a bogus art critic who leads the gullible astray, clearly references Wilde's long hair and mannerisms. Following the publication of *Poems,* Wilde was openly lampooned in Edward Linley Sambourne's cartoon *O.W. Oh, I feel just as happy as a bright Sunflower! Lays of Christy Minstrelsy:* "Aesthete of Aesthete! What's in a name? The poet is Wilde, But his poetry's tame" (**Figure 2**; *Punch,* vol. 80, 25 June 1881, p. 298).[2] With the publication of his poems Wilde had at last achieved celebrity. The sunflower frames Wilde's face like a lion's ruff; above all Wilde wanted to be one of society's lions. Du Maurier nicknamed those who courted the famous lion hunters. Alluding to the Greek myth of Clytie, the sunflower, an Aesthetic emblem since the 1860s, signalled "hopeless longing and unfulfilled desire." Wilde was now indelibly associated with the sunflower, alongside his talismanic lily. These associations would be mercilessly exploited by American satirists. Yet rather than derailing Aestheticism, the cartoons spawned a cult and gave the public readily identifiable stereotypes.

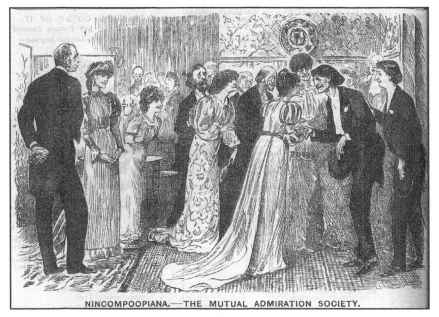

NINCOMPOOPIANA.—THE MUTUAL ADMIRATION SOCIETY.

Figure 1: George du Maurier,
Nincompoopiana—The Mutual Admiration Society; Punch,
Vol.78, February 14, 1880, 66.

" O. W."

" O, I feel just as happy as a bright Sunflower ! '
Lays of Christy Minstrelsy.

Æsthete of Æsthetes !
What's in a name ?
The poet is WILDE,
But his poetry's tame.

Figure 2: Edward Linley Sambourne, *O.W. Oh, I feel just as happy as a bright Sunflower! Lays of Christy Minstrelsy:* "Aesthete of Aesthetes! What's in a name? The poet is Wilde, But his poetry's tame"; *Punch*, Vol. 80, June 25, 1881, 298.

The "Mutual Admiration Society" acquired popular currency through Francis Burnand, the editor of *Punch*, who animated them on the stage in *The Colonel* (February 1881). By this time the public were familiar with dandies and their lovelorn acolytes, ensuring both the success of *The Colonel* and Gilbert and Sullivan's *Patience,* which opened shortly after in April 1881. *Patience* pitted two rival poets, Reginald Bunthorne and Archibald Grosvenor, for the affections of a chorus of "lovesick maidens"; many believed the effete Bunthorne was based on Wilde. These stage productions spawned popular music hall songs; *My Aesthetic Love* (1881, cover by Alfred Concanen, V&A) ridiculed aesthetic pretensions, especially their affected language: "She's utterly utterly consummate too too! And feeds on the lily and old china blue, And with a sunflower she will sit for an hour." The sunflower, the lily (purity), the peacock feather (eternal beauty) were aesthetic totems. Old Blue, Oriental blue and white porcelain, had acquired cult status through du Maurier's cartoon *The Six-Mark Teapot*, which was said to be based on Wilde's infamous claim "I find it harder and harder every day to live up to my blue china" (Ellmann 43):

THE SIX-MARK TEA-POT.

Æsthetic Bridegroom. "IT IS QUITE CONSUMMATE, IS IT NOT?"
Intense Bride. "IT IS, INDEED! OH, ALGERNON, LET US LIVE UP TO IT!"

Aesthetic Bridegroom: "It is quite consummate, is it not!"
Intense Bride: "It is, Indeed! Oh, Algernon, let us live up to it!"

Figure 3: The Six-Mark Teapot. *Punch*, vol 79, 30 Oct. 1880, p.194.

This in turn led to the so-called *Patience* or *Aesthetic* Teapot (1881, **Figure 4**), literally a limp-wristed and hand-on-hip caricature of Wilde and his coterie. Modeled by James Hadley for the Royal Worcester Company, one side features a long-haired effete artist, wearing sage green velvet, a floppy purple cap and sporting a sunflower, while on the other side a mournful maiden with a calla lily recalls Gilbert's "doleful train" of lovesick maidens. Inscribed "Fearful consequences through the laws of Natural Selection and Evolution of living up to one's teapot," the vessel took a swipe at Darwin's theories of evolution, as well as Wilde's famous aphorism. Rarefied and hype-sensitive aesthetes were apparently suffering from a surfeit of culture. Aesthetic men were hardly manly; perhaps they had evolved "too far," to the point of emasculation.

Figure 4: *Patience or Aesthetic Teapot,* James Hadley for the Royal Worcester Company; Art Institute of Chicago, 1881.

The Wildean type also circulated in fiction; Walter Besant and James Rice, *Monks of Thelema* (1878) gives us Paul Rondelet, a fellow of Lothian College, who writes "mystic and weird" poems, while Rhoda Broughton's Francis Chaloner in *Second Thoughts* (1880) is a "long pale poet" with a Botticelli head who holds a "lotus lily in one pale hand" (Broughton 135, 138). Maudle and Postlethwaite left the pages of *Punch* in May 1881; the joke was no longer funny, as Aestheticism had entered the mainstream. *Punch*, ever more hostile to aesthetic culture, now openly lampooned Wilde. Walter Hamilton attempted to defend aesthetic culture, publishing the movement's first history, *The Aesthetic Movement in England* (1882). For his part, Wilde believed he was the original of Maudle, while (A) Postlethwaite was a composite based on members of his aesthetic circle (Lewis and Smith 46). Leonée Ormond has convincingly argued that Wilde turned the tables and assumed aspects of du Maurier's characters to capitalise on the publicity generated by *The Colonel* and *Patience*. Small wonder Richard D'Oyly Carte chose Wilde to promote *Patience* in the United States. Fearing Americans were less familiar with aesthetic eccentricities, "Carte expected *Patience* to give a fillip to Wilde's lectures, and the lectures to give a fillip to *Patience*" (Ellmann 144). Burnand sarcastically observed: "From the constant mention of this well-known English entrepreneur's name and his entertainments, we are almost induced to believe that the gifted Aesthetic [Wilde] simply appears in America as a sort of peripatetic showman's advertisement for Mr Carte's numerous ventures" (*Punch*, vol. 82, 22 Apr. 1882, p. 192). The lecture tour was certainly a financial success; Wilde received a half-share of the profits of $11,210 (Ellmann 182).

Aestheticizing America

Wilde was 27 when he arrived in New York in January 1882. He was not the first to recognize the financial benefits of an American tour: Charles Dickens went before him in 1842. But he would also have been aware that Dickens found the "Americans were simply not English enough" (Meckier). What became known as his "Quarrel with America," Dickens resented how many tried to make money out of his fame; an enterprising barber claimed to be selling locks of his hair. Wilde was similarly exploited; the characters from *Patience* were used to sell everything from tea to cigars (**Figure 5:** Hegan Brothers Wallpapers, Louisville, c. 1882). The famous photographs of Wilde taken in New York by Napoleon Sarony on the eve of his tour were pirated for trade cards[3]; his face promoted "Neilson's Secret Mm Marie Fontaine Freckle Cure." Some of the images are not very kind; a trade card for "Mitchell's Prodigious Pharmacy" lampoons his stage attire, as well as his lust for money. Wilde's outrageous clothes and worship of the sunflower (now with a dollar sign on its face) was simply a money-making ploy; notoriety at any cost was better than invisibility. "Clark's O.N.T. Spool Cotton—the best thread for hand and machine sewing," has Oscar performing besides Jumbo the Elephant, billed as "the largest known animal in creation." Formerly a resident of London Zoo, Jumbo arrived in the United States in 1882, courtesy of another empresario, Phineas T. Barnum. As the star attraction of the Barnum and Bailey Circus, Jumbo, like Wilde, travelled the length and breadth of America. Mr Punch observed, "Mr Barnum having got Jumbo has refused D'Oyly Carte's offer of his Aesthetic Two-Twoness Oscar . . . Hail, Prince Barnum of Moneygo!" (*Punch*, 1882, vol. 81, p. 192). Jumbo's life came to a dramatic end being hit and killed by a train in 1885. The greatest show had to go on, so Jumbo was stuffed; "If I can't have Jumbo living, I'll have Jumbo dead, and Jumbo dead is worth a small herd of ordinary elephants," Barnum told the *New York Times*.

People are g ing " Wilde,"
(not)scar)
over our Æsthetic designs in
WALL PAPERS.

HEGAN BROS.,
348 Fourth Avenue,
LOUISVILLE, KY.

"Conceive me, if you can,
A matter-of-fact young man,
An alphabetical, arithmetical,
Every-day young man!"
PATIENCE.

Figure 5: Trade card 'Hegan Brothers Wallpapers, Louisville' based on a character from *Patience*, c.1882.

The most vicious attacks came from the cartoonist Thomas Nast, from whom it is said we get the term "nasty." Nast redrew du Maurier's cartoon *A Love Agony. Design by Maudle* (**Figure 6**; *Punch*, vol. 78, 5 June 1880, p. 254) with Wilde as a modern Narcissus, the voice of Echo ringing from the hills "He is an Aesthetic sham". [4] The sunflower clenched in his hand is inscribed Notoriety; in the reflection the sunflower bears a dollar sign, while Wilde's silhouette resembles a lion; "Mr O'Wilde you are not the first one that has grasped at a shadow" (c. 1882, British Library; **Figure 7**) Nast was not fond of the Irish. Several of the cartoons are racist; a foreign interloper, Wilde was an Irishman posing as an English gentleman. The six cards drawn by E. B. Duval offer us "National Aesthetics" depicting the aesthete as Irish ("Begorra and I belave I am Oscar himself"), Chinese, French, German, black and finally, as a white American who will sell anything. Confused by his "soft effeminate flesh," "graceful form" and "certain womanly air," newspaper critics even posed the question *Could he be a "she"?* (Mendelssohn 150). Interior decorating was hardly a manly pursuit.

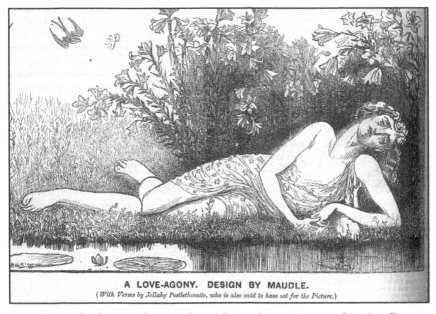

A LOVE-AGONY. DESIGN BY MAUDLE.
(*With Verses by Jellaby Postlethwaite, who is also said to have sat for the Picture.*)

Figure 6: George du Maurier, *A Love Agony: Design by Maudle*; *Punch*, Vol. 78, June 5, 1880, 254..

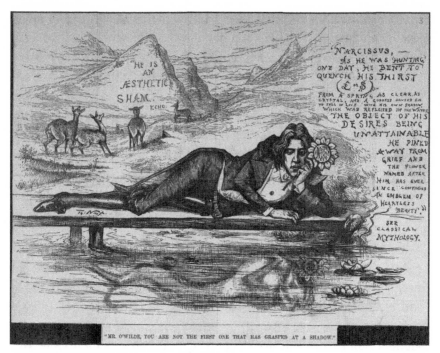

Figure 7: Thomas Nast, *Mr. O'Wilde, You Are Not the First One That Has Grasped at a Shadow*; British Library; c.1882

    Disliking the expression "Aesthetic Movement," Wilde began his tour with "The English Renaissance of Art," first given in New York on January 9, 1882. Wilde abandoned this lecture as it proved unpopular. Wilde was quick to switch his allegiance from the "inaccessible" higher arts to the popularist cause of home decorating. Kevin O' Brien considers Wilde picked an unpromising subject; but, in fact, this was far from the case (42). By the early 1880s taste had become a contentious issue. Interior decorating had been elevated to an art form. It was now considered equal to painting as a means of self-expression; arranging a room was likened to painting a composition or orchestrating a symphony. Objects, now strokes of color or musical notes, were valued for their tint and form; however, "a single false colour or false note destroys the whole" (Wilde, 915). The watch word was harmony, as *objet d'art*, a blue and white vase, piece of Venetian glass or a delicate embroidery, were to be arranged

          Critical Insights

to form a pleasing whole. No style or period was singled out; the antique could be blended with the modern, as taste was a matter of personal preferences. Above all a room was to be unique, reflecting the individuality and personality of the homeowner.

Lacking expertise, the wealthy could turn to an interior decorator, a profession that was just emerging. Many relied on the numerous domestic advice manuals that suddenly mushroomed; an expert on dress and interior décor, Mrs. Haweis declared "most people are now alive to the importance of beauty as a refining influence. The appetite for artistic instruction is even ravenous" (2). For his *House Beautiful* lecture Wilde requested copies of the Rev. William J. Loftie's *A Plea for Art in the Home* (1877) and Mrs. Haweis's *Art of Dress* (1879) from Colonel Morse, manager of the lecture tour.[5] O'Brien gives examples of Wilde's borrowings from Ruskin's *The Two Paths* (1859) and Morris's *Hopes and Fears for Art*, a lecture series given from 1878 to 1881, published in 1882 (150). He came close to plagiarizing Morris: "Have nothing in your house that is not useful or beautiful" (914). Wilde's lack of originality was noted at the time. Ambrose Bierce, whose stinging denunciation came in *The Wasp* (April 1882) declared "In Mr Wilde's lectures there is nothing to criticise, for there is nothing of his own."

The title of Wilde's lecture was apparently purloined from Clarence Cook's highly influential *House Beautiful: Essays on Beds and Tables, Stools and Candlestick6s* (Walter Crane, *frontis*, 1878; **Figure 8**). Cook, the rather caustic art critic of the *New York Tribune*, dedicated his book to his wife: "To Her whose happy union of head, hands and heart, has made one house beautiful through many chequered years." In the same league as Charles Locke Eastlake's influential *Hints on Household Taste* (1868), Cook's Anglo-Japanese aesthetic was more appealing to Wilde than Eastlake's neo-Gothic style. Wilde established his aesthetic credentials by roundly stating, "French furniture, gilt and gaudy, is very vulgar, monstrous and unserviceable" (919). Although he stressed "every home should wear an individual air in all its furnishings and decoration" and "should express the feelings of those who live in it," Wilde laid down certain broad principles (914). These broad principles were more like rules. The entrance hall should not be papered, as it was too close to the elements; wooden panelling was better. As regards floors, don't carpet at all. Secondary colours should be used on walls and ceilings. Large gas chandeliers should be replaced by side brackets with delicate shades to avoid glaring light. Ugly cast-iron heating stoves must give way to "the healthy, old-English open fireplace" (920). His grandson Merlin Holland likens Wilde's advice to a "Conran manifesto from the 1970s, advocating plain rather than heavy cut glass, the simple beauty of natural wood and if you cannot afford the finest and most expensive in Persian rugs, put down elegant rush matting . . . the message of beauty and simplicity" (20).

Figure 8: Walter Crane, *frontis*, Clarence Cook, *House Beautiful; Essays on Beds and Tables, Stools3 and Candlestick*; 1878.1878.

Back Home: Tite Street

Having done his part to civilize America, Wilde returned to England in January 1883. He attempted to launch his career as a playwright, staging *Vera*, his first play, in New York. It was initially well received by the audience, but the critics were lukewarm; the play closed a week after it had opened. The following years were given over to touring Britain offering audiences his *Personal Impressions of America, The Value of Art in Modern Life*, and *Dress*. The varnish and paint manufacturer Theodor Mander heard Wilde speak in Wolverhampton in 1884; three years later he began to build his own House Beautiful, Whitwick Manor, one of the finest surviving aesthetic houses. Engaged to Constance Lloyd in 1884, Wilde at last got the chance to create his own House Beautiful; fortuitously Constance was given £5000 in advance of her inheritance to lease and furnish a house. Wilde had pontificated for so long on the subject, he was expected to practice what he preached. As Whistler pointed out: "You have been lecturing to us about the House Beautiful; now is your chance to show us one" (Ellmann 234). Wilde turned to E.W. Godwin, Whistler's architect, "the greatest aesthete of them all"! A modest terraced house, No. 16, Tite Street, Chelsea, was duly renovated in seven months at considerable expense (**Figure 9**). Sadly, no images are known of the interiors Godwin created, although a full description survives (Hyde 1951). Godwin favored using tones of a single color when decorating a room; for Wilde he chose white. Wilde described the chairs for the dining room as "sonnets in ivory" and the table "as a masterpiece in pearl." Godwin's instructions were precise: "the whole of the woodwork to be painted enamel white and the walls pt [sic] in oils enamel white and grey to the height of 5ft 6 ins. The rest of the walls and ceiling to be finished in lime white with a slight addition of black to give a white greyish tone'" (Aslin 19). The dining room was "a study in lightness, delicacy and simplicity" (Hayes 47). Describing his own drawing room in terms of music, Godwin sought "tenderness" while "the ultra-refinement of the delicate tones of colour" were to form the background to a few "but unquestionable gems in the exquisitely sensitive room": "I say *sensitive* for a room has a character that may influence for good or bad the many who enter it, especially the very young" (Aslin 19). Judging from the raising of his own children, whose nursery walls were lined with Japanese prints and fans, Godwin was raising the next generation of aesthetes; Wilde's children would grow up in exceptionally artistic surroundings.

Figure 9: No. 16 Tite Street, Chelsea, Wilde home from c.1884 to 1895; Anne Anderson, 2018.

While Tite Street lay at the heart of bohemian Chelsea, many of Wilde's neighbors were from the highest echelons of Society. Following bankruptcy and loss of his precious White House, Whistler returned to Tite Street in 1881, residing in the ground floor apartment of a studio block (No. 33). Perhaps unable to stomach the reappearance of Wilde on his doorstep, by 1885 Whistler was living with his mistress Maud Franklin in The Vale, Chelsea. His place was taken in the Tite Street flat by John Singer Sargent, the most fashionable and highest paid portrait painter of the day. Other notable artists resided on Tite Street: Archibald Stuart Wortley, the Hon. John Collier, and Anna Lee Merritt. Along the Chelsea Embankment one could find the barrister Wickham Flower, who lived in the beautiful Swan House decorated by Morris & Co., Lord Monkswell, father of Hon. John Collier, the Marquis of Ripon and Ralph, and Lord Wentworth, Byron's grandson. Wilde had achieved his goal; paraphrasing Lord Illingworth, he had fitted himself to the "best society."

Notes

1. The Lindsays invested £150,000 of their own money, building a splendid gallery on New Bond Street, the smartest part of London.

2. Mendelssohn has shown that *Punch* put the words to *The Big Sunflower*, a time-honored minstrel song, in Wilde's mouth (285).

3. One of Sarony's portraits of Wilde (No.18,1882) became the subject of a U.S. Supreme Court case, *Burrow-Giles Lithographic Co. v. Sarony* 111 U.S. 53 (1884), in which the Court upheld the extension of copyright protection to photographs.

4 *Harper's Weekly* pirated du Maurier's cartoons.

5. "The House Beautiful" was apparently composed in Chicago and first given on March 11, when it was entitled "Interior and Exterior House Decoration." Looking for a more eye-catching by-line, the title may have been coined by the press.

Works Cited

Broughton, Rhoda, *Second Thoughts*. New York: Frank F. Lovell, 1880.

Gere, Charlotte. "The Art of Dress, Victorian Artists and the Aesthetic Style," *Simply Stunning: The Pre-Raphaelite Art of Dressing*, exhibition catalogue. Cheltenham: Cheltenham Art Gallery, 1996. pp.13–24.

Haweis, H.R. (Mary Eliza). *The Art of Decoration*. London: Chatto & Windus, 1881.

Hayes, Richard. "At Home, 16 Tite Street," Anne Massey and Penny Sparke (eds.) London and New York: Routledge, 2013. pp. 37–51.

Holland, Merlin. "From Madonna Lily to Green Carnation," *The Wilde Years: Oscar Wilde and the Art of His Time*, exhibition catalogue, edited by Tomoko Sato, and Lionel Lambourne. London: Barbican Centre, 2000. pp.10–27.

Holland, Merlin, and Rupert Hart-Davis, editors. *The Complete Letters of Oscar Wilde*. London: Fourth Estate, 2000.

Hyde, H. Montgomery. *"Oscar Wilde and His Architect." The Architectural Review*, 109, Mar. 1951. p.175.

Lewis, Lloyd, and Henry Justin Smith. *Oscar Wilde Discovers America* (1882). New York: Benjamin Blom, 1967.

Meckier, Jerome. *Dickens: An Innocent Abroad Charles Dicken's American Engagements*. Lexington: U P of Kentucky, 2014.

Mendelssohn, Michèle. *Making Oscar Wilde*. Oxford: Oxford U P, 2018.

O'Brien, Kevin. *Oscar Wilde in Canada: An Apostle for the Arts*. Toronto: Personal Library.

O' Sullivan, Vincent. *Aspects of Wilde*. London: Constable & Co., 1936.

Wilde, Oscar, "House Beautiful," *Collins Complete Works of Oscar Wilde Centenary Edition*, Glasgow: Harper Collins, 1999, pp. 913–25.

Oscar Wilde and George Bernard Shaw_____

Colin Cavendish-Jones

Ireland's two greatest playwrights, her most celebrated wits, perhaps her most recognizable and charismatic figures in any field of endeavor, were born within two years and two miles of each other in mid nineteenth-century Dublin. Both were members of the Anglo-Irish Protestant Ascendancy, and both made their homes and careers in England, where they moved in the highest social and literary circles, which fêted but never entirely accepted them: they were in society but not of it.

Oscar Wilde was born on October 16, 1854, at 21 Westland Row, which runs along the east side of Trinity College, Dublin. This was a solidly middle-class dwelling, but the following year the family moved to 1 Merrion Square, one of the grandest addresses in Dublin. The young Wilde grew up surrounded by aristocrats, politicians, and some of the most eminent professional men in Ireland, of whom his father, William, an ophthalmic surgeon and Oculist in Ordinary to Queen Victoria who founded and ran his own hospital, was one. His mother Jane, who had a great influence on Wilde's writing, was a poet, historian, folklorist and polemicist who wrote under the romantic pseudonym of Speranza and (quite erroneously) claimed descent from Dante.

In January 1864, William Wilde was knighted. Sir William and Lady Wilde sent their nine-year-old son away to board at Portora Royal School, one of Ireland's oldest and most distinguished public schools, established by King James I in 1608. From Portora, Wilde won a Royal Scholarship to read Classics at Trinity College, Dublin, where he proved an outstanding student, coming first in his class and winning the Berkeley Gold Medal, the University's highest award in Greek. In 1874, he went on to Magdalen College, Oxford, where he achieved a double first and won the prestigious Newdigate Prize for poetry.

George Bernard Shaw had a rather less auspicious start in life. He was born at 3 Upper Synge Street, in Portobello, a modest house in a lower-middle-class district of Dublin, on July 26, 1856. The Shaws, like the Wildes, were part of the Protestant Ascendancy, the dominant elite of landowners and professionals, but George Carr Shaw, Bernard Shaw's father, was one of its least successful members. He was pensioned off from the civil service before Bernard Shaw was born and quickly descended into a squalid existence of penury and alcoholism, from which his family and friends periodically attempted to rescue him.

The young George Bernard Shaw hated school and, unlike Wilde, received little formal education, although he later became an impressive autodidact. In 1871, at the age of 15, he left school and became a clerk in a firm of land agents where he worked hard for over four years and rose to become head cashier. In 1876, when Wilde was halfway through his career at Oxford, Shaw moved to London, where he spent the next few years educating himself in the British Museum Reading Room and struggling unsuccessfully to become a writer.

Wilde and Shaw are both best known as dramatists, but success in this field did not come quickly or easily for either of them. Wilde's first play, *Vera, or the Nihilists*, a melodramatic piece about Russian revolutionaries plotting to kill the Tsar, failed to find a producer in London[1] and later closed after a week in New York. His second, *The Duchess of Padua*, a blank-verse love tragedy heavily indebted to Victor Hugo, remained unperformed for eight years after he wrote it, then ran for only three weeks, again in New York. It was not performed in England until after his death.

Shaw's first play, *Widowers' Houses*, was staged only twice, in December 1892, and his next two, *The Philanderer* and *Mrs. Warren's Profession*, both written in 1893, had to wait until the twentieth century for stage productions. These three were later collected as *Plays Unpleasant*, the title signifying that they were written to vex or at least challenge rather than to entertain the audience, and were followed by the three more congenial *Plays Pleasant*: *Arms and the Man*, *Candida,* and *You Never Can Tell*. The first of these, *Arms and the Man,* produced in April 1894 at the Royal Avenue Theatre, was Shaw's first financial and popular success, although it was poorly received by the critics, who found its tone too cynical. It ran for three months in London, followed by a tour of the provinces and a production in New York, and earned enough money for Shaw to give up his job as a music critic.

Arms and the Man is a satirical comedy, deriding the conventions of war, love, and social class. In this sense, though Shaw labelled it a "pleasant" play, it is not markedly different from his "unpleasant" plays, which are also principally concerned with social ills and human failings. The characteristic Shavian drama is a problem play, and it is no coincidence that Shaw spent as much time and effort on his expository prefaces as he did on the plays that followed them. One standard edition of Shaw's dramatic works has two volumes: one containing the plays and the other the prefaces. They are of approximately equal length.

Oscar Wilde's first dramatic successes slightly preceded Shaw's. After his Biblical drama, *Salomé,* written in French and not performed either in English or in England until after his death, he wrote and produced a trio of social comedies: *Lady Windermere's Fan, A Woman of No Importance,* and *An Ideal Husband.* These were brilliantly successful, staged at London's leading theatres, the St. James's and the Haymarket, and extremely lucrative, each earning thousands of pounds to support Wilde's increasingly lavish lifestyle. These three social comedies are the most Shavian works Wilde ever wrote. In sending Shaw a copy of *Lady Windermere's Fan,* Wilde described it as "Op. 1 of the Hibernian School," going on to label Shaw's *Widowers' Houses* as Op. 2 and his own *A Woman of No Importance* as Op. 3. As Stanley Weintraub points out, this creation of a "Hibernian School" out of the works of two playwrights was partly a reference to the fact that Wilde and Shaw were the first Irish dramatists in decades to make an impact on the London stage (25) but it also highlights certain significant similarities of theme and treatment.

Wilde's social comedies are set in a rarefied social atmosphere, among lords and ladies in gilded Mayfair mansions or on the country estates of the aristocracy. Nonetheless, they begin as "problem plays" in the tradition of Shaw and Ibsen, concerned with social questions of injustice and inequality; and Wilde, like Shaw, uses certain characters to articulate his concerns. In *A Woman of No Importance*, the most damning criticism of fashionable English society comes from the puritanical American Hester Worsley. Her animadversions can sound rather strident, even hysterical, compared with the sophisticated wit of the other characters:

> Oh, your English society seems to me shallow, selfish, foolish. It has blinded its eyes and stopped its ears. It lies like a leper in purple. It sits like a dead thing smeared with gold. (Wilde CW 483)[2]

Yet Hester's criticisms are versions of the same points made by Lord Illingworth, the witty, detached dandy who criticizes polite society from within, or even the social critiques of Wilde himself in *The Soul of Man Under Socialism*, a long essay he had published in 1891, two years earlier. When Hester tells Lady Hunstanton: "If you throw bread to the poor, it is merely to keep them quiet for a season" (Wilde CW 483), she echoes Wilde in *The Soul of Man*, complaining that upper-class philanthropists "try to solve the problem of poverty . . . by keeping the poor alive; or, in the case of a very advanced school, by amusing the poor" (Wilde CW 1174), as well as Lord Illingworth, who has already told a pompous Member of Parliament that the East End of London "is the problem of slavery. And we are trying to solve it by amusing the slaves" (Wilde CW 471). While Hester's style of speaking puts her at odds with other characters in the play, the orientalizing acrolect of the "leper in purple" is one quite frequently employed by Wilde in other works. *Salomé* is written in this style (in French, admittedly, but the English version we now have of *Salomé*, while still attributed to Lord Alfred Douglas, is principally Wilde's own work). So are Wilde's two volumes of fairy tales, *The Happy Prince* and *A House of Pomegranates*, as well as certain sections of *The Picture of Dorian Gray*. Wilde never entirely abandoned this way of writing, and one can hear it still in the more high-flown passages of *De Profundis*.

Wilde told Herbert Beerbohm Tree, the actor who played Lord Illingworth in *A Woman of No Importance* that: "This witty aristocrat whom you wish to assume in my play is quite unlike anyone who has been seen on the stage before. He is like no one who has existed before. . . . He is a figure of art. Indeed, if you can bear the truth, he is MYSELF" (qtd. in Ellmann 380). There is no doubt that Lord Illingworth is one of a line of brilliant dandies who appear in Wilde's works looking and sounding like the author and expressing his views. Prince Paul Maraloffski in *Vera*, the Duke in *The Duchess of Padua*, Lord Henry Wotton in *The Picture of Dorian Gray*, Lord Darlington in *Lady Windermere's Fan*, Lord Goring in *An Ideal Husband* all seem to be similar alter egos for Wilde himself. Yet it is Hester and Mrs. Arbuthnot who appear in a position of moral authority at the end of *A Woman of No Importance*, while Lord Illingworth, in an ironic inversion of the play's title, is dismissed as a trivial and irrelevant man.

Bernard Shaw's dramas clearly contain a series of dominant characters paralleling Wilde's dandies, though they began to appear only after Wilde's career as a dramatist was already over. The first of them is arguably Julius Caesar in Shaw's 1898 play, *Caesar and Cleopatra*, although there are similar elements present in some earlier characters, such as General Burgoyne in *The Devil's Disciple* and the eponymous heroine of *Candida*. The same characteristics and ideas later appear in various Shavian heroes, such as the arms manufacturer Andrew Undershaft in *Major Barbara*, Professor Higgins in *Pygmalion* and, most obviously, Jack Tanner in *Man and Superman*. These characters are all paragons of willpower and intellect, contemptuous of social *mores* and moral codes, bending the other characters in the play to their inexorable will. In Act II of *Pygmalion*, Professor Higgins decides to satisfy his intellectual curiosity and demonstrate his brilliance by passing off Eliza, the flower seller, as a Duchess. He is met with a chorus of protest. His friend Colonel Pickering and his housekeeper Mrs. Pearce both implore him to "be reasonable." Mrs. Pearce protests that "you can't take a girl up like that as if you were picking up a pebble on a beach" (Shaw 724). Yet in the end, Higgins does just as he chooses, and everyone else does as he chooses too, for he is a force of nature. Exactly the same applies to Caesar, Undershaft, Tanner and the other Shavian Supermen.

Man and Superman is of special significance in discussing this phenomenon because the title refers directly to Friedrich Nietzsche's concept of the Übermensch, a notoriously difficult word to translate, but one which has often been rendered into English as "Superman." The Übermensch first appears in Nietzsche's 1883 work *Also sprach Zarathustra,* in which he is described as a great goal for humanity, a higher type of man who will be as far beyond us as we are beyond the apes, transcending the pettiness of commonplace people:

> Overcome for me, you higher men, the little virtues, the little prudences, the sand-grain sized considerations, the detritus of swarming ants, the pitiful contentedness, the "happiness of the greatest number"! (Nietzsche Zarathustra 233)

Nietzsche's Übermensch is superior in strength, courage and intellect to the men who preceded and surround him. However, Nietzsche explicitly rejects the notion of moral superiority, since he regards the Christian idea of goodness we have inherited as false and worthless, a euphemism for weakness.

The influence of Nietzsche on Shaw is a complex matter, and Shaw himself changed his mind several times over the course of a long career about what the German philosopher meant to him. In the preface to *Man and Superman,* he gives a list of kindred spirits, whose thinking he regards as broadly similar to his own: "Goethe, Shelley, Schopenhauer, Wagner, Ibsen, Morris, Tolstoy and Nietzsche." It seems almost an act of perversity to place Nietzsche's name last here, particularly as the list contains several names that few have thought to associate with Shaw, beginning with the Shakespeare-worshipping Romantics, Goethe and Shelley.[3]

The question of Nietzsche and Wilde is ostensibly much simpler, for there is no evidence that Wilde ever heard so much as Nietzsche's name, much less read his books. Wilde could not read German and Nietzsche's works did not begin to appear in English until 1895, the year of Wilde's imprisonment. However, several of

Wilde's contemporaries, including Bernard Shaw, noticed distinct similarities between the attitudes and aphorisms of the German philosopher and the Irish playwright. Max Nordau, a German physician and cultural critic, compared them and their writings in his popular study of European degeneracy, *Entartung* (1892), though he also notes that neither man could have heard of the other and concludes:

> The similarity, or rather identity, is not explained by plagiarism; it is explained by the identity of mental qualities in Nietzsche and the other ego-maniacal degenerates. (Nordau 444)[4]

The direct influence of Nietzsche on Shaw, and the lack of it on Wilde, goes some way towards explaining the differences in structure and tone between the two halves of the Hibernian School. Wilde's plays were initially structured as conventional melodramas. They ended either tragically, like *Vera* and the *Duchess of Padua*, or, in the case of the social comedies, with vice exposed and virtue rewarded. In both *Lady Windermere's Fan* and *A Woman of No Importance,* there is an unresolved tension caused by the fact that the most perceptive and thoughtful character in the play, who acts as Wilde's surrogate and spokesman, is not on the side of virtue. In Nietzschean terms, the characterization is beyond good and evil, while the plot is not. It is only in *An Ideal Husband* that Wilde decides to place his own mouthpiece, Lord Goring, on the side of the angels.

Modesty is not a quality often associated with Wilde, but it does suggest a complete lack of self-righteousness or spiritual pride that it took most of his dramatic career for him to realize that the spokesman for his own views and values in the play need not necessarily be a villain, no matter how many dramatic or philosophical compromises this entailed. Lord Goring is introduced in just the same terms as Wilde's other dandies. His father, Lord Caversham, and Sir Robert agree that he is idle, sybaritic and obsessed with appearances. Yet as Wilde's stage directions warn, "He is fond of being misunderstood. It gives him a point of vantage" (Wilde CW 521). In terms of his conduct, and even his advice to his friends, the Chilterns, Lord Goring is unimpeachably moral. He tells Sir Robert that "no man should have a secret from his own wife" (Wilde CW 535). He condemns the corrupt financier Baron Arnheim as a "damned scoundrel," opposing the seductive "philosophy of power" and "gospel of gold" that Sir Robert has learned from him (Wilde CW 537). His offer of help to Lady Chiltern echoes that of Lord Darlington to Lady Windermere, but whereas Lord Darlington is in love and wants to separate the lady from her husband, Lord Goring does everything he can to repair the Chilterns' marriage and protect their honor, even putting his own romance with Mabel Chiltern in jeopardy to do so. Even Lady Chiltern is surprised by his sincerity:

> LORD GORING: All I do know is that life cannot be understood without much charity, cannot be lived without much charity. It is love, and not German philosophy, that is the true explanation of this world, whatever may be the explanation of the next. And if you are ever in trouble, Lady Chiltern, trust me absolutely, and I will help you in every way I can. If you ever want me, come to me for my assistance, and you shall have it. Come at once to me.
> LADY CHILTERN (*looking at him in surprise*): Lord Goring, you are talking quite seriously. I don't think I ever heard you talk seriously before. (Wilde CW 543)

Anne Varty detects in this speech an echo of Wilde's favorite moral philosopher and anarchic individualist, who was such a central figure in his work from "The Selfish Giant" to *De Profundis*.

> Lord Goring's . . . speech drops the dandy's mask, in order to reveal a Christ figure beneath. "Love your neighbour like yourself"; "Come unto me those who are weary and heavy laden and I will give you rest" are the *dicta* of the Gospels which he puts into action. (Varty 187)

Varty is right to hear echoes of Christ in Lord Goring, but this does not mean that his dandyism is merely a mask or a pose. At this point in his career, Wilde was developing his ideas about aesthetics and ethics to come up with a philosophy more nuanced than the anti-ethical ideas of Shaw and Nietzsche. There is clearly a difference between seeing the flaws in the conventional morality of one's time and proclaiming, as Nietzsche does that "there are absolutely no moral facts" (Nietzsche Anti-Christ 183). Nietzsche and Shaw are both inclined to neglect the very idea of morality as slavish hypocrisy and cant. Their Supermen are intellectually and aesthetically superior to ordinary people, but have no moral dimension.

Wilde's view is more complex and is best articulated by Gilbert in his Socratic dialogue "The Critic as Artist":

> Aesthetics are higher than Ethics. They belong to a more spiritual sphere. . . . Aesthetics, in fact, are to Ethics in the sphere of conscious civilisation, what, in the sphere of the external world, sexual is to natural selection. Ethics, like natural selection, make existence possible. Aesthetics, like sexual selection, make life lovely and wonderful, fill it with new forms, and give it progress, and variety and change. (Wilde CW 1145)

The first sentence of this passage is sometimes quoted out of context (as John Carey does in *The Intellectuals and the Masses*) to suggest that Wilde does not care about ethics. Wilde's Darwinian analogy, however, makes it clear that he regards ethics as vital. Aesthetics are higher than ethics because they are more comprehensive, applying to everything in the universe. Ethics descend from aesthetics: one might say that they are a branch of aesthetics, a specifically human form of beauty. Where Nietzsche and Shaw place aesthetics and ethics in opposition to one another, Wilde places them in relation.

The first of Wilde's dandies, Prince Paul Maraloffski in *Vera*, is as anti-ethical as any Shavian Superman. His successors become increasingly benign until Lord Goring appears as the Messiah in faultless evening dress. Wilde thus shows a clear philosophical progress in which he develops a subtler philosophy than Nietzsche without having heard of Nietzsche and transcends the Shavian Superman before Shaw had even thought of such a being. How far Wilde came from the melodrama and the problem play is evident from his final perfect work of drama and Shaw's curiously obtuse reaction to it.

The Importance of Being Earnest has always tended to exhaust the superlatives of its critics. It has all the qualities of a soap bubble: light, iridescent, glittering, glassy, ungraspable. W. H. Auden (often a perceptive critic of Wilde) called it "perhaps the only pure verbal opera in English" (Auden 322) and the contemporary reviewer William Archer also seized upon the analogy of music, calling the play "a sort of *rondo capriccioso*, in which the artist's fingers run with crisp irresponsibility up and down the keyboard of life" (Archer 56).

Almost the only critic who remained entirely unimpressed by Wilde's final play was George Bernard Shaw. In a contemporary review he insisted that *Earnest* was a revamped piece of juvenilia dating from the 1870s (at which time Wilde had not, in point of fact, written any plays, or anything at all apart from some undergraduate essays and a handful of poems) and concluded:

> On the whole I must decline to accept *The Importance of Being Earnest* as a day less than ten years old; and I am altogether unable to perceive any uncommon excellence in its presentations. (qtd. in Beckson 222)

Later, in a letter to Frank Harris, Shaw called the play "essentially hateful" and said that "Clever as it was, it was his first really heartless play" (Harris 333). These comments not only tell us far more about Shaw than they do about Wilde, but serve to illustrate, perhaps better than any of the homages he received from sympathetic critics, the completeness of Wilde's success.

Shaw understood and praised such plays as *A Woman of No Importance* because they were, at least in terms of structure and incident, problem plays in the Ibsenite, Shavian tradition. *The Importance of Being Earnest* is an attempt to create a perfect world, in which the only possible problems are not only ludicrous, but so eminently soluble that they disappear as soon as they arise, like soap bubbles blown into the air. The heartlessness to which Shaw objects is a symptom of this perfection. The characters in *The Importance of Being Earnest* are not actually cruel. When Jack believes that Miss Prism is his mother, and a fallen woman, he offers instant forgiveness, in sharp contrast to the puritanical Lady Windermere and Hester Worsley:

> Unmarried! I do not deny that is a serious blow. But after all, who has the right to cast a stone against one who has suffered? Cannot repentance wipe out an act of folly? Why should there be one law for men, and another for women? Mother, I forgive you. (Wilde CW 415)

What would undoubtedly have been a serious problem in one of Wilde's earlier plays, or in any play by Shaw, is resolved immediately, then turns out not to have been a problem in the first place. Whereas Gerald Arbuthnot in *A Woman of No Importance* suffered a real disadvantage from his father's abandonment of him (becoming a bank clerk in a third-rate provincial town instead of enjoying an effortless passage through Eton and Oxford into fashionable society and independence), Jack Worthing was no sooner lost by his nursemaid than discovered and adopted by a wealthy and charitable old gentleman, who bestowed on him approximately the same social advantages he would have enjoyed with his mother and father. The sad virtues, pity, compassion, charity, stoicism, are not necessary in a perfect world. That is why Shaw thought the play heartless, because he was always striving towards a Socialist Utopia. It never occurred to him, as it did to Wilde, simply to behave as if he had already found it. Wilde's final play is the perfection of his adjuration in *The Soul of Man Under Socialism*, to behave and write as though the Beloved Republic were already in being.

Shaw lived more than twice as long as Wilde and was a vastly more prolific writer. He died in 1950, perhaps the most famous playwright in the world, an Academy Award winner and a Nobel Laureate who would certainly have been even more loaded with honors if he had not steadfastly refused to accept any recognition from the British crown. His success and renown are a direct contrast with the circumstances of Wilde's death, half a century earlier, in exile and disgrace in a dingy Paris hotel room for which he was unable to pay the bill, which was not settled until two years after he died.

For much of the twentieth century, Wilde's name was a byword for sin and depravity. He was denounced from pulpits and a scarlet pamphlet of pornographic photographs entitled *The Sins of Oscar Wilde*, ambitiously priced at $20, enjoyed a wide circulation on college campuses. Only recently, following the Gay Rights Movement and the decriminalization of homosexuality, has Wilde come to be regarded as a figure of moral authority, a philosopher, even a prophet and a sage. Both Wilde and Shaw now enjoy this status among a considerable number of acolytes and admirers; but I would argue that Wilde, despite his drastically shorter lifespan and lower output, has more to teach us about art and morals. Shaw, for all his genius, does not develop. Professor Higgins is no more than Caesar in a frock coat. He went on writing the same play, making the same points, for decade after decade; superbly eloquent, magnificently cutting, a great intellect and a fine wit, but learning nothing.

Wilde, in sharp contrast, is constantly developing and refining his ideas. Even the social comedies, which superficially seem similar, display a remarkable development in treatment and theme over the course of a few years. The idea of a morality derived from beauty, an aesthetic basis for ethics is perhaps the subtlest and most satisfactory of all the ideas the Victorians found to replace conventional religion. In his first play, Wilde wrote that "in good democracy, every man should be an aristocrat" (Wilde CW 699). By the end of his career, he was very much more ambitious for his readers. He wants us not only aristocrats, but philosophers, aesthetes, and artists. As long as we continue to have such ambitions for ourselves, to consider, appreciate and create beauty, Wilde will be a crucial figure for us, and his works an indispensable guide.

Notes

1. Wilde's timing was unfortunate. On March 1, 1881, just as Wilde had finished writing *Vera*, Tsar Alexander II was assassinated by a group of Nihilist revolutionaries. While undeniably topical, the play was deemed too politically sensitive to be staged that year.

2. Richard Ellmann suggests that these lines were the cause of the booing at the end of the first performance (Ellmann 381). If this was the case, the audience probably regarded Hester, to some extent, functioning as the author's mouthpiece in her criticism of English society.

3. Shaw disliked Shakespeare and particularly loathed the cult of "Bardolatry" or Shakespeare-worship, even going so far as to write a short puppet play, *Shakes versus Shav*, in which he argues his own claims to be regarded as the superior dramatist.

4. Wilde actually refers to Nordau's book in a petitionary letter he wrote to the Home Secretary from Reading Gaol on July 2, 1896, referring to "the intimate connection between madness and the literary and artistic temperament" and continuing: "Professor Nordau in his book *Dégénérescence* published in 1894 having devoted an entire chapter to the petitioner as a specially typical example of this fatal law" (Wilde CL 656). Wilde is mistaken both in saying that an entire chapter is dedicated to him, and in the thrust of Nordau's argument. In the light of this, and the obvious uncongeniality of the book to Wilde, it seems quite probable that he merely glanced at it, heard about it, or read a review in which his own name was mentioned. Bernard Shaw certainly did read Nordau's book and wrote a brilliant polemic in response: *The Sanity of Art* (1895).

Works Cited

Archer, William. Review of *The Importance of Being Earnest, The World*, 20 Feb. 1895, sites.broadviewpress.com/lessons/DramaAnthology/ArcherOnWilde/ArcherOnWilde_print.html.

Auden, Wystan Hugh. *Forewords and Afterwords*. New York: Random House, 1973.

Carey, John. *The Intellectuals and the Masses: Pride and Prejudice Among the Literary Intelligentsia 1880–1939*. London: Faber and Faber, 1992.

Ellmann, Richard. *Oscar Wilde*. New York: Knopf, 1988.

Harris, Frank. *Oscar Wilde*. New York: Carroll & Graf, 1992.

Nietzsche, Friedrich, *The Anti-Christ, Ecce Homo, Twilight of the Idols*, edited by Aaron Ridley and Judith Norman. Cambridge: Cambridge U P, 2005.

_____. *Thus Spoke Zarathustra*, edited by Adrian Del Caro and Robert Pippin. Cambridge: Cambridge U P, 2006.

Nordau, Max, *Degeneration*, edited by George L. Mosse. Lincoln, Nebraska: U of Nebraska P, 1993.

Shaw, George Bernard. Complete Plays. London: Constable & Co., 1931.

Varty, Anne. *A Preface to Oscar Wilde*. London: Longman, 1998.

Weintraub, Stanley. "'The Hibernian School': Oscar Wilde and Bernard Shaw." *Shaw:* vol. 13, 1993, pp. 25–49. *JSTOR*, www.jstor.org/stable/40681506.

Wilde, Oscar. *The Critical Heritage*, edited by Karl E. Beckson. London: Routledge, 1997.

_____. *The Complete Letters of Oscar Wilde*, edited by Merlin Holland and Rupert Hart-Davis. London: Fourth Estate, 2000.

_____. *Complete Works*. London: Collins, 2003.

"Myriad Meanings": Oscar Wilde's Critical Afterlives

Benjamin Hudson

"Myriad Meanings"

Contemporary culture revives Oscar Wilde at an astonishing pace. In the fall of 2018, while I was teaching an upper-level seminar on Wilde, a scholarly, full-life biography of Wilde was published by Matthew Sturgis; Rupert Everett's film *The Happy Prince,* which surveys the years after Wilde's imprisonment, received its North American release; my students enlightened me of the virtual oeuvre of Natalie Wynn, dubbed "the Oscar Wilde of Youtube" that fall for her incisive videos excoriating right-wing fascist ideology with wit, style, and—like Wilde—a Platonic knack for the genre of philosophical dialogue; at least two adaptations of *Dorian Gray* with a female lead were then in development for film and television; and there were two local, Central Florida productions of the Moisés Kaufman play *Gross Indecency* about the trials that sent Wilde to prison. These coincidences made my job a lot easier, of course; while some students in my courses have struggled to see the relevance of some nineteenth-century texts and authors to their lives today, none could pretend that Wilde was a relic of the past. He was omnipresent and in many different guises.

The critical tradition on Wilde is not dissimilar from that in popular culture. Surveying the landscape of scholarly approaches to Wilde's work can be a daunting task. Some traditions emphasize his Irish heritage and sympathy with Irish republicanism, others look at patterns of Christian martyrdom, European philosophy, or socialist critique in his work. Some all but ignore Wilde's marriage to focus on the homosexual adventurism that sent him to prison, and yet others wonder if that adventurism and what seems like its concomitant marital deceit is evidence of his misogyny, or if his portrayals of women are proto feminist. Other critical camps focus on his mastery of the epigram and other literary forms, showcase his borrowings and appropriations from other writers, or illuminate the material and financial circumstances of writing and celebrity in the England of the 1880s and 1890s. These various critical traditions have sometimes been hostile to each other, leading one prominent scholar to label them "the Wilde wars" (Killeen 424). In sum, the critical attention to Wilde over the last 40 years especially might give us a slight feeling of vertigo as we survey its volume and variety, and, rather than creating a single unifying image of the author and his work, this critical diversity expands our image of the man prismatically into many different Wildes. In this sometimes-contradictory critical composite, Wilde becomes, like his character Dorian Gray, "a complex multiform creature" rather than a static and stable historical or literary figure (Wilde *Uncensored Picture* 174).

The diversity of critical opinions about Wilde has interesting parallels to several of his fictions about literary interpretation. In the riotously digressive fictional dialogue "The Critic as Artist," Wilde's most sustained examination of the function of criticism, the character Gilbert instructs his slow-witted interlocutor Ernest that criticism is, in fact, a higher calling than artistic creation, for criticism "treats the work of art simply as a starting-point for a new creation. It does not confine itself [...] to discovering the real intention of the artist and accepting that as final. [...] Nay, it is rather the beholder who lends to the beautiful thing its myriad meanings, and makes it marvelous for us, and sets it in some new relation to the age, so that it becomes a vital portion of our lives" ("The Critic as Artist" 239). In effect, the author licenses the dizzying array of critical Wildes we have now before us. He invites criticism to remake his work in the varied interests of the critic's current moment.

Although "The Critic as Artist" may be Wilde's most elaborate theory of criticism, it is in fact his short story "The Portrait of Mr W. H." that may help us wrap our minds around what Wilde thinks of the tendency of critical appraisals of authors that balloon into often contradictory critical stances and legacies. "The Portrait of Mr W. H." is a story of the search for the mysterious addressee of Shakespeare's sonnets, known only as "Mr W. H." from a dedication printed in the first edition of the sonnets by publisher Thomas Thorpe in 1609. In the 1880s and 1890s, the progenitors of today's literature professors were feverishly hunting for the real-life identities behind the "Fair Youth" and "Dark Lady" of Shakespeare's sonnets.[1] In "Portrait," Wilde has a good deal of fun at their expense.

In brief, the story charts a literary theory concocted by the young actor Cyril Graham who determines that Shakespeare's addressee and the "Fair Youth" of the sonnets was a beautiful young man and actor like himself named Willie Hughes. The story follows the development of Cyril's theory, which he imagines perfect from close reading alone, to Cyril's attempt to convince his skeptical older friend Erskine by soliciting a forged portrait of the Renaissance actor from a starving artist in Holborn, when no historical evidence of Willie Hughes's existence can be found. When Erskine detects the forgery, Cyril martyrs himself in protest to his friend's skepticism. The novel's outer frame plots the attempts of an unnamed narrator to verify Cyril's hypothesis when he hears the story of the portrait from Erskine. The narrator himself becomes "converted" to the Willie Hughes theory, contemplates it for several months, and finally puts "all of his enthusiasm" into a letter to Erskine that attempts to re-recruit the older man into a plan of publication (Wilde "Portrait" 35, 94). This letter drains belief in Cyril's theory from the narrator but succeeds in Erskine's reconversion. After an impassioned disagreement, Erskine leaves England to try and verify the theory in the historical archives of the Continent. Several years later, the narrator receives a letter from Erskine announcing that he, too, will martyr himself for the theory, so he rushes to the Côte d'Azur to rescue his friend. In Cannes, he discovers that Erskine has died of consumption, and the threat of suicide, like the portrait, was another forgery. Erskine's mother delivers the fatal portrait to the narrator, noting that her son had "begged" her to turn it over to the younger man (Wilde "Portrait" 100). As the novella ends, the portrait sits in the narrator's library where "it is very much admired by [his] artistic friends," and he concludes his tale, noting that "sometimes, when I look at it, I think there is really a great deal to be said for the

Willie Hughes theory of Shakespeare's Sonnets" (Wilde "Portrait" 100–01).

"The Portrait of Mr W. H." has been a lodestone, as you can imagine, for queer readings of Wilde's legacy. Long before, the story even came up in Wilde's infamous trial, when opposing counsel asked the author on the stand if he had "written an article pointing out that Shakespeare's sonnets were practically sodomitical" (Holland 93). Under the threat of criminal punishment, Wilde countered that of course he had done the opposite and hedged on the fact that Cyril's theory is indeed not historically proven. Wilde's performance in the courtroom begins to look a bit disingenuous when we turn our attention to the reminiscences of his contemporaries and his own historical record. The artist Charles Ricketts, from whom Wilde commissioned his own fraudulent portrait of Willie Hughes to use as a frontispiece to an extended version of the story that never appeared, recalled that Wilde hoped that "Our English homes will totter to their base when my book appears," an admission that cleanly places Wilde's story in opposition to English domesticity and its attendant narratives of heterosexual marriage and reproduction (33). Famously, "Portrait" was conceived with Wilde's dear friend and likely first homosexual lover Robert Ross over dinner; in his correspondence, Wilde reminds Ross, "the story is half yours" and solicits a new theory from the younger man after the story appeared: "Write to me a letter. Now that Willie Hughes has been revealed to the world, we must have another secret" (*Complete Letters* 407–08). Wilde's letter is somewhat misleading, for commentary on Shakespeare's male addressee had been in print for over a century (Chedgzoy 152). Yet, by proposing the story as the public revelation of a secret shared between the two men, the letter suggests how the story's interest in queer ways of knowing literary history extends outside its frame to the society of Wilde's own life. So, what does today's scholar of Wilde rely on? His statement at the trial, when he might have faced criminal punishment for a "sodomitical" text, or his statements to his friends and lovers? In the end, our search to pin down the "sodomitical" truth of "Portrait" might turn us into sleuths like Erskine, desperate for scientific certainty. Wilde's story, instead, asks its readers to consider the benefits of a critical pose like the narrator's, who has enjoyed the pleasures of thinking about the theory but who ends the story content to rest "sometimes" in an occasional belief of its merit.

Wilde's story shows a clash between critical methods of interpreting an artist's work and legacy. "Working purely by internal evidence," Cyril is a close reader, who believes that all the necessary information to detect the figure of the addressee is within the sonnets themselves (Wilde "Portrait" 37). Erskine, however, indebted to the scientific rigor associated with his alma mater Cambridge, demands "some independent evidence about the existence of the young actor" (Wilde "Portrait" 43). He argues for the necessity of the historic record. When Cyril first outlines his theory, Erskine counters "that the name of Willie Hughes does not occur in the list of the actors of Shakespeare's company as it is printed in the first folio" (Wilde "Portrait" 42). He reserves judgment until they have found the historic evidence that confirms the theory fully "beyond the reach of doubt or cavil" (Wilde "Portrait" 44). It is the narrator, who, like Wilde, matriculated at Oxford and is similarly shaped by his educational upbringing, wavers between these two views. Like Erskine, he hunts for "absolute verification," but like Cyril, he becomes imaginatively fascinated and convinced by the internal evidence of Shakespeare's sequence: "I could almost fancy that I saw [Willie Hughes] standing in the shadow of my room, so well had Shakespeare drawn him" (Wilde "Portrait" 70, 58). Ultimately, he decides that, although he is not convinced wholeheartedly of the existence of the elusive Willie Hughes, "sometimes," when gazing at a knowingly forged portrait of the young man, he believes the theory has merit.

The narrator's critical stance might seem naïve or knowingly contradictory, but it has a legacy much like Erskine's skepticism. As Cambridge became associated in the nineteenth century with rigorous empiricism and the hard facts of science, Oxford, on the other hand, was known for developing a more philosophical equilibrium, or what the scholar Linda Dowling has called "a disposition to play with ideas" (xv). Wilde asks us to take our cue from the narrator, as we survey a diverse and sometimes contradictory critical legacy.

We should not fool ourselves into thinking that Wilde or his work—or Shakespeare's, for that matter—has ever a singular exclusive meaning, but we should, like his narrator, let ourselves be seduced by a variety of interesting and compelling arguments. As Gilbert cautions, we should resist the urge to determine "the real intention of the artist and accepting that as final;" rather we should open ourselves up to "myriad meanings" (Wilde "The Critic as Artist" 239). With "a disposition to play with ideas," we can wade into the troubled waters of the Wilde wars with curiosity and openness to contradiction and the fruitful possibilities of critical nuance and "sometimes" certainties.

Over the next sections of this essay, I will trace with very broad strokes some central concerns in Wilde studies, those that have been most significant to my students. I hope to give you a sense of some of the principal preoccupations of contemporary criticism and places you might go to investigate further. Of course, this summary is by no means exhaustive, and there are other established avenues in Wilde studies like the place of evolutionary science in his work and his theories of personhood as performance that do not appear here. But the following three categories of sex and gender, politics and the marketplace, and religion should offer you a sense of some of the dappled, variegated Wildes in contemporary criticism.

Quare Wilde: Identitarian Readings and the Question of Wilde's Feminism

One of the most voluminous investigations into Wilde's life and art has been a several-pronged investigation into his life and work through the lens of sexuality. While some had for much of the second half of the twentieth century championed Wilde as a kind of gay genius and martyr, Richard Ellmann, the well-regarded biographer of Irish literary icons like James Joyce and William Butler Yeats, is largely responsible for inaugurating the scholarly attention to Wilde's sexuality (and national origin as well) with his Pulitzer Prize-winning biography in 1988. Despite some inconsistencies in scholarship, Ellmann brought attention to Wilde's affair with Lord Alfred Douglas as a "consuming passion" and foundation for the spectacular highs and lows of Wilde's final decade (384). In Ellmann's wake, critical interest in Wilde's sexuality, its influence on modern culture as perhaps the most public account of modern homosexuality in England as a result of journalistic fascination with his trials, and the sexual dynamics of his published works flourished.

Perhaps the most epochal work that examined Wilde under the rubric of sexuality studies was Eve Sedgwick's *Epistemology of the Closet*, a monograph that built on work she'd already completed about how English literature of the eighteenth- and nineteenth-centuries revealed a "homosocial" world where men triangulated their unconscious desire for each other through their relationships with women. In *Epistemology of the Closet*, Sedgwick hones in on *The Picture of Dorian Gray* (1890–1891), a text that has since been extraordinarily productive for exploring queer themes in Wilde's work. In her extraordinarily incisive reading, the novel "takes a plot that is distinctively one of male-male desire, the competition between Basil Hallward and Lord Henry Wotton for Dorian Gray's love, and condenses it into the plot of the mysterious bond of figural likeness and figural expiation between Dorian Gray and his own portrait" (Sedgwick 160). Sedgwick argues that this conversion was advantageous for Wilde, who was well aware of the legal prohibition of "gross indecency"—a legal euphemism for homosexual behavior—under which he would be found guilty and sent to prison in 1895. The collapse of the competition between the older characters for Dorian's affection into a competition between Dorian and his portrait discloses, according to Sedgwick, "the protective/expressive camouflage it offered to distinctly gay content" (161). Sedgwick's dense, provocative prose paved the way for a sustained academic attention from the queer theorists who followed in its wake.

In her later work, Sedgwick cautions us to respect the complexities of sexuality in Wilde's work and life. Although it can be tempting to think of Wilde as a repressed gay man in an excessively repressive homophobic culture, scholarship has since understood that what we think of as a *gay man* was a category under construction at the time of Wilde's trials, and the publicity of those trials very much influenced the cultural figure we now think of as gay.[2] It is undeniable that Wilde's works develop interest in sexual and romantic relations between men, but we must also recognize the historical complexity of his particular moment and the other necessary facts of his biography. As Eleanor Fitzsimons notes, "his sexuality is complex. It seems that from the early 1890s onward, he was attracted exclusively to men, a realization that his grandson Merlin Holland senses came as a relief to him in many ways. That said, there is little doubt that his love for his wife, Constance, was genuine" (12). Constance's recent biographer Fanny Moyle even wonders "how closely the Wildes may have worked on certain projects" and suggests that "The Selfish Giant," one of Wilde's best loved stories for children, may be "a genuine collaboration" between the man and wife (135–36). The relative happiness of Wilde's early marriage, then, and the outsized influence of the trials, suggests the need for "myriad meanings" in considerations of Wilde and sexuality.

Ellmann's career as a chronicler of the lives of Irish literary greats also encouraged an important growth in critical attention to Wilde's national identity. Ellmann unearthed a rumor, for instance, that though Wilde had been christened as Anglican shortly after his birth in 1854, his mother, who later wrote Irish nationalist poetry pseudonymously as Speranza, had a reformatory chaplain baptize him again as Catholic several years later in the country south of Dublin (19). A Catholic baptism might be a powerful symbol in a country of Catholics who had been historically discriminated against from holding legislative authority and beholden to the machinery of English control through its Anglo-Irish Protestants. In fact, both of Wilde's parents showed an interest in Irish patriotism and folklore, and though Wilde left his country, which had suffered nearly 700 years of colonial rule by England, to make his way in England, scholars have drawn attention to the significance of his Irish birth and the republicanism he likely inherited from his mother. Perhaps the most significant intervention in this regard is Declan Kiberd's *Inventing Ireland*, which casts Wilde as an influential figure in the modern Irish literary tradition. For Kiberd, Wilde understood that in order to subjugate its colonies, England needed to create and maintain binary fictions about itself and the people it colonized. Because the English needed to believe that Ireland required its direction, the Victorian popular press published images of the Irish as childlike and apelike; these images provided reinforcement for England's belief in its fitness to administrate Irish lives and affairs. If Englishmen believed themselves masculine and rational, the people it colonized, Kiberd argues, needed to be thought of as effeminate and emotional. Such are two binaries, Kiberd shows, that Wilde exploded in "an art of inversion" that "applies to gender stereotypes above all." In *The Importance of Being Earnest*, for instance, Wilde's male characters "lounge elegantly on sofas and eat dainty cucumber sandwiches" while "the women in the play read heavy works of German philosophy and attend university courses" (Kiberd 39). For Kiberd, this "art of inversion" punctures the ideological fictions that England creates for itself to legitimize its control over its colonies and helps us to identify a strain of anti-Imperialism in Wilde's work. The work that has followed in Kiberd's wake looks to Wilde's art of conversation, his children's fiction, and his relationships with other Irish nationalists to make the case for the importance of his national identity.

For Kiberd, Wilde's gender inversions signal his distaste for English chauvinism, but this topic has also encouraged fruitful debate from feminists and critics interested in the gendered politics of Wilde's work. While Wilde may argue against restrictive social hypocrisies that disadvantage women in *A Woman of No Importance* and "The Harlot's House," *Dorian Gray*, on the other hand, excises women characters altogether with the death of Sybil Vane, in what feminist critic Elaine Showalter calls "an escalating contempt for women" (176), and the playwright's take on the Biblical legend of Salomé squares too cleanly with misogynist fears of a seductress who uses men's lust to trouble divine order and the gendered hierarchy of the state. Yet, in Wilde's early professional life, he was committed to early feminist issues as editor of *The Woman's World* from 1887–1889, and critic Laurel Brake has painstakingly showed how he helped to reshape the periodical's focus from traditionally feminine concerns like gossip and fashion to those of modern and "serious readers who want (and need) education and acculturation" (142). In Eleanor Fitzsimons's estimation, as editor, Wilde "demonstrated a nuanced and progressive attitude towards gender expectations and control" (14). Similarly, critic Sos Eltis defends Wilde's "progressive politics" through his plays, which reveal him to be, she argues, "a consistent champion of women's rights both in his life and his work, supporting all the primary demands of late nineteenth-century feminism" (7). In sum, paradox and contradiction are a mainstay not only in Wilde's work but also our thinking about it. As "a complex, multiform creature," Wilde is many things at once.

Wilde and the Market: Professionalism and Politics
Josephine Guy and Ian Small have cast doubt on critical interpretations of Wilde that privilege psychological, queer, and anti-imperialist readings of his writings. In *Oscar Wilde's Profession*, they argue that Wilde's career instead testifies to his navigation of the *fin-de-siècle* "culture industry," a complex of "material constraints" that structure and limit the institutional dissemination of any printed or theatrical text. In their introduction, Guy and Small suggest that "the expressive qualities, which the 'gay' and 'Irish' [critical] paradigms attribute to Wilde's works, are not always compatible with the material details of their textual histories—of the histories of their composition and publication" (7). Guy and Small reveal a commercially troubled Wilde, whose poor sales figures reflect his difficulty determining the appetites of his audience. Guy and Small represent a diverse body of critics who are interested in how Wilde's work and life intersect with the vicissitudes of the Victorian marketplace.

Because Wilde lived and worked at a time when England's colonial exploitation of its territories around the globe redistributed value domestically, the economic and cultural force of the bourgeoisie sat atop the new wealth generated by the Industrial Revolution, the working class stirred the imaginations of Victorian sages like Matthew Arnold and the philosophies of Karl Marx, and socialism was becoming an intellectual and cultural interest, critics have been drawn to the economic implications of Wilde's work. In a brief and insufficient survey, for example, Dorian Gray's fastidious, exotic collecting seems indicative of a newly possible kind of exploitative global consumerism at the nineteenth century's close, and Wilde's essay "The Soul of Man Under Socialism" invites us to consider his economic and political philosophy, which, in that essay, argues paradoxically that socialism is a necessary step on culture's advance to a utopian, perfect individualism. Moreover, the social worlds of the comedies are almost wholly aristocratic, hypocritical, and irredeemably mercenary, and Wilde's distaste for selfish property-ownership animates the moral of Christian charity in his fairy tale "The Selfish Giant." Thus Wilde's writings reflect his varied engagements with economic realities and theories and respond to the ideas of his time.

Wilde's various and often paradoxical poses in relation to economic philosophy (and in general) have been explained by Regenia Gagnier as a responsiveness to the diverse audiences that he addressed. With regard to the scandal occasioned by the appearance of *The Picture of Dorian Gray*, for example, Gagnier notes, "here, as in most cases of scandalous works, it is probably more useful to look at the audience scandalized than to look at the work" (7). It was in the journalists' best interest to resist the aestheticism of Dorian Gray, since the novel toyed with the idea of an art indifferent to social concerns, and their livelihoods depended on their position as the arbiters of what art was socially acceptable. Though Wilde is frequently confrontational with bourgeois values in his work and demands artistic freedom from the moral limitations of journalists and their scrupulous standards of decency, Gagnier reveals how Wilde's many paradoxical stances show his strategic navigation of several distinct audiences. The goal of the comedies, Gagnier illustrates, had the biaxial aim "to be commercially competitive and critical"—to make money, of course, but also to chastise the bourgeois society he parodied (8). Gagnier's attention to the differing networks and responsiveness of Wilde's audiences situate Wilde as a savvier maneuverer through the late Victorian artistic and economic sphere than Guy and Small suggest. Gagnier has since overseen critical attention to Wilde in the marketplace that plays close attention to the dynamics of consumption; for these critics, the dandy, who like Dorian Gray voraciously collects art objects from all over the world, is a symbol of a new kind of acquisitive hunger at the end of the nineteenth century.

Christ and Catholicism

Whether or not he was baptized in an unorthodox second ceremony as Roman Catholic in his childhood, Wilde continued to be fascinated with Catholicism and its myths throughout his life, a fact that has been significant not only for scholars interested in tracing a commitment to Ireland in his work, but also scholars of religion as well. Wilde considered a Catholic conversion while he was at Oxford and even traveled to Italy to attempt one. Years later, after he was released from prison, he adopted the pseudonym of the martyred "Sebastian," a commentary on his own persecution at the altar of Victorian respectability, and returned to Italy where he was blessed by the pope at least seven times (Frankel 267–68). In his work, his first volume of poetry records a struggle between Christian orthodoxy and the pleasures he associates with a Classical pagan tradition; the speaker of the sonnet "Hélas," for example, wonders whether he will "lose a soul's inheritance" for touching "the honey of romance" (*Complete Works* 864). Another, "Humanitad," closes with the line "That which is purely human, that is Godlike, that is God" (*Complete Works* 876), and "The Ballad of Reading Gaol," his most successful poem, invites its readers to find the Christlike in the criminal. Wilde's fascination with Catholicism is not only traced in his poetry, though; his most important prose similary engage with its themes. In the opening of *Dorian Gray*, Wilde alludes to the fall of man as Lord Henry's intellectual seduction of Dorian—a disclosure of "life's mystery" that transforms the young man—takes place in Basil's garden (77). But Wilde did not only rework Old Testament themes. Notably, "The Soul of Man Under Socialism" and *De Profundis* radically theorize Jesus as an aesthete; in the "Soul of Man," Wilde writes, "the message of Christ to man was simply, 'Be thyself.' That is the secret of Christ" (135). And *De Profundis*, a letter written to Alfred Douglas from prison, enlists Christ as a perfect artist who made his life a perfect work of art. In his short fictions, martyrdom and Christlike self-sacrifice is an inescapable theme, and *Salomé*, of course, rewrites a Biblical story through the prism of decadence. In effect, as Frederick Roden has claimed, "Christian theology dominates the Wilde corpus" (136).

Ellis Hanson is one critic who has sensitively traced the importance of religion to Wilde's life and work. Although it may seem surprising that Wilde, who fought against moralistic proscriptions for art, would be drawn to the church, Hanson reconceives how Catholicism might have appeared to Wilde and his aesthetic circle:

> The Church is itself a beautiful and erotic work of art [. . .]. It is like a great museum in its solemn respect for art and its extraordinary accumulation of dead and beautiful things. It is a relic of itself, and like all saintly relics it commands devotion. The sheer excess of the Church—its archaic splendor, the weight of its history, the elaborate embroidery of its robes, the labrynthine mysteries of its symbolism, the elephantine exquisiteness by which it performs daily miracles— has always made it an aesthetic and festishistic object of wonder. (6)

Here, Catholicism seems like a natural fit for Wildean decadence and an obvious subject for Wilde's consideration; as a "beautiful and erotic work of art," the Church, like Shakespeare's sonnets or Basil's painting, is at home in Wilde's catalog.

The meditations on Christ in *De Profundis* are Wilde's most sustained engagement with and interpretation of the Gospels, and the image of Christ therein can be categorized as twofold—artist and lover. According to Hanson, "Christ is valorized as an aesthete, a mouthpiece for Wilde's own theories about art, individualism, imagination, love, sorrow, and faith" (237). In casting Christ's as the most sympathetic imagination, Wilde upholds him as a supreme artist: "the very basis of his nature was the same as that of the nature of the artist—an intense and flamelike imagination" (*Complete Letters* 741). In celebrating Christ as a supreme artist—and the pinnacle of imaginative possibility—Wilde demonstrates his agenda to close any supposed gap between religious orthodoxy and his own aestheticism. Yet, Wilde also celebrates Christ as a perfect lover;

in Roden's estimation, "The theology of *De Profundis* is amatory" (150). Wilde writes, "if [Christ's] place is among the poets, he is the leader of all the lovers. He saw that love was that lost secret of the world for which the wise men had been looking, and it was only through love that one could approach either the heart of the leper or the feet of God" (*Complete Letters* 743–44). Wilde enlists Christ, the "leader of all the lovers" with a passionately sympathetic imagination, to defend himself against the contempt of a hypocritical Victorian public.

Wilde believed that Christ was a perfect artist because "he realised in the entire sphere of human relations that imaginative sympathy which in the sphere of Art is the sole secret of creation" (*Complete Letters* 741). We might apply this lesson of "imaginative sympathy" also to the contradictions and arguments of the Wilde wars and the conflicting sincerities of its critics. Wilde's oeuvre, like the man himself, is a "complex multiform creature"; it explores sex and gender, nationalism, politics, the marketplace, and religion from various, complex perspectives. Wilde's reading of Christ reminds us that we would be unwise and ungenerous to fix, like Erskine and Cyril, a final or singular meaning to his life and work. Instead, as we survey the variety and volume of Wilde's critical legacy, we should open ourselves up to the pleasure of paradox and variability in our thinking about this very complicated man and the diverse afterlives of his writings.

Notes

1. Shakespearean scholar Samuel Schoenbaum describes the 1880s as a period when "the literature produced by the fantastic quest for identities achieved a volume out of all proportion to its significance" (*Shakespeare's Lives* 317).

2. The most important scholarship in this regard is Ed Cohen's *Talk on the Wilde Side* and Alan Sinfield's *The Wilde Century*. Both Cohen and Sinfield take the philosopher Michel Foucault's insight in the first volume of *The History of Sexuality* that the late nineteenth century was a moment in time that was transforming, through medical, legal, and psychological discourses, the idea of sodomy from a sexual act anyone might perform to one indicative of a certain kind of

personality, with an identifiable set of personality traits. In this regard, Wilde's trials, and the excessive attention from an exuberantly hostile press, help to form the modern public image of the sodomite or male homosexual. If Wilde seems so obviously queer to us today, Cohen argues, it is because "the newspapers effectively (re)produced the possibility for designating Wilde as a kind of sexual actor" (Cohen 131). In effect, the stereotypes of male homosexuality we have today were created, in part, from the hostile Victorian press.

Works Cited

Brake, Laurel. *Subjugated Knowedges: Journalism, Gender and Literature in the Nineteenth Century*. Houndsmills: The Macmillan P, 1994.

Chedgzoy, Kate. *Shakespeare's Queer Children: Sexual Politics and Contemporary Culture*. New York: Manchester U P, 1995.

Cohen, Ed. *Talk on the Wilde Side: Towards a Genealogy of a Discourse on Male Sexualities*. New York: Routledge, 1993.

Dowling, Linda. "Introduction." Wilde, Oscar. *The Soul of Man Under Socialism and Selected Critical Prose*, edited by Linda Dowling. New York: Penguin Books, 2001, pp. vii–xxvii.

Ellmann, Richard. *Oscar Wilde*. New York: Vintage Books, 1988.

Eltis, Sos. *Revising Wilde: Society and Subversion in the Plays of Oscar Wilde*. Oxford: Clarendon P, 1996.

Fitzsimons, Eleanor. *Wilde's Women: How Oscar Wilde Was Shaped by the Women He Knew*. New York: Overlook Duckworth, 2016.

Frankel, Nicholas. *Oscar Wilde: The Unrepentant Years*. Cambridge: Harvard U P, 2017.

Gagnier, Regenia. *Idylls of the Marketplace: Oscar Wilde and the Victorian Public*. Stanford: Stanford U P, 1986.

Guy, Josphine, and Ian Small. *Oscar Wilde's Profession: Writing and the Culture Industry in the Late Nineteenth Century*. Oxford: Oxford U P, 2000.

Hanson, Ellis. *Decadence and Catholicism*. Cambridge: Harvard U P, 1997.

Holland, Merlin. *Irish Peacock and Scarlet Marquess: The Real Trial of Oscar Wilde*. New York: Fourth Estate, 2003.

Kiberd, Declan. *Inventing Ireland: The Literature of the Modern Nation.* London: Vintage, 1995.

Killeen, Jarlath. "The Greening of Oscar Wilde: Situating Ireland in the Wilde Wars." *Irish Studies Review*, vol. 23, no. 4, 2015, pp. 424–50, doi: 10.1080/09670882.2015.1085672.

Moyle, Fanny. *Constance: The Tragic and Scandalous Life of Mrs Oscar Wilde.* New York: Pegasus, 2011.

Ricketts, Charles. *Recollections of Oscar Wilde.* London: Pallas Athene, 2011.

Roden, Frederick. *Same-Sex Desire in Victorian Religious Culture.* New York: Palgrave Macmillan, 2002.

Schoenbaum, Samuel. *Shakespeare's Lives.* Oxford: Clarendon P, 1971.

Sedgwick, Eve Kosofsky. *Epistemology of the Closet.* Berkeley: U of California P, 1990.

Showalter, Elaine. *Sexual Anarchy: Gender and Culture at the Fin de Siècle.* New York: Penguin Books, 1990.

Wilde, Oscar. *The Complete Letters of Oscar Wilde*, edited by Merlin Holland and Rupert Hart-Davies. New York: Henry Holt, 2000.

_____. *The Complete Works of Oscar Wilde.* London: HarperCollins, 2003.

_____. "The Critic as Artist." *The Soul of Man Under Socialism and Selected Critical Prose*, edited by Linda Dowling. New York: Penguin Books, 2001, pp. 213–79.

_____. "The Portrait of Mr W. H." *The Soul of Man Under Socialism and Selected Critical Prose*, edited by Linda Dowling. New York: Penguin Books, 2001, pp. 31–101.

_____. *The Uncensored Picture of Dorian Gray*, edited by Nicholas Frankel. Cambridge: The Belknap P, 2012.

Queer Wilde

Nikolai Endres

Oscar Wilde, the queer martyr, was convicted of "gross indecency," sent to prison for two years with hard labor, and passed away, aged 46 years, in 1900. However, Wilde was also a happily (for a while) married husband—"'O execrable facts, that keep our lips from kissing, though our souls are one'" (qtd. in Frankel 26), Wilde wrote to Constance after their wedding—and proud father of two sons. While he had a reputation as quite a ladies' man in Great Britain (fighting, for example, for the affections of Florence Balcombe, who to Wilde's chagrin instead married Bram Stoker, the future author of *Dracula*, or writing love sonnets to actress Ellen Terry), on his visit to the United States he flaunted a queer persona with his outrageous costume, wit, and carnations. Some of his greatest literary creations are females, notably the fabulous women of his comedies or the *femme fatale Salomé*, and even his dandies have questionable heterosexual credentials: "Men marry because they are tired; women, because they are curious; both are disappointed," Lord Henry Wotton muses in *The Picture of Dorian Gray* (46).[1] After his release from prison, it was his gay friends who pushed for a reconciliation with Wilde's estranged wife; after her premature demise, they kept on badgering Wilde to remarry for respectability, to which he replied the following: "'I am quite sure that you will want me to marry this time some sensible, practical, plain, middle aged boy, and I don't like the idea at all'" (in Frankel 245). And for a century now, people from all over the world have flocked to his grave in the Père Lachaise cemetery in Paris, where brightly colored lipstick marks (by men, women, gays, lesbians, none of the above, all of the above?) did such damage to his tombstone that the authorities had to cordon it off. Queer, isn't it?

Queer Theory

What is a queer reading? Probably the most famous exponent of queer theory is Paul-Michel Foucault, who changed how we look at sexuality. During the Victorian period, which was far from Puritanical or repressed but actually produced a proliferation of sexual discourses, various professionals became interested in "the homosexual." Up until then, there had been homosexual acts (sodomy)—now sexuality became an identity:

> The nineteenth-century homosexual became a personage, a past, a case history, and a childhood, in addition to being a type of life, a life form, and a morphology, with an indiscreet anatomy and a possibly mysterious physiology. Nothing that went into his total composition was unaffected by his sexuality. It was everywhere present in him: at the root of all his actions because it was their insidious and indefinitely active principle; written immodestly on his face and body because it was a secret that always gave itself away. It was consubstantial with him, less as a habitual sin than as a singular nature. (Foucault 43).

Eve Sedgwick was one of the pioneer theorists that applied Foucault's findings to literature, defining queerness as "the open mesh of possibilities, gaps, overlaps, dissonances and resonances, lapses and excesses of meaning when the constituent elements of anyone's gender, of anyone's sexuality aren't made (or can't be made) to signify monolithically" (*Tendencies* 8). Specifically about the Victorian period, she writes:

> With respect to the homosocial/homosexual style, it seems to be possible to divide Victorian men among three rough categories according to class. The first includes aristocratic men and small groups of their friends and dependents, including bohemians and prostitutes; for these people, by 1865, a distinct homosexual role and culture seem already to have been in existence in England. [. . .] This role is closely related to—is in fact, through Oscar Wilde, the antecedent of—the particular stereotype that at least until recently has characterized American middle-class gay homosexuality, namely "effeminacy, transvestism, promiscuity, prostitution, continental European culture, and the arts" (Sedgwick *Between Men* 172–73).

However, Wilde could only hint at those stereotypes, for as he famously termed it in court, homosexuality was "The Love that dare not speak its name" (Hyde 236). How, then, can one convey sexual identity without naming it? Actually, we do it all the time. Think of asking the following questions: Have you seen movies such as *Mommie Dearest, Call Me by Your Name,* or *Brokeback Mountain*? Are you a fan of ABBA, Cher, or Lady Gaga? Do you like *Teletubbies, Queer as Folk,* or *Will & Grace*? Have you read *Simon vs. the Homo Sapiens Agenda*? Wilde uses a similar code.

A queer lens on Wilde, therefore, must take into account not only how his culture constructed homosexuality—what Richard Kaye calls "the restrictions, aspirations, and expectations of the Victorian literary and theatrical marketplace" (196)—but also how Wilde defied the censor by conveying the love that dare not speak its name. Let us start with *Dorian Gray*, followed by his comedy *The Importance of Being Earnest* and the fairy tale "The Happy Prince."

Queer Dorian

We begin with Dorian's questionable masculine credentials. He faints, commodifies himself in the painting, exposes himself to the masculine gaze, and spends most of his time indoors—all of which would have been gendered as feminine. Add to that Dorian's predilection for cross-dressing: "On one occasion he took up the study of jewels, and appeared at a costume ball as Anne de Joyeuse, Admiral of France, in a dress covered with five hundred and sixty pearls. This taste enthralled him for years, and, indeed, may be said never to have left him" (120). Then there is Dorian's predilection for crossing continents. Queer travel has a time-honored tradition. Even nowadays, announcing a trip to Key West, San Francisco, or Amsterdam could convey someone's sexuality. Wilde does the same. Paris, city of light and lust (homosexuality had been decriminalized in France by the Napoleonic Code), lured Wilde as well as Dorian and Basil (who is catching a train to France when Dorian kills him). In Venice, Dorian remembers "a wonderful love that had stirred him to mad delightful follies. There was romance in every place" (121).

Every winter, Dorian sojourns with Lord Henry in Northern Africa, with its easy availability of Arab boys.

Another queer destination is the classical world, Greece and Rome. Lord Henry recommends that Dorian "forget all the maladies of mediaevalism, and return to the Hellenic ideal" (28). What ideal is he talking about? The medieval maladies are the Christian strictures of morality, but things were different in Athens. The relationship between Dorian and Lord Henry, between a younger and older man, recalls Greek pederasty, where an older man taught his protégé, who, in turn, provided the beauty that inspired the older man. In many ways, Lord Henry is a surrogate father to the orphan Dorian. "I was a schoolboy when you knew me," Dorian tells Basil, but thanks to Lord Henry "I am a man now" (87). And it is in his old schoolroom, the painting's hiding place, that Dorian remains unspoiled. Add to that Dorian's first name, unusual in English, which recalls the Dorian tribe, often credited with "inventing" pederasty. British university students would have read about Greek love in the Socratic dialogues, notably the *Symposium* and the *Phaedrus*. Plato remained dear to Wilde's heart, as he revealed in his famous courtroom speech: "'The Love that dare not speak its name' in this century is such a great affection of an elder for a younger man as there was between David and Jonathan, such as Plato made the very basis of his philosophy, and such as you find in the sonnets of Michelangelo and Shakespeare. It is that deep, spiritual affection that is as pure as it is perfect" (Hyde 236). Wilde had prefigured this speech in *Dorian Gray*, "It was such love as Michael Angelo [Michelangelo] had known, and Montaigne, and Winckelmann, and Shakespeare himself" (92), with all his examples having a reputation for homoerotic attraction.

As a result, Dorian appropriates a queer canon, reading about Roman same-sex love in Petronius' *Satyricon* and in Suetonius' queer biographies of Roman emperors such as Tiberius, Caligula, or Nero. Basil's compliment to Dorian as Antinous evokes Emperor Hadrian's great love, just as the mythological signifiers of Adonis, Hylas, or Narcissus convey divinely sanctioned homoeroticism. Closer to home hits Dorian's avid lecture on Shakespeare and his attraction to the mysterious Mr W. H. (which is elaborated on in Wilde's "The Portrait of Mr W. H."), and about King Edward II's love for Piers Gaveston in the eponymous play by Christopher Marlowe.

Speaking of Rome, Catholicism has always attracted queer writers: the pope's flowing robes, naked cherubs, male celibacy, the tangibility of Christ's body, the spectacle of mass, the suffering on the cross:

> [Dorian] had a special passion, also, for ecclesiastical vestments, as indeed he had for everything connected with the service of the Church. In the long cedar chests that lined the west gallery of his house, he had stored away many rare and beautiful specimens of what is really the raiment of the Bride of Christ, who must wear purple and jewels and fine linen that she may hide the pallid macerated body that is worn by the suffering that she seeks for, and wounded by self-inflicted pain. (105)

The main saint Dorian worships is Sebastian, long known as patron of the LGBTQ population (Sebastian supposedly helped Christians in an age of persecution, thereby "coming out" as a religious deviant himself, just as later Sebastian became a healer of plague victims, an important gay icon in the age of AIDS), who was shown full of arrows, his body profanely tortured; yet painters reveal this gorgeous Roman soldier as experiencing orgasmic bliss, as willingly succumbing to this act of penetration.

Yet, there is someone in the novel that doesn't come across as very queer. In fact, that person is very flesh and blood, very beautiful, very much in love with Dorian, and she is a woman. Sybil Vane seems to resist a queer approach. Although much of our queer analysis relies on, let's say, circumstantial evidence, we cannot overlook the fact that Dorian asks Sybil to marry him. But that is the beauty of a queer reading; it questions even the most obvious. Sybil is an actress, specializing in the Bard: "Lips that Shakespeare taught to speak have whispered their secret in my ear. I have had the arms of Rosalind around me, and kissed Juliet on the mouth," Dorian muses (65). But Dorian is no Romeo. First of all, as we saw earlier, Wilde had already queered Shakespeare's love of the mysterious "W. H." Second, in Elizabethan times, Dorian would have kissed a male on the mouth, for all roles were played by men. Third, Rosalind (and it is only when she plays Rosalind, not after having watched Sybil play Juliet and Imogen in *Cymbeline* the first two nights, that Dorian proposes) is one of Shakespeare's queerest roles: in *As You Like It*, a male actor would have dressed up as Rosalind, who on stage puts on "man's apparel" to play a character called Ganymede, in mythology a beautiful Trojan shepherd who was abducted by Zeus and became his cupbearer, and who asks Orlando to accept them (to use a non-binary pronoun) for what they are, a male, a Ganymede, a boy actor. It seems fair to say that such a role could have been conceived of only by a queer author, now christened Shakesqueer (see Menon). Of course, Sybil acts one more time, good old Juliet again, and Dorian is so horrified by this heterosexual travesty that he breaks off the engagement (and Sybil plays Juliet to the very end, committing suicide).

We might as well ask now what Dorian signifies to the twenty-first century. If pederasty were the dominant paradigm, it would come across as pretty dated. Nowadays, we value equality and reciprocity in gay relationships, and we do find that here. True, Dorian is initially schooled by Basil and Henry, but since he never grows up or old and because throughout the text he is interested in "young men" (as, for example, Basil asks him: "Why is your friendship so fatal to young men?" 112), Wilde prefigures the peer relationships of our time. In fact, this might be Wilde's most radical idea. In 2019, we have forcefully moved on from homosexuality to gay marriage—and maybe, if Sybil was really a boy, Dorian was asking for his hand. And there is something else that matters to millennials: porn.

Let us finish with *Gluttony* (part of the series *The Seven Deadly Sins*) subtitled *The Porno Picture of Dorian Gray*. In the year 2000, an undergraduate film student named Cyril Vane (played by Tanner Hayes) becomes obsessed with a porn star from thirty years before, Dorian (Eric Hanson), who performed in what we call the beefcake era. Later Dorian turned to directing, using the anagram Ian Rod as his title. Eternally young, he never did a sexual repeat, tried his hands at being a chef, and set the record as one of world's most voracious pickle eaters (1757 pickles in three hours, according to the *Guinness Book of World Records*). Under another pseudonym, Dan Roi, Dorian made a compilation of cum-shots, *Forever Cum*, spurred on by the music of Richard Wagner's "Ride of the Valkyries." Yet another video is called *Lick It Up*, where Dorian intended to depict "an orgasm that went on forever." Here Cyril notices a mirror in one of the scenes, in which he sees director Dorian in all is his spotless beauty. Interviewing the person who claims to have discovered Dorian, Cyril finds out that Dorian's first movie, *Narcissus Rising*, was never released, for it allegedly "captured his soul." Like Basil's painting, there is only one copy. The filmmaker eventually meets his idol, perfectly perfect, and asks about *Narcissus*. Dorian commands him to switch off the camera, takes him up to his attic, and plays the fabled video. In *Narcissus*, Dorian is an old and wrinkled man (though still muscular and by no means entirely unattractive). After Cyril confesses his love for Dorian—"I love you"—which Dorian dismisses as nothing he hasn't heard before—they have sex. After the climax, with the reel dramatically ending and fate-like breaking, Dorian grows old, while the movie restores its pristine actor. Wilde, isn't it?

Queer Earnest

In *The Importance of Being Earnest,* Wilde continues his queer project, and he does so in two ways. He subverts three pillars of Victorian respectability—family, marriage, patriarchy—and plants various queer signifiers.

The Victorian family, modelled on the queen's nine children and her beloved husband Albert, collapses spectacularly in *Earnest*. In the famous handbag episode, Jack seems to think that Miss Prism is his mother (albeit a "fallen women"); when she indignantly denies that suggestion, he conflates his aunt, Lady Bracknell, with his mother. Rather than being Algernon's cousin, Cecily is actually his niece, while earlier Jack claimed that she was his aunt, who calls Jack her uncle. The Victorian standard of two parents seems in

---

short supply: "To lose one parent, Mr. Worthing, may be regarded as a misfortune; to lose both looks like carelessness" (Act 1, p. 18).[2] Brothers die and rise from the dead; strangers call each other "sisters"; best friends turn out to be family; and handbags become mothers. Sedgwick, in her chapter "Tales of the Avunculate: Queer Tutelage in *The Importance of Being Earnest*," even goes so far as to contend "Forget the Name of the Father. Think about your uncles and your aunts" (*Tendencies* 59). In French, a language Wilde spoke fluently, *une tante* translates as, for example, "drag queen," while "uncle" denotes the older man in a same-sex relationship (similar to the pederastic paradigm we saw in *Dorian Gray*). *The Importance of Being Earnest* hints at a family of drag queens, sugar daddies, and, above all, aunts: "Some aunts are tall, some aunts are not tall. That is a matter that surely an aunt may be allowed to decide for herself. You seem to think that every aunt should be exactly like your aunt! That is absurd!" (Act 1, p. 9).

Although Queen Victoria lost her husband early, she remained earnestly devoted to him, donning the widow's black garb of woe until her dying day. No such longevity exists here. Asked why bachelors serve better drinks,

> LANE: I attribute it to the superior quality of the wine, sir. I have often observed that in married households the champagne is rarely of a first-rate brand.
> ALGERNON: Good heavens! Is marriage so demoralising as that?
> LANE: I believe it *is* a very pleasant state, sir. I have had very little experience of it myself up to the present. I have only been married once. That was in consequence of a misunderstanding between myself and a young person. [. . .]
> ALGERNON: Lane's views on marriage seem somewhat lax. Really, if the lower orders don't set us a good example, what on earth is the use of them? They seem, as a class, to have absolutely no sense of moral responsibility. (Act 1, p. 6, emphasis in original)

A few lines later, Algernon adds his own two cents: "You don't seem to realize, that in married life three is company and two is none" (Act 1, p. 12). Lady Harbury, her hair turned to gold from grief, looks twenty years younger since her poor husband's death; thanks to the help of a French maid, Lord Lancing fails to "know" his wife. Gwendolen expresses grave scepticism about the sacrament of matrimony: "Ernest, we may never be married. From the expression on mamma's face I fear we never shall. [. . .] But although she may prevent us from becoming man and wife, and I may marry someone else, and marry often, nothing that she can possibly do can alter my eternal devotion to you" (Act 1, pp. 22–23).

Presiding over the Victorian family is the towering figure of the father, providing financially, governing subjects, fighting wars, laying down the law, all serious business—not so Gwendolen's papa: "Outside the family circle, papa, I am glad to say, is entirely unknown. I think that is quite as it should be. The home seems to me to be the proper sphere for the man. And certainly once a man begins to neglect his domestic duties he becomes painfully effeminate, does he not? And I don't like that. It makes men so very attractive" (Act 2, p. 39). There is a lot "wrong" with this passage, not least the attractiveness of effeminate men. In any case, the fathers of *Earnest*, where are they? Lord Bracknell is an invalid, cloistered in domesticity; Jack and Algernon's father, General Moncrieff, "was essentially a man of peace, except in his domestic life" (Act 3, p. 58), becoming an early casualty of his belligerent nature; the only other "father," Canon Chasuble (who is High Church, or Anglican approximating Catholic ritual), is accused of entertaining Miss Prism as his mistress.

Queer theory thus finds alternative family constellations, marriage as severed from morality and downgraded in favor of something we might call love, and fathers that act suspiciously like uncles. Are there no real men, then, in *Earnest*?

Victorian masculinity entailed self-control. Stoicism, avoiding all forms of extravagance, of public emotion, of excessive leisure, of sexual insecurity . . . was an important guiding protocol. "[He] has a strong upright nature. He is the very soul of truth and honour. Disloyalty would be as impossible to him as deception," so Gwendolyn's ideal of Ernest, but she foresees trouble: "But even men of the noblest possible moral character are extremely susceptible to the influence of the physical charms of others" (Act 2, p. 39). The play begins with Algernon, in a "luxuriously and artistically furnished" room, devouring cucumber sandwiches until none are left, later washed down with Perrier-Jouët, Brut, '89 (the champagne of high society, priced accordingly), drowned by the noise of "Wagnerian" music (the epitome of decadence); clothed in "Bunbury suits," these gentlemen will be traveling with three portmanteaus, a dressing-case, two hat-boxes, and they will love "wildly, passionately, devotedly, hopelessly" (Act 2, p. 35). Christopher Craft puts it well: the play's "gluttony that, by axiomatically transposing sexual and gustatory pleasures (cucumber sandwiches, muffins, breads: buns— Banbury or Bunbury—everywhere), operates as a screen metaphor for otherwise unspeakable pleasures" (148).

The most unspeakable pleasure, of course, is "bunburying," which is definitely queer: leading a double life, inventing fictitious friends, searching out pleasure in obscure locales, refusing to call a spade a spade. Kerry Powell proposes: "Whether *Earnest* is 'about' homosexuality or not, some recent research makes clear that there was certainly a flourishing homosexual subculture in London (and elsewhere) in the 1890s, and that Wilde and his contemporaries were equipped with an interpretative framework enabling them to 'read' homosexuality in life and representations of it on stage, even if theatrical depictions of homosexuality were necessarily inexplicit under the watchful eye of state censorship" (112). He then lists some queer locales that Wilde mentions, such as Victoria Station or Oxford Street, sites of cruising and departures to places of frivolity. Piccadilly Circus is the gateway to notorious theater-land, and the Albany, Jack's address, hosted queer poet Lord Byron. Craft notes Wilde's possible pun on "urning"/ "earnest" (162), with *urning* connoting a gay male in the Nineties, just as Wilde would have known J. G. Nicholson's 1892 book of homoerotic poems, *Love in Earnest*.

With all this queerness, we are not surprised that Wilde's best play now features all-male productions. Emulating immortal performances by Edith Evans or Margaret Rutherford, Quentin Crisp, Brian Bedford, David Suchet, or Geoffrey Rush have all tried their hands at Lady Bracknell. How about the men of *Earnest*? They would fit right into the new millennium, for they are proto-metrosexuals. According to Mark Simpson, "The typical metrosexual is a young man with money to spend, living in or within easy reach of a metropolis—because that's where all the best shops, clubs, gyms and hairdressers are. He might be officially gay, straight or bisexual, but this is utterly immaterial because he has clearly taken himself as his own love object and pleasure as his sexual preference" ("Meet the Metrosexual"). Algy, in particular, seems to have taken himself as his own love object, for until he meets Gwendolyn, we hear nothing about a significant other in the play (unlike Jack, whose cigarette case gives him away). Aunt Agatha finds that "Algernon is an extremely, I may almost say an ostentatiously, eligible young man. He has nothing, but he looks everything. What more can one desire?" (Act 3, p. 52). Algy, conversely, casts a queer eye on frumpy Jack: "I never saw anyone take so long to dress, and with such little result" (Act 2, p. 34). Simpson concludes: "Metrosexuality is, in a paradox that Wilde would have relished, not skin deep. It's not about facials and manbags, guyliner and flip flops. It's not about men becoming 'girly' or 'gay'. It's about men becoming everything. To themselves. Just as women have been encouraged to do for some time" ("The Metrosexual is Dead"). What more can one desire?

Queer Fairies

Queer theory also casts its eyes on fairy tales. Consider Maurice Sendak's global blockbusters. Sendak was gay but closeted for most of his life, wisely realizing that a gay author of children's book would arouse suspicion. However, according to Jesse Green, "The traditions of children's literature, in which toddlers are presexual and often not even human, provided the camouflage they needed to write about real things without offense." Sendak, for example, gave Mickey, the naked toddler from *In the Night Kitchen* (1970), the first penis in the history of fairy tales. And imagine what a recipe for disaster Mickey's baking into a cake by three burly men with red noses and big spoons in the dead of night would have been in an adult story, or as Sendak recalls: "'the lusciousness of cooking, of kneading with your hands, of undressing and floating in this sensuosity of milk . . . and thus driving every librarian crazy!'" (qtd. in Cott 53; ellipsis in original). Nowadays, queer children's books seem pretty standard. Random House just brought out another one by Rob Sanders, author of *Pride: The Story of Harvey Milk and the Rainbow Flag*, this time about the seminal LGBTQ event of the past century: *Stonewall: A Building. An Uprising. A Revolution*, targeted at children from five to eight. Yet, long before Sendak and Sanders, Wilde published his own queer fairy tales. We will look at "The Happy Prince."

Queer Princes
A swallow is left behind by his companions hibernating in Egypt and flies to the statue of the late Happy Prince. While alive, the prince was happy, sheltered from the outside world in his palace. Now, from his new vantage point, he is overwhelmed by the sorrows of his people and asks the swallow to take the treasures of his monument to the poor. As the prince loses his beauty and the swallow freezes to death, both are consigned to a dustheap, from where an angel takes them to heaven.

Critic John-Charles Duffy identifies five queer themes in Wilde's fairy tales:

1. devoted friendship between men (most fully developed in Wilde's "The Devoted Friend"),
2. non-reproductive sex (such as the love between the fisherman and a mermaid in "The Fisherman and his Soul" or the seemingly self-pleasuring title character of "The Young King," who finds himself "on the soft cushions of his embroidered couch, lying there wild-eyed and open-mouthed, like a brown woodland Faun, or some young animal of the forest newly snared by the hunters," 213),
3. aestheticism (a philosophy rejecting Victorian utilitarianism, which defined things by their usefulness),
4. pederasty (as Duffy discusses at length in "The Selfish Giant"), and
5. "the Unblessed, Unnatural, Unnameable" (homosexuality as sinful, unnatural, unspeakable).

The devoted friendship between the swallow (gendered as male) and the prince grows more and more intimate, with the prince constantly begging for yet another night, and the fact that the swallow initially loved a (female) Reed just serves as his cover (as it did for the Wilde, the married husband). Is their relationship more than Platonic? It is hard to see all the drops falling on the swallow as just tears, for there must have been mighty many to "drench" the bird, just as the swallow feels "warm" despite the frigid temperatures. The swallow's end is heartbreaking: "And he kissed the Happy Prince on the lips, and fell down dead at his feet" (276), with "death" possibly connoting an orgasm (as it often does in Shakespeare). Moreover, Duffy's aestheticism pervades the tale, beginning with the statue, "He was gilded all over with thin leaves of fine gold, for eyes he had two bright sapphires, and a large red ruby glowed on his sword-hilt" (271), and after the prince divests himself of his precious ornaments, the swallow promises him "The ruby shall be redder than a red rose, and the sapphire shall be as blue as the great sea" (275).

The Victorian discourse of homosexuality as depravity is belied by the sacrifices the swallow and the prince make. We might as well go so far and call this story a Christian moral of a queer couple feeding the poor, covering the naked, visiting the sick, and looking out for their own kind: "Under the archway of a bridge two little boys were lying in one another's arms to try and keep themselves warm" (275–76). Are we surprised that God redeems them? "'Bring me the two most precious things in the city,' said God to one of His Angels; and the Angel brought Him the leaden heart and the dead bird. 'You have rightly chosen,' said God, 'for in my garden of Paradise this little bird shall sing for evermore, and in my city of gold the Happy Prince shall praise me'" (277). Next, their love is patently unnatural, between a bird and a man, but unnatural things do happen, as the Professor of Ornithology notes: "A swallow in winter!" (273). Profound love between two males (one older, one younger), possibly including sex, intense aesthetic reciprocity, and everlasting salvation—"'I will stay with you always,' said the swallow, and he slept at the Prince's feet" (275)—Wilde names it all.

One of the reasons I chose "The Happy Prince" is its adaptation in the 2018 movie *The Happy Prince*. Director Rupert Everett covers Wilde's years after the release from prison—and he fully queers them. Theoretically, prison was supposed to "cure" Wilde of his homosexuality; judged by that standard, Reading Gaol failed spectacularly. Nicholas Frankel, who recently published a biography of Wilde's post-jail years, argues that Wilde remained "unapologetic, unrepentant, and even defiant about the crimes that sent him to prison in the first place" (10); rather, Wilde's "amours were always conducted with joy, affection, and good humor; and he clearly inspired the devotion of young lovers" (297). The movie begins with Wilde narrating "The Happy Prince" to his sons Cyril and Vyvyan, but story time is also bedtime, and ten years later, Wilde has transferred his affections to the French rent boy Jean and his younger brother Leon, who impatiently waits outside the bedroom for Wilde to finish his business with Jean and continue his tale. Wilde's powers of potency gradually waning, just as the Happy Prince is stripped bit by bit of his prestige, he remains the consummate story teller. And while he loves Jean and Leon, he never forgets his Cyril and Vyvyan (as we see in the movie's cutbacks), one big queer family.

The Open Mesh of Possibilities

Relating his tale of Cecily's guardianship and invention of a brother, Jack concludes: "That, my dear Algy, is the whole truth pure and simple," to which Algy replies: "The truth is rarely pure and never simple" (Act 1, p. 10). The same goes for Oscar Wilde, whose life, whose texts, whose movies defy truth pure and simple. It even goes for queerness itself: "If queerness can be defined, then it is no longer queer" (Menon 7). That is the open mesh of possibilities.

Notes

1. All references (except for *The Importance of Being Earnest*) are to the *Collins Complete Works of Oscar Wilde*.
2. All references are to *The Importance of Being Earnest: Authoritative Text, Backgrounds, Criticism*.

Works Cited

Cott, Jonathan. *There's a Mystery There: The Primal Vision of Maurice Sendak*. New York: Doubleday, 2017.

Craft, Christopher. "Alias Bunbury: Desire and Termination in *The Importance of Being Earnest*." In *The Importance of Being Earnest: Authoritative Text, Backgrounds, Criticism*, edited by Michael Patrick Gillespie. New York: Norton, 2006, pp. 136–66.

Duffy, John-Charles. "Gay-Related Themes in the Fairy Tales of Oscar Wilde." Victorian Literature and Culture, vol. 29, no. 2, 2001, pp. 327–49.

Foucault, Michel. *The History of Sexuality, Volume I: An Introduction*. Tr. Robert Hurley. New York: Random House, 1980.

Frankel, Nicholas. *Oscar Wilde: The Unrepentant Years*. Cambridge, Massachusetts: Harvard U P, 2017.

Green, Jesse. "The Gay History of America's Classic Children's Books." *New York Times Style Magazine*, 7 Feb. 2019, www.nytimes. com/2019/02/07/t-magazine/gay-children-book-authors.html.

The Happy Prince. Dir. Rupert Everett. Perf. Rupert Everett, Colin Firth, Emily Watson, Colin Morgan. Maze Pictures, 2018.

Hyde, Montgomery H. *The Trials of Oscar Wilde*. London: William Hodge, 1948.

Kaye, Richard A. "Gay Studies / Queer Theory and Oscar Wilde." In *Palgrave Advances in Oscar Wilde Studies*, edited by Frederick S. Roden. Basingstoke and New York: Palgrave Macmillan, 2004, pp. 189–223.

Powell, Kerry. *Acting Wilde: Victorian Sexuality, Theatre, and Oscar Wilde*. Cambridge: Cambridge U P, 2011.

Sedgwick, Eve Kosofsky. *Between Men: English Literature and Male Homosocial Desire*. New York: Columbia U P, 1985.

_____. *Tendencies*. Durham, North Carolina: Duke U P, 1993.

Shakesqueer: A Queer Companion to the Complete Works of Shakespeare, edited by Madhavi Menon, Durham, North Carolina: Duke U P, 2011.

The Seven Deadly Sins: Gluttony (aka *The Porno Picture of Dorian Gray*). Dir. Wash West [Westmoreland]. Perf. Eric Hanson, Tanner Hayes, Tony DeAngelo, Chi Chi La Rue. All Worlds Video, 2000.

Simpson, Mark. "Meet the Metrosexual." *Salon*, 22 July 2002, www. salon.com/2002/07/22/metrosexual/.

_____. "The Metrosexual is Dead. Long Live the 'Spornosexual.'" *Telegraph*, 10 June 2014, www.telegraph.co.uk/men/fashion-and-style/10881682/The-metrosexual-is-dead.-Long-live-the-spornosexual.html.

Wilde, Oscar. *Collins Complete Works of Oscar Wilde*. Glasgow: Harper Collins, 1999.

_____. *The Importance of Being Earnest: Authoritative Text, Backgrounds, Criticism*, edited by Michael Patrick Gillespie. New York: Norton, 2006.

CRITICAL
READINGS

Imagining Greatness: The Staging of Oscar Wilde in America_____

Annette M. Magid

Imagine being in your mid-twenties and having a famous musical team, comprised of a composer and a lyricist, decide that you were the perfect person to influence people to see a musical they have written. The theme of their musical is a subject about which you absolutely love writing and talking. In fact, the musical seems to be about some things you did in your life, including winning a prestigious prize for a folio of poems you wrote at college. Next, continue to imagine that the same musical team decides that you would be the perfect person to promote their musical in a different country. Finally, imagine that the musical team actually paid for your trip, and a new wardrobe, to go to a country on the other side of the Atlantic Ocean and serve as the key spokesperson for their musical. Those incidents are exactly what happened to Oscar Wilde when he was sent from his native home of Ireland to America in 1881. Not only did Oscar Wilde promote the musical, *Patience*, throughout a well-planned itinerary established by Gilbert & Sullivan's promotion director, Wilde also took the opportunity to promote himself.

When the promoters of Gilbert and Sullivan's operetta, *Patience,* were worried that Americans, whom Oscar Wilde labeled during one of his early speaking engagements at the Brooklyn Academy of Music "as ignorant as they were insolent" (Morris 87) would not understand the subtlety of the satirical tone of the operetta, glib-tongued, poetic, decadent Oscar Wilde was their first choice to conduct an extensive speaking engagement in order to help Americans understand the subtlety of the satirical tone of the operetta. Londoners considered themselves more sophisticated than Americans. *Patience* was a highly successful Gilbert and Sullivan operetta in London's Savoy Theatre.

In December 1881, Wilde sailed for New York with a pre-paid ticket to travel across the United States at the expense of the operetta's promoters and deliver a series of lectures on Aesthetics. The fifty-lecture tour was originally scheduled to last four months, but it stretched to nearly a year, with over 140 lectures given in 260 days. Wilde agreed to lecture in the United States and Canada in 1882, announcing on his arrival at customs in New York City that he had "nothing to declare but his genius." Despite widespread criticisms in the press regarding his languid poses and aesthetic costume of velvet jacket, knee breeches, and black silk stockings, Wilde for twelve months exhorted the Americans to love beauty and art. In their comic operetta *Patience,* Gilbert and Sullivan based the character Bunthorne, a "fleshly poet," partly on individuals like Wilde who loved beauty, art, and poetry. Wilde's American lecture tour as the self-proclaimed "Professor [or Apostle] of Aesthetics" (Nicholls 9) incorporated his disdain for conventional morality and his relentless pursuit of celebrity.

Ralph Keyes claims in *The Wit and Wisdom of Oscar Wilde,* "Wilde's life was an ongoing performance starring himself" and "writing was merely an ongoing vehicle propelling him toward his real goal: the dramatization of Oscar Wilde" (3). Therefore, Wilde was a perfect choice for the production's promotion. Wilde originally came to America on an all-expense paid tour at the behest of Richard D'Oyly Carte, the producer in New York of Gilbert and Sullivan's operetta, to serve as a living "poster" through a series of lectures across America in order to promote and popularize the Gilbert and Sullivan's operetta, *Patience; or, Bunthorne's Bride.* The entire trip to America fit into Oscar's life philosophy:

> "to be forever curiously testing new opinions and courting impressions, and never acquiescing in the facile orthodoxy . . . To burn always with this hard, gemlike flame, to maintain this ecstasy is success in life." (qtd. in Lambourne 7)

When he arrived in America, Wilde cleverly embraced the media and talked freely to a variety of local newspaper reporters providing himself with his own publicity as he traveled by train throughout the United States. Wilde's whirlwind tour of America was a complex media event. He even became his own advance man by talking to reporters about his upcoming lectures and promoting himself as the spokesman for the Aesthetic Movement, which he labeled as "the science of the beautiful" (Morris 2).

From the moment Wilde landed on the dock in New York harbor, reporters took the opportunity to offer the public the image they saw. When an interviewer from the *New York World* asked, "Will you lecture?" Wilde responded, "That will depend considerably upon the encouragement with which my philosophy meets." Evidently, he met with very strong approval of his philosophy since he was able to espouse his science of Aestheticism to large, receptive, audiences. Several of the initial interviewers filled the first few paragraphs of their interview with precise descriptions of Wilde's appearance: everything from his nearly six foot-three height, to his "broad shoulders," "deep blue eyes, and long arms" (Hofer and Scharnhorst 13). Many interviewers commented on his "bottle green dressing gown, trimmed in fur, the length of which is at his feet" (Hofer and Scharnhorst 15).

His custom-made clothes were photographed and commented upon repeatedly and matter-of-factly. Most reporters made observations regarding his long, "flowing, wavey [*sic*] hair," but the color shifted from "light" to dark brown. Several references were made regarding his "shoulder-length tresses." Beside the "hundreds of times he was asked to define aesthetic," American reporters learned that appearances that were to have represented the man, such as demonstrated through Wilde's foppish clothing, were deceiving since he had "a firm handshake, boundless energy, unquenchable good humor and unexpected ability to out-drink any and all challengers" (Morris 3). His ability to drink and his quick wit quickly won over his American hosts, who "were naturally predisposed to appreciate rugged individualism in even its most exotic forms" (Morris 3). Even though some audiences came to his lectures to laugh, many stayed to be entertained and at times enlightened. It should be noted that it was never Wilde's intention to talk down to his audience. He told one reporter from Philadelphia that he regarded his talks as a casual conversation between friends (Morris 3). Regarding his real purpose for being in America, *Patience* turned out to have a fairly successful run in New York City, and it was somewhat successful in other east coast cities such as Philadelphia.

Despite widespread ridicule in the press of his languid poses and aesthetic costume of velvet jacket, knee breeches, and black silk stockings, Wilde for twelve months exhorted the Americans to love beauty and art. His audiences were comprised mostly of American middle-and upper-class women who were interested in making their homes and themselves aesthetically pleasing. It should be noted that Oscar Wilde would not have been the man he became without the encouragement and gene pool into which he was born. A brief overview of his parentage is necessary when studying Oscar and his promotional trip to America. It helped that he came from a prestigious family, attended the best schools, and was an excellent student at every school he attended, earning honors throughout his educational experience.

Sometimes studying a person's family may offer an important observation platform to enable someone to understand how he became the person he was. During the nineteenth century the concept of a family's influence on the future lives of their children was particularly important. For Wilde, merely observing his family and his life growing up in his unusual household seems to have a strong influence on the man he became. Until he was nine, Oscar Wilde was educated at home, where he learned to read, write, and fluently speak French from his French nursemaid; and he had an equally intense immersion in German from his German governess. He then attended Portora Royal School in Enniskillen, County Fermanagh, Ireland from 1864 to 1871. Until his early twenties, Wilde summered at the villa, Moytura House, his father built in Cong, County Mayo, Ireland. At Moytura House, he and his older brother Willie played with George Moore, who in adulthood became a famous painter, short story writer, poet, and art critic. Not only did Moore have an influence on Willie and Oscar Wilde, Moore was said to have been a strong influence on James Joyce.

Wilde's home was a constant whirl of activity. He was raised in a home where his mother held literary salons, also called soirées, where as a young child he was expected to "entertain" the guests.

His mother, who always wanted to have a daughter, had Oscar and his older brother wear beautiful dresses and stand in the center of the room and recite poetry. Just from this detail one can see how Oscar's love of beauty and flamboyance developed.

His mother, who called herself "Speranza," an Italian word meaning "hope," claimed that she had Italian ancestry. She was well-educated and came from an upper middle-class family. Speranza was an excellent poet who wrote revolutionary poems for the Young Irelanders to support Irish independence from England. She frequently read Young Irelanders poetry to her sons, which enhanced their love of poetry. She also read American poet Walt Whitman to her children. Whitman's poetry with its keen observation of nature and human interaction gave Wilde an appreciation for the beauty in all that was around him. Speranza loved paintings and statues of ancient Greeks and Romans, which helped him to establish his skills in drawing as well as his interest in mastering the Greek language. Wilde's mother was an authority on Celtic myth and folklore.

Oscar Wilde's mother did attain her wish for a daughter, and Wilde's sister, Isola, was born in 1857. Sadly, Isola died from meningitis at the age of nine. Wilde was a teenager when she died, and he wrote a poem called "Requiescat" in her memory. After her death, Wilde carried the poem and a lock of her hair with him until the day he died.

His father, Sir William Wilde, was Ireland's leading ear and eye surgeon, who published *Aural*, a comprehensive tome on the treatment of the ear.[1] Sir Wilde was constantly travelling to small towns in Ireland to treat patients, so in order to spend some time with his sons, he occasionally took one son at a time with him while he made his rounds to his patients. Oscar heard folktales from various people during his trips with his father. All the exposure to Ireland's rural people added to his interest in storytelling and language usage.

From Oscar's father's dedication to his profession, the son learned that in order to be successful, one must be sure of oneself and not to stray from his/her opinion. This thinking helped him when he was chosen to be the spokesperson for *Patience*. He believed in

Aestheticism and was able to carry the message to many people in America.

Wilde, like his father, mother, and paternal grandfather, was knowledgeable about nearly every topic. His remarkable eidetic memory, inherited, no doubt, from his father Sir William (Magid 114) enabled him to speak cleverly about whatever topic arose, at times borrowing witticisms from others which, as Richard Ellmann suggested in his book *Eminent Domain*, seemed to be common practice among eminent writers such as Yeats, Wilde, Joyce, Pound, Eliot, and Auden. Wilde readily offered his opinion about whatever popped into his fertile mind; and what he didn't know, he made up with such eloquence that even the cleverest listener thought Oscar was incorporating precise facts into his lectures.

Not only was Oscar a wonderful wit, perfect with his quick repartees and excellent with comedic timing, he was also a great speaker with a familial attribute of a melodious voice which the famous actress Lily Langtry identified as "one of the most alluring voices that [she had] ever listened to" (Morris 16). Even though Langtry was enticed by his voice, a reporter from the *Philadelphia Inquirer* found that the "most noticeable peculiarities about his talk were a singsong division of words into a species of blank verse of his own" (Hofer and Scharnhorst 17).

Oscar Wilde's appreciation for the idea that clothes make the man also fit into the role that Gilbert and Sullivan etched into their musical. Oscar himself once complained to a friend that he might have to stop going out to dinner so often because it took so long to dress for the occasion. In fact, it usually took Oscar almost five hours to dress in what he identified as proper attire, which included a pressed jacket, perfectly creased and pressed slacks, a contrasting and pressed vest, a pressed top coat, clean underwear, cleaned and pressed shirt, matching (and, if necessary, darned) socks, a pressed silk cravat, a steamed wool hat, matching leather gloves, and mirror-polished shoes. The group of friends who also prepared and dressed in this manner were called "decadents."

Margaret Kennedy reinforces a key point related to a person such as Oscar Wilde serving as a perfect promotional representative for

Patience. Kennedy states that "Art teaches people how to live; it is the way out of despair, towards a better life. Wilde may not be so direct, but this connection between art and social reform . . . is embedded in his work" (102). Without Wilde's observations, criticisms and his observations following his tour of America, the modern view of the Victorian era would be vastly different.

Oscar Wilde's tour of America in 1882 occurred at a highly opportune moment for an English (or Irish) celebrity since transatlantic relationships were at an all-time high following the marriage a few years earlier of New York socialite, Jennie Jerome, to Lord Randolph Churchill, a union that produced the future Prime Minister of England, Winston Churchill. While other British literary luminaries such as Charles Dickens, who visited America a generation earlier, viewed Americans with distain, Wilde seemed to enjoy his encounters with the American public and the journalists in the daily press (Morris 3). According to Wilde, "Interviewers are a product of American civilization, whose acquaintance I am making with tolerable speed" (Hofer and Scharnhorst 1). Wilde further commented to a group of interviewers, "We have no interviewing in England" (Hofer and Scharnhorst 1). Wilde was clever enough to realize that it was through the press and its agents that his notoriety would flourish. He needed the vehicle of the press to launch his philosophy, which was to provide a venue for his promotional tour as well as a means of promoting himself as a poet and as an Aesthete.

Wilde also knew that the interactions he established through the promotion of *Patience* might serve as contacts for his own plays that he hoped to write and produce for an American audience. The two classes of people Wilde hoped to reach in America were "the handicraftsmen and the artists" (Morris 51). This group of people was not the audience whom Gilbert and Sullivan had in mind as a potential audience who might see their play. Wilde did not seek to speak to that group because he did not feel he could teach the idle rich anything.

Wilde came to America seventeen years after the end of the Civil War, a time when Lloyd Lewis and Henry Justin Smith in their 1936 book *Oscar Wilde Discovers America* note that "wealth had become fluid and the economy had suddenly, violently accelerated the industrial progress . . . [which] overwhelmed the agrarian civilization and made the United States . . . the greatest manufacturing nation in the world" (42). "Ready money" in America was impressing Wilde just as it had impressed, awed, or outraged almost every foreigner who had visited America since 1862. America was a civilization of the stock exchange and the corporation. In New York, Wilde saw the great collectors and possessors of mountainous cash, owners of vast properties that could be transformed quickly into currency (Lewis and Smith 42).

Perhaps in response to some of the barbs audience members made about Wilde's appearance, Wilde often took the opportunity during his lectures to insult some of the areas most treasured edifices such as the famous Water Tower in Chicago about which he said that he was "amazed that any people could so abuse Gothic art." He also said that the White House in Washington, DC more resembled an oversize bunkhouse than a residence fit for a president. Wilde even criticized one of America's National Landmarks, Niagara Falls. He had several unflattering comments about the "unnecessary amount of water going the wrong way," but his most memorable was when he wrote: "Every American bride is taken there, and the sight of the stupendous waterfall must be one of the earliest, if not the keenest, disappointments in American married life." In Cincinnati, Wilde saw a "no smoking" sign in the hall in which he was booked to lecture. Wilde, an enthusiastic smoker, complained, "Great heaven, they speak of smoking as if it were a crime. I wonder they do not caution the students not to murder each other on the landings." He went on with his diatribe against Cincinnatians by saying, "You have no architecture, no scenery [here] . . . I wonder no criminal has ever pleaded the ugliness of your city as an excuse for his crimes" (Friedman 167).

When Wilde went to Louisville, even though there were several other major events going on at the same time, he drew a nearly sold-out house. The excellent attendance for his lecture is a tribute to his success with American audiences. Oscar's tour to a multiplicity of cities and towns across America helped him to influence many female members of his audiences. Since the Industrial Revolution was moving swiftly in America, there was a glorification of mechanical objects and an enormous focus on progress; yet American women still sought beauty in their personal lives (Morris 28). Post-Civil War, many women's magazines and special interest newspapers covered topics such as how to be a good wife and mother and how to produce the perfect pastry. Wilde was aware of American editor Mary Eliza Haweis's publications such as *The Art of Beauty* (1878), *The Art of Decoration* (1881), and *Beautiful Houses* (1882), to name a few, and he consulted her work while preparing his own lecture, "The House Beautiful," for American audiences. His goal was to help women to open their eyes to beauty in all its forms and price ranges. "Women have natural art instincts," he would tell them, "which men usually acquire only after long special training and study; and it may be the mission of the women of this country to revive decorative art into honest, healthy life" (Wilde 913). For Wilde, America offered freedom to present himself as a dandified, aesthetic celebrity using his wit and rapier tongue without the constraints of the mannered and restrained society into which he was born. Through his lectures he enhanced the audiences', especially women's, overall appreciation of beauty. Oscar Wilde's lectures may have been among the sparks that helped encourage the establishment of the Arts and Crafts movement in America. This moved American homes during the Gilded Age from being functional to being beautiful.

Note

1. Some of the information included in Sir Wilde's book is still taught in British Medical Schools.

Works Cited

Archer, Linda. "Oscar Wilde and the Passion of the Absurd." *Quintessential Wilde: His Worldly Place, His Penetrating Philosophy and His Influential Aestheticism*, edited by Annette M. Magid. Newcastle upon Tyne: Cambridge Scholars P, 2014, pp. 2–15.

Conrad, Peter. *Imagining America*. New York: Oxford U P, 1980.

Ellmann, Richard. *Eminent Domain. Yeats Among Wilde, Joyce, Pound, Eliot, and Auden.* New York: Oxford U P, 1967.

_____. *Oscar Wilde.* New York: Alfred A. Knopf, 1988.

French, Bryant Morey. *Mark Twain and the Gilded Age: The Book That Named an Era.* Dallas: Southern Methodist U P, 1965.

Friedman, David M. *Wilde in America: Oscar Wilde and the Invention of Modern   Celebrity.* New York: W. W. Norton & Company, 2014.

Haweis, Mrs. H. R. *The Art of Beauty.* New York: Harper & Brothers, 1878.

_____. *The Art of Decoration.* Piccadilly, London: Chatto and Windas, 1881.

_____. *Beautiful Houses: Being a Description of Certain Well-Known Artistic Houses* London: Sampson Low, Marston, Searle & Rivington, 1882.

Kennedy, Margaret S. "Wilde's Cosmopolitanism: The Importance of Being Worldly," *Wilde's Wiles: Studies of the Influence of Oscar Wilde and His Enduring Influences in the Twenty-First Century,* edited by Annette M. Magid. Newcastle-upon-Tyne, England: Cambridge Scholars, 2013, pp. 90–113.

Lambourne, Lionel. *The Aesthetic Movement.* New York: Phaidon P, 1942.

Lewis, Lloyd, and Henry Justin Smith. *Oscar Wilde Discovers America* [1882] New York: Benjamin Bloom, 1936.

Magid, Annette M. "Wily William: A Study of William Robert Wills Wilde." *Wilde's Wiles: Studies of the Influence on Oscar Wilde and His Enduring Influences in the Twenty-First Century.* Newcastle upon Tyne: Cambridge Scholars P, 2013, pp. 114–37.

Morris, Roy, Jr. *Declaring His Genius.* Cambridge, Massachusetts: The Belknap P of Harvard U P, 2013.

Nicholls, Mark. *The Importance of Being Oscar: The Wit and Wisdom of Oscar Wilde Set Against His Life and Times.* New York: St. Martin's P, 1980.

Pappas, Dennis G., M. D. "Sir William Wilde: A Historical Review." *Ear, Nose & Throat Journal,* vol. 62, no. 6, 1983, pp. 321–24.

Wilde, Oscar. *Oscar Wilde in America: The Interviews,* edited by Matthew Hofer and Gary Scharnhorst. Urbana and Chicago: U of Illinois P, 2010.

_____. *The Complete Works of Oscar Wilde*. London: HarperCollins, 2003.

_____. *The Wit & Wisdom of Oscar Wilde: A Treasury of Quotations, Anecdotes, and Repartee*, edited by Ralph Keyes. New York: HarperCollins, 1996.

"His Warmest Admirers": Oscar Wilde and His Interactions with Women_____

Eleanor Fitzsimons

If you were asked to identify a man you would not readily associate with women, you might think first of Oscar Wilde. The penalties imposed upon him as a gay man—imprisonment, impoverishment, and ignominy—have ensured that his life has been examined largely through the prism of his relationships with men, Lord Alfred Douglas in particular. Yet, Wilde had a genuine fondness for women, and they in turn were drawn to him. As his close friend and biographer Vincent O'Sullivan explained in *Aspects of Wilde:*

> I have always found, and find today, his warmest admirers among women. He, in his turn, admired women. I never heard him say anything disparaging about any woman, even when some of them required such treatment! (57)

Wilde's admiration for women as friends, fellow writers, performers, and campaigners had its roots in his close relationship with his remarkable mother, Lady Jane Wilde. A wit, a beauty, a revolutionary poet, an essayist and an accomplished translator, a loving wife and mother, and a quixotic campaigner for women's rights, she was also an incorrigible snob and a brilliant conversationalist. She was famous long before he was. Wilde admired her considerable intellect and her prodigious appetite for life. She had a profound influence on his writing and his character. Through her example, he understood that women could be just as creative and intelligent as men.

In her youth, Jane Elgee, as she was before marriage, campaigned fiercely for Irish liberty in defiance of her unionist family who believed that Ireland should remain loyal to the British monarch. Although she was exceptionally bright and eager to learn, she was denied a formal education, like most women of her time.

As a consequence, she was largely self-taught. In an interview published towards the end of her life, she recalled:

> I was always very fond of study, and of books. My favourite study was languages. I succeeded in mastering ten of the European languages. Till my eighteenth year I never wrote anything. All my time was given to study. (*Hearth and Home* 6)

Jane Elgee wrote revolutionary poetry as "Speranza," the Italian word for hope. In 1847, during the height of the Irish famine, her words had a galvanizing effect: "a nation is arising from her long and ghastly swoon," she declared (J. Wilde *Poems* 37). In "The Famine Year," she condemned the arrival of "stately ships to bear our food away" (J. Wilde *Poems* 5). In "The Exodus," she lamented the "million a decade" (J. Wilde *Poems* 55) forced to flee, many of them starting new lives in America, where her writing was hugely popular. Speranza's most celebrated composition was "The Brothers," a rousing ballad eulogizing Henry and John Sheares, one a lawyer, the other a barrister, both United Irishmen hanged for their part in the rising of 1798. In tone and theme, it resembles her son's *Ballad of Reading Gaol*, and it was taken up by the street balladeers of Dublin. Charles Gavin Duffy, editor of *The Nation*, the weekly nationalist newspaper in which Speranza's poems were published, believed that her poetry "represented a substantial force in Irish politics, the vehement will of a woman of genius" (95). Alexander Martin Sullivan, who took over as editor in 1855, described how "her personal attractions, her cultivated mind, her originality and force of character, made her a central figure in Dublin society" (75). Although Wilde's eponymous heroine in his first play, *Vera; or, the Nihilists*, was inspired by Russian revolutionary Vera Zasulich, she also resembles his idealistic mother during her freedom-fighting youth.

In 1882, when Wilde, aged twenty-seven, embarked on a lecture tour of America, he was the scarcely-known author of a slight collection of poetry, and an emerging leader of the Aesthetic Movement. The revolutionary credentials of his formidable mother persuaded influential women like Anne Lynch Botta, a prominent patron of the arts, to invite him into their homes. Lynch Botta's father, Patrick Lynch, a rebellious Dubliner, had been imprisoned then deported from Ireland after the failed rising of 1798. His daughter's literary gatherings, held at her brownstone salon at 25 West 37th Street, were attended by every major poet, artist, and musician of her day, among them Emerson, Irving, Trollope, Thackeray, Horace Greeley, Fanny Osgood, and Margaret Fuller. She introduced Edgar Allan Poe, virtually unknown in New York, to her influential circle and encouraged him to read aloud from early versions of *The Raven*. Wilde benefited from her support, and the support of other influential American women, among them the formidable newspaper proprietor Mrs. Frank Leslie, who later married his brother Willie; Jane Tunis Poultney Bigelow, an important figure in the New York literary scene; Marietta Paran Stevens, of whom it was said "probably no woman in New York has launched a greater number of ambitious young men and women into the social maelstrom" (Fitzsimons 104); influential journalist Kate Field, who had covered Charles Dickens's tours; and Jane Cunningham Croly, founder of the Women's Parliament, "Sorosis," America's first professional woman's club, and the General Federation of Women's Clubs.

In 1851, when Jane Elgee married Dr. William Wilde, later Sir William Wilde, an eminent surgeon and collector of Irish folklore, she gave up revolution and devoted herself to her husband and their three children: Willie, Oscar, and Isola. She did not stop working and earned a reputation as an accomplished translator of scholarly works. When Sir William Wilde died in 1876, he left his widow in poverty as a result of his poor financial management. She had no option but to move to London, where she made a meager living from her writing. Wilde introduced her to the women he had befriended there, among them celebrated actresses Ellen Terry and Sarah Bernhardt, "professional beauty" Lillie Langtry, and accomplished artist Louise Jopling. At that time, he was collaborating with several women, and celebrating others by writing sonnets about them. He translated a poem with Polish actress Helena Modjeska, who had fled her native Poland as a result of political persecution, and he provided advice and funding to enlightened American actress Elizabeth Robbins, who brought the plays of Ibsen to England and staged them herself.

In her erudite articles, Lady Wilde was bitter in her condemnation of the neglect of women. Harnessing her finest revolutionary rhetoric, she raged:

> Women truly need much to be done for them. At present they have neither dignity nor position. All avenues to wealth and rank are closed to them. The state takes no notice of their existence except to injure them by its laws. (Fitzsimons 29)

Lady Wilde's progressive, albeit slightly erratic views on the position of women in society were uncompromisingly frank. In "The Bondage of Women," she expressed her despair at the universal disregard shown for the intellect of women: "For six thousand years," she wrote, "the history of women has been a mournful record of helpless resignation to social prejudice and legal tyranny" (J. Wilde *Social Studies* 23). She ended with an exceptionally powerful passage:

> Genius never yet unsexed a woman, or learning or culture ever so extended; but the meanness of her ordinary social routine life, with all its petty duties and claims, and ritual of small observances, degrades and humiliates her, for it deprives her of all dignity, and leaves her without any meaning in God's great universe. (J. Wilde *Social Studies* 23)

Lady Wilde campaigned vociferously for women to be granted greater access to formal education, a theme taken up by her son Oscar. In "Venus Victrix," from her collected essays *Social Studies*, she insisted:

> It is impossible to believe that woman will be less attractive because educated, less tender and devoted because learned, less loving because she can attain the high station, honour, dignity and wealth, which hitherto only marriage could confer, by her own unfettered intellect and genius (J. Wilde 95).

She welcomed the Married Women's Property Rights Act of 1882 as "an important and remarkable epoch in the history of women," and she expressed relief that a woman would no longer enter marriage "as a bonded slave, disenfranchised of all rights over her fortune" (J. Wilde *Gentlewoman*). Yet, Lady Wilde was contradictory in her approach to marriage. She was adamant that a loyal wife should accommodate her husband's indiscretions; certainly Sir William Wilde had given her ample opportunity to put this philosophy into practice. In May 1884, when Oscar, aged twenty-nine, married Constance Lloyd, her new mother-in-law, who regarded her as a "very nice pretty sensible girl-well-connected and well brought up" (Fitzsimons 147), advised her that unwavering support for her husband was the key to a happy marriage.

Letters Wilde exchanged with Constance and testimony provided by several of their friends confirm that he was blissfully happy during the early years of his marriage. Lillie Langtry, who was one of his closest confidantes, recalled how he "often talked rapturously" (Fitzsimons 146) about Constance. Ada Leverson, a staunch supporter after his arrest and imprisonment, recalled: "'When he was first married, he was quite madly in love, and showed himself an unusually devoted husband'" (qtd. in Moyle 90). Even Lord Alfred Douglas, the love of Wilde's later life, characterized Wilde's marriage in *Oscar Wilde: A Summing Up* as "a marriage of deep love and affection on both sides" (93).

Constance, who had a troubled adolescence, was far less flamboyant than her husband and could appear shy and lacking in confidence. In fact, she was a bright, progressive, and politically active woman, who spoke excellent French and Italian, and was an accomplished pianist. Newspaper accounts pay tribute to her beauty and praise her aptitude as a public speaker. Her speech "Home Rule for Ireland," delivered at the Women's Liberal Federation annual conference of 1889, was applauded in the *Pall Mall Gazette*. She campaigned vociferously for greater participation of women in public life. As a member of the Chelsea Women's Liberal Association, she was instrumental in having Lady Margaret Sandhurst elected to the London County Council. Her strong views on dress reform, which she shared with her husband, led her to join the committee of the Rational Dress Society in order to campaign for an end to the ridiculous, restrictive fashions that prevented women from leading fulfilling lives. In "Clothed in Our Right Minds," a lecture she delivered to the Rational Dress Society in 1888, she advocated the wearing of divided skirts, insisting that, as God had given women two legs, they should have the freedom to use them.

The couple's elder son, Cyril, was born shortly after they celebrated their first wedding anniversary. His brother, Vyvyan, followed seventeen months later. Wilde, who was beginning to acknowledge that he was sexually attracted to young men, had grown restless by then. Increasingly, he sought opportunities to escape what he regarded as the stultifying constraints of his Victorian marriage. Although he grew disillusioned with married life, his empathy with the women he admired never wavered. His eagerness to collaborate with progressive women was never more evident than when he accepted the editorship of society magazine *The Lady's World* in April 1887, a magazine he regarded as "a very vulgar, trivial, and stupid production" (Holland and Hart-Davis 332) In the face of strong opposition from publishers Cassell and Company, Wilde insisted on renaming the magazine *The Woman's World*. In a letter to general manager Thomas Wemyss Reid, he undertook to transform it into "the recognised organ for the expression of women's opinions on all subjects of literature, art, and modern life" (Holland and Hart-Davis 297). Wilde vowed that, under his editorship, *The Woman's World* would "take a wider range, as well as a high standpoint, and deal not merely with what women wear, but with what they think, and what they feel" (Holland and Hart-Davis 297).

It is often assumed that Wilde accepted this role simply to secure a regular income. Certainly, as a married man of thirty-two with a young family to provide for and exquisite tastes to gratify, he found it impossible to fund the lifestyle he desired out of his unreliable earnings as a freelance reviewer and occasional lecturer. He had written little of note at that time. Although Constance brought a modest allowance to the household, by 1887 their resources were falling distressingly short of their outgoings. The weekly salary of six pounds was very welcome, but it does not account for Wilde's insistence on changing the content of the magazine so radically when he could have left it largely as it was. A committed individualist, Wilde believed that women should be allowed far more autonomy than they were afforded by patriarchal Victorian society. As a regular contributor to several popular periodicals, he would have realized how badly served intelligent, ambitious women were by the plethora of new magazines claiming to represent their interests. In response, he used his platform at *The Woman's World* to highlight the more absurd aspects of gender discrimination, and to facilitate debate on the issues faced by women who attempted to enter the public sphere. Literature was a key focus. One of Wilde's most rewarding tasks was the commissioning of new works of fiction from emerging and radical women writers. In "Literary and Other Notes," he gave what he called "special prominence" (Holland and Hart-Davis 327) to books written by women. In "Oscar Wilde as Editor," an article published in *Harper's Weekly* in 1913, Arthur Fish, the young man Cassell appointed as Wilde's sub-editor, insisted that the "keynote" of *The Woman's World* under Wilde's editorship was no less than "the right of woman to equality of treatment with man" (18). He also attested that articles on "women's work and their position in politics were far in advance of the thought of the day" (18). Fish never doubted Wilde's commitment to *The Woman's World*, and he described how ferociously his boss fought to retain editorial control:

> Sir Wemyss Reid, then General Manager of Cassell's, or John Williams the Chief Editor, would call in at our room and discuss them [women's issues] with Oscar Wilde, who would always express his entire sympathy with the views of the writers and reveal a liberality of thought with regard to the political aspirations of women that was undoubtedly sincere. (Fish 18)

The first issue of *The Woman's World* under Wilde's editorship appeared in November 1887. A fresh cover design featured his name prominently with key contributors listed below. In a significant departure from convention, each article was attributed to its author by name. Wilde relegated fashion to the back pages and opened a debate on gendered dress codes by declaring that, in time, "dress of the two sexes will be assimilated, as similarity of costume always follows similarity of pursuits" (*WWI* 40). He castigated the "absolute unsuitability of ordinary feminine attire to any sort of handicraft, or even to any occupation which necessitates a daily walk to business and back again in all kinds of weather" (*WWI* 40). Gone entirely were "Fashionable Marriages," "Society Pleasures," "Pastimes for Ladies," and "Five o'clock Tea." Instead, Wilde promoted literature, art, travel and social studies. In his "Literary and Other Notes," he demonstrated unequivocal support for the greater participation of women in public life. He campaigned for them to be granted access to education and the professions, and he argued that the "cultivation of separate sorts of virtues and separate ideals of duty in men and women has led to the whole social fabric being weaker and unhealthier than it need be" (*WWII* 390). For his first issue, he commissioned a lengthy article from Eveline, Countess of Portsmouth on "The Position of Women." Like Lady Wilde, who also contributed to *The Woman's World*, she welcomed amendments to marriage law designed to reform an institution that, in her view, "might and did very often represent to a wife a hopeless and bitter slavery" (*WWI* 8). In "The Fallacy of the Superiority of Man," published the following month, Laura McLaren, founder of the Liberal Women's Suffrage Union, asked: "If women are inferior in any point, let the world hear the evidence on which they are to be condemned" (*WWI* 54).

Education was another key focus of *The Woman's World*. Wilde commissioned articles on the women's colleges in the universities of Oxford and Cambridge, and on Alexandra College, an all-girls institution of higher education in his native Dublin. He also published articles encouraging the few women who had benefited from access to higher education to explore opportunities opening up to them in the professions: medicine, law, and education. Many less fortunate women lived in dire poverty along with their children. Several articles in *The Woman's World* drew attention to their plight and proposed solutions that went far beyond the usual ineffectual charitable works. In "Something About Needlewomen," trade unionist Clementina Black, who helped establish the Woman's Trade Union Association, encouraged needlewomen unable to earn a living wage from the piecework they were given to combine into cooperatives. Irish journalist Charlotte O'Connor Eccles drew attention to the alarming conditions endured by Dublin's women weavers, and insisted that their poverty should be alleviated through education and training. Emily Faithfull, a member of the Society for Promoting the Employment of Women, insisted that society had a duty to educate all girls in some trade, calling, or profession.

Wilde tackled the contentious issue of women's involvement in politics head-on. He was unequivocal in his support for their greater participation. In his review of *Darwinism and Politics*, by Scottish philosopher David George Ritchie, he praised that author's rebuttal of Herbert Spencer's contention that, should women be admitted to political life, they might do mischief by introducing the ethics of the family into affairs of state; "If something is right in a family," Wilde countered, "it is difficult to see why it is, therefore, without any further reason, wrong in the state" (*WWII* 390). He commissioned several articles on the campaign for women's suffrage. He also assisted his wife in helping Lady Margaret Sandhurst in her controversial bid to be elected to the London City Council by publishing in full a speech she delivered in January 1889, in which she expressed sympathies for the Home Rule cause in Ireland, thus echoing one of his mother's key concerns.

In *Oscar Wilde and his Mother*, published in 1911, Wilde's friend Anna de Brémont declared: "Society began to take Oscar Wilde seriously when he became editor of *The Woman's World*" (73). The press response was similarly positive: "Mr Oscar Wilde has triumphed," declared the *Nottingham Evening Post*, "the first number of the 'Woman's World' has already appeared, and has, I believe, been sold out" (Fitzsimons 169). Praising Wilde for "striking an original line," the *Times* hailed *The Woman's World* as "gracefully got up . . . in every respect" (Fitzsimons 169). Yet, Wilde's tenure as editor of *The Woman's World* was short-lived. Much of his disenchantment was born of frustration rather than lack of commitment: "I am not allowed as free a hand as I would like"

(Holland and Hart-Davis 325), he told his friend Helena Sickert. In a letter to Scottish writer William Sharp, he complained: "The work of reconstruction was very difficult as the Lady's World was a most vulgar trivial production, and the doctrine of heredity holds good in literature as in life" (Holland and Hart-Davis 332). In April 1889, Wilde informed the Board of Inland Revenue that he would be leaving Cassell & Co. in August. By October 1889, his name was gone from the cover.

Wilde had not neglected his own writing during his two-year tenure as editor. Dozens of his poems, reviews, essays and stories were accepted by various periodicals during this time, and he also published and promoted *The Happy Prince and Other Tales,* his first collection of stories. The break with *The Woman's World* heralded an exceptionally productive period that saw the publication of two further collections of short stories, *Lord Arthur Savile's Crime and Other Stories* and *The House of Pomegranates*, and a collection of essays titled *Intentions*. He was keen to write something longer. One of his contributors to *The Woman's World*, bestselling novelist Ouida, born Maria Louisa Ramé, had a profound influence on *The Picture of Dorian Gray*, the only novel he ever wrote. Ouida's decadent novels celebrated a lush aristocratic existence, and her aesthetic style kicked against the fetters imposed by Victorian notions of prudence, rationality, and worth. She pioneered a new style of language, studded with witty epigrams, which allowed her characters to indulge in the most subversive behavior imaginable. Her paeans to beauty earned her a devoted following amongst Aesthetes and Pre-Raphaelites, but she was also hugely popular with the shop girls and footmen who frequented the circulating libraries or saved up for six shilling, single-volume reprints of her latest novel. Reviewing Ouida's "amazing romance" *Guilderoy* in the *Pall Mall Gazette*, Wilde christened her "the last of the romantics"; his admiring verdict was "though she is rarely true, she is never dull" (Fitzsimons 197).

Ouida popularized the indolent male dandy connoisseur. Her women were strikingly beautiful, aristocratic socialites, loyal to no one but themselves, who spoke in epigrammatic language reminiscent of Wilde's. Her influence should not be overstated, but critics recognized something of her style in Wilde's work. In a review of *The Picture of Dorian Gray*, the *St. James' Gazette* opined that while "the style was better than Ouida's popular aesthetic romances the erudition remained nonetheless equal" (Fitzsimons 199). Their critic concluded, "the grammar is better than Ouida's—the erudition equal; but in every other respect we prefer the talented lady" (Fitzsimons 199). Writing in *McBride's Magazine*, Julian Hawthorne, journalist son of Nathaniel, claimed:

> "Mr. Wilde's writing has what is called 'colour,'—the quality that forms the main-stay of many of Ouida's works,—and it appears in the sensuous descriptions of nature and of the decorations and environments of the artistic life." (qtd. in Fitzsimons 199)

Ouida's short play *Afternoon*, published in 1883, introduced "Aldred Dorian," a collector of beautiful objects and a painter of portraits.

Although Wilde attracted notoriety, and considerable admiration, after *Dorian Gray,* he never wrote another novel. During the 1890s, he was drawn once more to writing plays. In 1892, he worked on two very different manuscripts: *Salomé*, a Biblical tragedy in one act, and *Lady Windermere's Fan*, a brilliant social comedy that remains popular to this day. Sadly, he never saw *Salomé* performed since it was refused a licence by the English Examiner of Plays. It was staged during his lifetime when Aurélien Lugné-Poë, founder of the experimental Théâtre de l'Oeuvre in Paris, premiered it in February 1896, while Wilde was in prison in England. In contrast, *Lady Windermere's Fan* became the first in a series of glittering social comedies that exposed the deep-rooted double standards characterising patriarchal Victorian society.

Every play Wilde wrote was named for a woman: from his first, *Vera; or, the Nihilists*, to his last, *The Importance of Being Earnest*, which had the working title "Lady Lancing" in early drafts. In between came *The Duchess of Padua*, which he wrote for American actress Mary Anderson; *Lady Windermere's Fan*, which had the working title "A Good Woman;" *Salomé*, which was to have Sarah Bernhardt in the titular role; *A Woman of No Importance*, which was

"Mrs. Arbuthnot" in early drafts; and *An Ideal Husband*, which he called "Mrs. Cheveley" for a time. Wilde's attitudes towards women slipped into his plays. Since he believed passionately that women should enjoy the same rights and freedoms as men, and that no one should be prevented from doing anything one wished, he reserved his most biting commentary for puritanical women who sought to impose harsh moral strictures on women and men alike. In *A Woman of No Importance*, which he described as "a woman's play" (Holland and Hart-Davis 558), prim American Puritan Hester Worsley irritates fellow house guests by insisting that everyone should adhere to an unbearably strict code. Wilde considered Puritanism to be "'the real enemy of modern life, of everything that makes life lovely and joyous and coloured for us'" (qtd. in Fitzsimons 225). When the newspaper *The Sketch* interviewed him about *A Woman of No Importance*, he quipped: "'It is indeed a burning shame that there should be one law for men and another law for women. I think . . . I think there should be no law for anybody'" (qtd. in Fitzsimons 226).

Wilde often based his women characters on people he was close to. He created Mrs. Erlynne in *Lady Windermere's Fan* for Lillie Langtry. When he offered her the role, she was horrified at his willingness to reveal the existence of a daughter she had kept secret for many years, and turned him down. The delightfully droll Mrs. Allonby in *A Woman of No Importance* is Wilde's tribute to Ada Leverson, whose wit often matched his. She inspired several lines in the play; "Nothing spoils a romance more than a sense of humour in a woman and the lack of it in a man," she quipped (Fitzsimons 249). Wilde pilfered this for an exchange between Lord Illingworth and Mrs. Allonby. In *The Importance of Being Earnest*, he created four wonderful women characters. The imperious Lady Bracknell considers herself the most reliable arbiter of taste and probity in England. Her insistence on upholding absurd standards while at the same time demonstrating naked avarice recalls the duplicity of the society women who presided over London's most fashionable and influential drawing rooms. These women fêted Wilde while he entertained them but would never admit him into their inner circle. His instincts in lampooning them were well founded since they abandoned him in adversity. Dutiful governess Miss Prism causes the confusion at the center of the play when she struggles to reconcile her domestic duties with her ambition to write a three-volume novel, a dichotomy familiar to many Victorian women who felt unfulfilled in their domestic role. Miss Prism's charge, Cecily Cardew, and a second young woman, Gwendolen Fairfax, are alarmingly frank and self-possessed but let themselves down by favoring triviality over substance.

Before *The Importance of Being Earnest* was performed, Wilde cut several lines that seem to address the reason his marriage was failing. He had Algernon declare: "My dear fellow, all women are too good for the men they marry. That is why men tire of their wives" (qtd. in Böker, Corballis and Hibbard 16). As his celebrity grew, Wilde was increasingly absent from home and much of that time was spent in hotel rooms with a series of young men. Shortly after *The Importance of Being Earnest* opened to huge acclaim, Wilde was persuaded to pursue a libel action against the Marquis of Queensberry, father of his lover Lord Alfred Douglas. This rash act was prompted by a note left by Queensberry at the Albemarle Club accusing Wilde of "posing as a somdomite [*sic*]". The case was abandoned halfway through when the defense team presented damning evidence of Wilde's liaisons with various young men. Within weeks, he was arrested, tried, and convicted of gross indecency. He was sentenced to two years imprisonment with hard labor.

Constance Wilde's world fell apart after her husband was imprisoned. Obliged to flee abroad and to change her family name to Holland to protect their young sons, Cyril and Vyvyan, she did as much as she could to assist her husband, including paying him an annual allowance. Tentative attempts to reconcile with him came to an end when she died as a result of a botched operation performed in an Italian clinic in April 1898. She was thirty-nine years old. Regrettably, she is often portrayed as a figure of pity. In reality, she was strong and courageous, warm and true, and she met the many challenges she faced, including debilitating health problems, with steely determination.

When his popularity was at its height, Oscar Wilde was fêted and adored by women from every walk of life. Many of them abandoned him during the time he spent in prison and the few years that remained to him after he was released. He did benefit from the extraordinary loyalty shown to him by women who are largely forgotten today: the witty author and satirist Ada Leverson, who allowed him to stay in her house when he was being hounded; and the extraordinarily generous heiress Adela Schuster, who provided him with funds while he was in prison, allowing him to pay for his mother's funeral. Some of the warmest and most revealing accounts of Wilde were written by women who remained loyal to the end. Rather than remembering him as a brilliant but broken man who paid the highest price for being who he was, we should think of him as his friend Helena Swanwick, neé Sickert, feminist and pacifist, did when she wrote: "His extravaganzas had no end, his invention was inexhaustible, and everything he said was full of joy and energy" (65).

Works Cited

Böker, Uwe, Julie A. Hibbard, and Richard Corballis, editors. *The Importance of Reinventing Oscar: Versions of Wilde During the Last 100 Years*. Amsterdam: Rodopi, 2002.

Brémont, Anna Dunphy (comtesse de). *Oscar Wilde and his Mother*. London: Everett & Co., 1911.

Douglas, Lord Alfred Bruce. *Oscar Wilde, A Summing Up*. London: Richards P, 1961.

Fish, Arthur. "Oscar Wilde as Editor." *Harper's Weekly*, vol. 58, 4 Oct. 1913, p.18.

Fitzsimons, Eleanor. *Wilde's Women*. London: Duckworth, 2015.

Gavan Duffy, Charles. *Four Years of Irish History*. London, New York: Cassell, Petter & Co., 1883.

Hearth and Home magazine, 30 June 1892, reproduced in *Freeman's Journal,* 6 Feb. 1896, p. 5.

Moyle, Franny. *Constance: The Tragic and Scandalous Life of Mrs Oscar Wilde*. London: John Murray, 2012.

O'Sullivan, Vincent. *Aspects of Wilde*. London: Constable & Company Limited, 1936.

Sullivan, A. M. *New Ireland*. Glasgow: Cameron and Ferguson, 1877.

Swanwick, Helena. *I Have Been Young*. London: Victor Gollancz, 1935.

Wilde, Lady Jane. "A New Era in English & Irish Social Life." *Gentlewoman*. January 1883.

Cited in Melville, Joy. "Wilde, Jane Francesca Agnes, Lady Wilde (1821–1896)." *Oxford Dictionary of National Biography*. New York: Oxford University Press, 2004.

_____. *Poems*. Dublin: J. Duffy, 1864.

_____. *Social Studies*. London: Ward and Downey, 1893.

Wilde, Oscar. *Complete Letters of Oscar Wilde,* edited by Merlin Holland and Rupert Hart-Davis. London: Fourth Estate, 2000.

Women's World, Volume I (WWI). London: Cassell and Co., 1888.

Women's World, Volume II (WWII). London: Cassell and Co., 1889.

Sex, Love, and the Nineteenth Century: The Case of Lady Windermere_____

Melissa Knox

The degree to which nineteenth-century culture suppressed sexuality shows in Oscar Wilde's letter of May 20, 1885 regarding the impending birth of his first son: "My wife has a cold but in about a month will be over it." "I hope it is a boy cold, but will love whatever the gods send" (261). These lines, among Wilde's milder attacks on the social customs of concealing, minimizing, and denying sexual feelings and behaviors, characterize a culture far less comfortable with sexuality than previous periods. Without a good grasp of the depths of sexual secrecy, fear, and repression in the nineteenth century, it is not possible to understand the reforming vision of Oscar Wilde, whose ideas about sexual identity and sexual freedom are commonplace today, but were misunderstood and punished during his lifetime. When he died of an ear infection, probably worsened by a longstanding infection of syphilitic origin, in 1900 at age 46 (Gordon, 1209)[1], he reportedly remarked: "If another century began and I was still alive, it really would be more than the English could stand" (Harris, 348). Now regarded as a leading intellectual of his day, a philosopher passionately devoted to human rights, a great wit, a writer known for his comedies, and a visionary who helped open the door for the acceptance of same-sex love, Wilde was, until the nineteen-sixties, shunted aside by most critics as a trivial plagiarist and poseur.

In 1885, the year Wilde's first son, Cyril, was born, and for nearly seventy subsequent years, pregnancy remained hidden and unmentionable. When the American comedian Lucille Ball, a 1950s version of Ellen DeGeneres, became pregnant in 1952, she wanted her hit show, *I Love Lucy,* to continue, and daringly televised the announcement of her pregnancy. But the network didn't dare to let her use that word. Directing her co-star and husband to read a letter from a supposed member of his audience saying, "my husband and I are having a blessed event," Ball created a scene whose humor relied on embarrassment provoked by the idea of pregnancy. Pregnant women have a long history of being fired, though legal protections in most of the European Union and America have existed since 1978. The present writer remembers the era of Second-Wave Feminism (early 1960s to late 1970s) as a time when at least one young woman in her middle-school class believed her parents had only had sex once or twice, to produce her and a sibling, and imagined she was dying of cancer when menstruation began. Her mother had explained nothing, the school's sex education unit started too late, and social media did not yet exist to fill in the gaps.

Wilde's snide quip referring to his wife's pregnancy as a "cold" displays, like many of his remarks, a longing for greater openness about sexual acts, thoughts, and feelings. He was well aware that sexuality had not always proven so problematic a topic, that the ancient Greeks embraced the same-sex love that his contemporaries found unspeakable. Until the nineteenth century, sexuality had been less deliberately suppressed. The eighteenth-century English artist William Hogarth's most famous work, "The Rake's Progress," portrays a young man coming into money and then abandoning the pregnant woman he promised to marry. He stands being measured for a new suit; she stands sadly holding the wedding band she won't get to wear. Hogarth's series of paintings (later engravings) shows the young man squandering his wealth on drink, prostitutes, gambling—the syphilitic sores of the prostitutes prominent, the limply dangling sword an indication of impotence caused by drink and sexually transmitted diseases. In the seventeenth century, Andrew Marvell joked in "To His Coy Mistress" about what a waste he considered virginity (in the grave, he points out, "worms shall try [that is, eat] that long preserved virginity") (lines 27–28). In the sixteenth century, John Donne's poem, "To his Mistress Going to Bed," includes these lines: "License my roving hands, and let them go, / Before, behind, between, above, below" (25–26). In the fourteenth century, Geoffrey Chaucer cheerfully wrote of a woman being grabbed by the "queynte," ("priveley he caught hire by the queynte," line 3276) a word then suggesting the equivalent of "the family jewels" as well as a four-letter vulgarism beginning with "c," but which at the time was less crude and more anatomical. She sticks her buttocks out a window in the dark, so that an unwanted lover kisses an orifice he believes to be her mouth: "And at the wyndow out she putte hir hole, /And Absolon, hym fil no bet ne wers / But with his mouth he kiste hir naked ers" (lines 624–26). The unlucky lover finds out he's wrong when her preferred boyfriend sticks his bottom out the window and farts in the other man's face: "anon leet fle a fart," a loud one, characterized as a thunderbolt (3806).

In other words, English art, literature, and culture freely displayed sexual and bodily feelings and situations for centuries before the Victorian Age (1837–1901). Why things changed so much in the nineteenth century, such that pregnancy became unmentionable, homosexual behavior criminal, masturbation a disease, female arousal so frightening that by 1866, Dr. Isaac Baker Brown was "curing" it by performing clitoridectomies, has never been completely clarified. The rise of evangelical Christianity in England has been blamed, along with increasing death rates from syphilis. Greater possibilities for education meant emphasis on categorizing, and with categories came pigeonholes, and ultimately many, often moral, condemnations. As Jeffrey Weeks has documented, by 1867 a series of labels for types of sexual beings, "homosexual" among them (79, 84) had been coined, and with these new coinages came a deluge of theories, classifications, and dire warnings. Without a higher standard of living for most people, such classifications might never have existed, because more pressing needs, like finding food, clothing, fuel, and fresh water, took precedence.

In other words, leisure, including the luxury of indoor plumbing and education, which had become possible for more people, came with dangers: the proverbial warning often attributed to the Puritans, that "idle hands are the work of the devil," also points to the number of cruel and crackpot ideas about sex and sexuality that arose when people had enough time on their hands to study the subject. Sexuality became forbidden, dirty. Exceptions to the rule could always be found—Prince Bertie, Queen Victoria's son, owned a custom-made chair on rockers that facilitated his sexual encounters with two women at once (Smithsonian).

But the Victorian middle and upper classes represented the polar opposite of Bertie. In 1865, the influential physician William Acton wrote that "the majority of women (happily for them) are not very much troubled by sexual feeling of any kind" (*Function and Disorders*). Like Wilde's Lady Windermere in his social comedy, *Lady Windermere's Fan*, they were taught, as she puts it, "what the world is forgetting, the difference that there is between what is right and what is wrong" (387). For her, the notion of a married woman acknowledging attraction to a man who was not her husband, even if she never acts on her feelings, was unthinkable or, as she puts it, "vile" (388). The safest strategy, the one she is schooled by her stern aunt to incorporate into her entire way of looking at the world, is to substitute disgust for arousal; she prides herself on having "something of the Puritan in me" (387), on allowing "no compromise" (387).

The chief influence on nineteenth-century marriage, the cult of true womanhood, established four expected virtues for women: piety, purity, domesticity, and submissiveness. In other words, "good" women were expected to devote themselves to Christian self-sacrifice; to be "pure" in the sense of virginal when they married, ignorant of and suspicious of sexual desire, often even of the basics of human reproduction; to be devoted housewives and mothers, and unquestioningly to obey every demand of their husbands. It was taken for granted that women had no desires and ambitions of their own apart from the wish to be wives and mothers. In any case, women could not vote and had few legal rights. English women could not, for example, enter the medical profession until 1867, and they could not vote in national elections until 1918. Middle- and upper-class women usually did not work outside the home until the nineteen-seventies. Before 1882, when the "Married Women's Property Act" was made law, a divorced woman could lose her property and the right to see her children. Common law dictated that she was the property of her husband, not a person with civil rights distinct from his. Victorian art and culture strongly reinforced the cult of true womanhood, emphatically in Coventry Patmore's famous poem, "The Angel in the House," first published in 1854, the year in which Oscar Wilde was born.

This lengthy poem espouses the notion of women as suited only to the domestic sphere, idealizing and restricting them to the role of angelic servants to and protectors of their husbands and children. A woman could never become angry unless her husband failed, in return for his wife's submissiveness and housewifely virtues, to protect and remain faithful to her. Not even then, typically—but Wilde's heroines are revolutionary in their resentment of men who cheat on them.

Believing they have an actual right to faithful husbands, they represent the views of the New Woman, a late nineteenth-century emergent social construct moving in the direction of equality between the sexes. "New Women" took jobs as "typewriters" or typists, wrote for newspapers, pursued university degrees, or explored clothing styles less restrictive than whalebone corsets and full-length skirts. They wanted the right to vote, and they represented an increased desire for agency and power strongly feared in novels written by men in the final decades of the nineteenth century. Henry Rider Haggard's *She* and *King Solomon's Mines*, for instance, bestsellers, showcase all-powerful females who supernaturally live for centuries, commit murders, and possess secret knowledge about female sexuality. Grant Allen's 1895 novel, *The Woman Who Did,* scandalously suggested that marriage is bad for women, that "free unions" were better. This is not a point of view taken by Wilde's heroine Lady Windermere, however—who is far more conventional. Allen was far from being the only male writer propounding such views—Thomas Hardy and George Gissing were among the better known male authors writing about passionate women—but their views were hardly shared by Lady Windermere.

II

I introduced Oscar Wilde to my students not just as a great wit but as a public figure: he practically invented personal branding or image management, he daringly or suicidally promoted respect for same-sex love between men at a time when English culture preferred to pretend only one form of sexuality existed: the married kind, between what we would now call a cisgender man and a cisgender woman. "Bad" women—those who declined to conform to the cult of true womanhood—were acknowledged. In *Lady Windermere's Fan*, one of the men, Cecil Graham, remarks, "Wicked women bother one. Good women bore one. That is the only difference between them" (415). But Lady Windermere insists that women "who have committed what the world calls a fault . . . should never be forgiven" (388), until she comes pretty close to committing such a fault herself.

Even Wilde was careful not to be too direct, not, for instance, to use the term "prostitute" or to name socially unaccepted forms of sex, preferring to speak in a coded fashion, using "bimetallism" to refer to bisexuality (a term invented in 1892) in *The Importance of Being Earnest*. An earlier term, "heterosexual," has, like "homosexuality," had a checkered career, its meaning evolving over the decades from a pathologically lustful interest in the opposite sex to a "normal" interest in the opposite sex. Of course, "normal" begs the question of the meaning of the term, and of course both these terms presume the existence of only two genders. The array of terms now commonly used to convey sexual identity, from LBGTQ to asexual to fluid to genderqueer to non-conforming—and more— would have bewildered and disgusted the Victorians. Categories implied restriction, and restriction moral control. A situation in which restriction and control are seen as impediments would have been anathema.

The need for control may be seen in the new and growing field of sexology, in which two groups fought for authority: those who thought a "third sex" ought to be recognized, and those who pathologized most forms of non-reproductive sex apart from mouth kissing. Labels for the third sex included "homosexual," used by both groups, "urning," used by gay men, "sexual invert" used mostly by psychologists who saw the third sex as "deviant" sufferers, and "sodomite," an insult and a term invoking Biblical and legal condemnation. Both groups wrote books and pamphlets, some advocating tolerance but others defining homosexuality as a cause of criminal behavior or of "degeneration," a mistily defined deterioration suggesting the reverse of evolution.

The late Victorians—persons living in the last decades of the nineteenth century—had two broad categories for thinking about sex, one of which was "married" and the other of which was "gay," a term then meaning any kind of sexuality that was either illegal or morally transgressive or both. The nearest online etymological dictionary states that: "The word gay by the 1890s had an overall tinge of promiscuity—a gay house was a brothel," and the *Oxford English Dictionary*, a multi-volume comprehensive history of the English language, records that between about 1795 and the mid-1890s, and on a few later occasions the term meant a woman "living by prostitution" or a place serving as a brothel. The numerous phrases used to document this definition include, in 1799, "she keeps a gay house," and in 1890, "the gay ladies on the beat."

The female prostitutes who danced on the pavement in front of the building where Oscar Wilde was on trial and soon to be convicted of "indecent acts"—a legal term at the time meaning any kind of sexual behavior between men that did not include anal penetration—felt happy because the man whom they experienced as competition in the sex work business was about to go to prison. These women wanted to monopolize the prostitution market, so they resented men who were, like them, paid for sex. The trial and Wilde's subsequent two-year sentence had the desired effect for the women prostitutes: many men left England or refrained from paid sexual encounters with other men as a result.

The initial reaction of my students to Wilde's *Lady Windermere's Fan* was "Oh! There's no sex in this play." Because I had presented Wilde as a figure in the vanguard of the gay rights movement, my students were expecting something more direct, even something sexually salacious. I suggested that indeed this play was filled with sex—just not the kind of sex they were used to thinking about.

"Isn't it the case," I asked, "that you are all well aware of whom and what you find erotically interesting? Isn't it true that if you have any concerns or consider yourself inexpert at a particular sexual technique, that you can just ask someone or watch YouTube videos on the topic?"

"Yes, of course," they answered unanimously. "Naturally we're aware." They assumed everyone had always been just as aware of these things as they are.

I urged my students to imagine a time—the nineteenth century and long after—in which instant information was neither available nor considered desirable. Women especially were seen as in need of protection from certain forms of knowledge—in the case of Wilde's Lady Windermere, from the knowledge that her own mother is a divorced woman who had an affair.

Wilde alludes to a broad lack of knowledge about sexuality in his novel, *The Picture of Dorian Gray:* "Men marry because they are tired; women, because they are curious. Both are disappointed" (48). He meant that men were tired of going to prostitutes for sex and imagined marriage as a source of constantly available sexual encounters, and that women just wanted to get some idea what sex would feel like. Middle-class Victorian women—and women living long after the Victorian age—were often kept ignorant not just of sexual feelings but of the mechanics of human reproduction.

III

Discovering that her husband is giving large sums of money to the mysterious Mrs. Erlynne—the name apparently suggested by a popular sensation novel of 1860, *East Lynne*[2], about a woman who like Mrs. Erlynne leaves her husband for a lover—Lady Windermere upbraids him for insulting her honor. She complains,

> you who have loved me, you who have taught me to love you, [have passed] from the love that is given to the love that is bought. Oh, it's horrible! . . . And it is I who feel degraded! *You* don't feel anything. I feel stained, utterly stained . . . every kiss you have given me is tainted. (Wilde 394)

Before her marriage, Lady Windermere seems to be claiming she experienced no sexual feelings. Desire doesn't come naturally. She had to be "taught" by her husband. Sexual feeling was something a husband explained to a wife under the protection of marriage, and marriage alone. Reproduction, not pleasure, was the chief purpose of sexuality. Therefore, because he appears to have indulged in sex that is "bought" for pleasure, he is dirty ("stained") and so she feels dirty as well. "Stained" may also carry a more sinister medical connotation—during this period, and until the mid-nineteen-forties, sexually transmitted diseases were not curable. They were treated with a host of remedies, mostly metals like bismuth and mercury, that suppressed some symptoms but caused extremely toxic side effects, among them loss of teeth and kidney failure. Wilde is known to have been treated with mercury for a presumed syphilitic infection, and to have had grayish teeth as a result.

The sexual tension in the opening scene between Lady Windermere and Lord Darlington, before Lady Windermere has learned of any presumed infidelity on the part of her husband, is palpable. When her butler asks whether she's "at home" for visitors, informing her that the visitor in question is Lord Darlington, she hesitates before telling the servant to show Lord Darlington up, and reminds the butler she's home to any visitor who appears. The impression that she hopes visitors will appear in order to dilute whatever tensions already exist between herself and Lord Darlington is strong. Even before Lord Darlington walks into Lady Windermere's drawing room—and he is properly announced by the butler, as was the custom—her unease is evident, her wish for the interview to be over and done obvious. She says, "It's best for me to see him before tonight. I'm glad he's come" (Wilde 385).

By admitting to her morning-room a man of whom she disapproved, she put herself in no physical danger: her butler and other male servants are on the premises. But she was facing a guest who spoke to her on topics not admissible to polite society, about which a lady was expected to remain unaware. When Lady Windermere says, "I'm glad he's come," she seems conscious only of steeling herself for an encounter that she will find unpleasant— but not of one that may titillate her. The arousal is only clear in her responses to him, in her lack of humor. The modern viewer sees that Lady Windermere cannot face her attraction to him and knows that fighting can be foreplay. Lord Darlington exploits Lady Windermere's well-meaning pity and desire to save his soul.

The scene begins with apparent innocence, Lord Darlington on his best behavior, asking, "How do you do?" and getting the boilerplate response, same. But then Lady Windermere announces that she "can't shake hands" (Wilde 385), offering the excuse that her hands are wet with the roses she's arranging. Shaking hands would mean exposing herself to the arousal conveyed in a hand squeeze lasting a moment too long, to any touch conveying lust. The scene is often staged with Lady Windermere standing as far from Lord Darlington—his name implying he could be her secret darling if she'd only notice him—as she dares. Lord Darlington's desire to be her darling is hardly deterred: his next move is to ask about the "wonderful" fan he sees on the table and to ask to look at it. He doesn't mean to gaze at it. He means to touch it: she's prevented him from taking her hand, but he can fondle that fan suggestively, and she can try to ignore the way he is handling it: the dialogue is wide open to an actor's interpretation.

In Act Two, when Lady Windermere's birthday ball is in full swing, she—mistakenly believing her husband to be having an affair with Mrs. Erlynne—hands that brand-new fan to Lord Darlington, asking him to hold it for her. That gesture signals her wish to place herself, body and soul, in Lord Darlington's hands—but also suggests her helplessness. Even though she asks for the fan back, insisting she'll use it to strike Mrs. Erlynne across the face, the threat proves idle, its dramatic purpose to put Lord Darlington in charge: when the fan, along with all her resolve, slips from her hands and falls to the floor, he retrieves it and hands it to her. Lady Windermere has the typical limitations of the Victorian woman: she cannot imagine leaving either her husband or Lord Darlington behind and going off by herself.

But before Lady Windermere knows anything about her husband's supposed affair, she denies all feelings for Lord Darlington, aware only of her anger and discomfort. On the surface, all is politesse: Lady Windermere informs Lord Darlington that she received the fan as a birthday present from her husband, and that it has her name on it. She even lets him know that she is "of age" on this particular birthday—meaning that she had moved legally from childhood to adulthood. Lord Darlington pounces on this piece of information, apparently relieved she's not jail bait, saying: "I wish I had known it was your birthday, Lady Windermere. I would have covered the whole street in front of your house with flowers for you to walk on. They are made for you" (Wilde 386). Stage directions offer "a short pause" after this dynamite declaration.

A woman willing to admit to herself that she feels flattered, even aroused, by his attentions, might have laughed them off and indicated that he ought to find himself a nice, unattached girl. Such a woman knows the difference between a thought and an action. But if Lady Windermere understood that distinction, the play would be entirely different. That Lady Windermere remains unaware of her attraction, the attraction ever stronger because of her need to repress feelings that could only lead to self-condemnation, emerges in her anger. She tells Lord Darlington that he "annoyed" her "last night at the foreign office," that she is afraid he is "going to annoy" her again (386). What annoys her is clear: he stirs up feelings whose existence she doesn't want to acknowledge. He unsettles her.

Darlington speaks with the sangfroid of Miss Piggy: "I, Lady Windermere?" he asks, pretending innocence and, as the butler and footman enter and arrange the tea cups and sandwiches, professing to be miserable and requesting that she tell him what he did (386). For him, she appears to be a conquest—the less aware she is, the better, because the easier to manipulate. She forges ahead as she pours his tea, complaining of the "elaborate compliments" he paid her (386). She wants him to show solemn regret, because then the two of them could bury their sexual attraction under a pile of moral platitudes, pretend no feelings between them ever existed. But no such luck. With each flirtatious response, Lord Darlington edges her toward recognition of her feelings, like a skilled cat playing with a very naïve mouse. To her complaint that he paid her "elaborate compliments," he, instead of embarrassedly apologizing for his louche behavior, banters: "Ah, nowadays we are all of us so hard up, that the only pleasant things to pay ARE compliments. They're the only things we CAN pay" (386). He's confessing to being poor ("hard up" for cash) and equating paying compliments with paying bills, the former more fun, because free (Wilde 386).

Lady Windermere beseeches him to take her seriously— apparently because the less he does, the more she becomes aware that the two of them are engaged in a flirtation. Increasingly irritated, she lectures: "No, I am talking very seriously. You mustn't laugh, I am quite serious" (Wilde 386). His refusal to take her moral ideas seriously distresses her, making it more difficult for her to ignore their mutual attraction. But she tries: "I don't see why a man should think he is pleasing a woman enormously when he says to her a whole heap of things that he doesn't mean" (Wilde 386). She is character trapped by the sexual mores of his times to deny her natural sexual feelings; Wilde's representation of her is a wake-up call for Victorian audiences.

At this point, Lady Windermere leaves herself wide open for the response that is so difficult for her to face: "Ah, but I did mean them," Lord Darlington says, and the reader can almost imagine him drooling at the thought of seducing his prey (386). She gravely reproves him: "I should be sorry to have to quarrel with you, Lord Darlington. I like you very much, you know that. But I shouldn't like you at all if I thought you were what most men are. Believe me, you are better than most other men, and I sometimes think you pretend to be worse" (Wilde 386).

By expressing her belief in the double standard of the day— that women were innocent of sex and sexual feeling, and men sexual predators—Lady Windermere gives Lord Darlington all the ammunition he needs. With these remarks, as with her earlier ones, she begs him again and again to backtrack, to say he didn't mean to announce his attraction to her, to pretend that nothing indiscreet has been discussed. He's not taking that bait, and the discussion quickly moves to his wish for Lady Windermere—not "the world"—as she hopes, to take him seriously.

This is just what she will not do because ultimately what drives her, and the play, is her love for her husband and child, along with a love that she finally feels from her own mother, Mrs. Erlynne.

Although Lady Windermere cannot bear to admit their relationship, denying it with anger, the same emotion with which she renders herself unaware of erotic feeling, she allows Mrs. Erlynne to help her. Meeting Mrs. Erlynne in Lord Darlington's rooms, to which Lady Windermere has fled under the erroneous impression that her husband is having an affair with her, Lady Windermere initially resists Mrs. Erlynne's attempts to hustle her out of the room so the men don't see her: "There is something about you that stirs the wildest—rage within me" (Wilde 411). Lady Windermere says, revealing that she recognizes the person who abandoned her twenty years earlier, back when she was a baby, "a fright in flannel" (Wilde 407) as Mrs. Erlynne had characterized her at the ball.

Both women retreat from the recognition in order to be able to feel love without enduring too much sorrow from the mother's original betrayal. In a letter postmarked 23 February 1893, Wilde explained what he termed the "psychological" idea for the play, namely that of a woman dominated by newly discovered love for the child she had abandoned and who finds her love for her daughter unbearable, "makes [her] suffer too much." In a sketch for a play he never wrote but was working on at the same time as *Lady Windermere's Fan*, Wilde wrote: "I want the sheer passion of love to dominate everything" (600). In the end, Lady Windermere, dominated by this sheer passion for her husband and son, gives the impression of returning to the conventions of her day, conforming to the cult of true womanhood. But it is she who insists to her husband that Mrs. Erlynne is a very good woman—not a bad one, as he now believes. She has, in fact, transcended the social structures that dominated women of her day, the structures Wilde targets in his social comedies.

Wilde's subversive message comes across: Lady Windermere now understands more than her husband. She has moved toward self-determination and intellectual independence, achieving what Wilde wished for his culture. As Lord Windermere's horizons contract to visions of women as "good" or "bad," exactly his wife's categories at the play's beginning, her horizons expand: "There is the same world for all of us, and good and evil, sin and innocence, go through it hand in hand" (Wilde 429), she explains. Even though she and Mrs. Erlynne agree to pretend they don't recognize each other, even to repress the recognition, Lady Windermere is strengthened by accepting her mother's past, and could handle worse men than Lord Darlington with tact and humor. When her husband acidly dismisses Mrs. Erlynne as "clever," his wife takes his hand and calls her "a very good woman" (Wilde 430). In Lady Windermere's redefinition of this term lies Wilde's tacit deconstruction of the cult of true womanhood, of inequalities between husband and wife, and of the rigidities of Victorian morality. Pioneering what we tend to take for granted today, art as an expression of personal or political vision, art for its own sake, he consistently undermined the Victorian belief that art had to conform to visions of morality he found absurd. In his preface to *The Picture of Dorian Gray*, he asserted, "Vice and virtue are to the artist materials for an art" (17)—not, in other words, moral categories.

Notes

1. Neil McKenna suggests (446–47) that Wilde had contracted gonorrhea, also incurable before antibiotics became available. Wilde's venereal infections did not improve his health—or his chances of recovering from the ear infection, whatever its immediate cause.

2. A number of writers have suggested connections between these names, among them Colin Nicholson, Kerry Powell, and Susan Balée.

Works Cited

Acton, Sir William. "The Functions and Disorders of the Reproductive Organs in Youth," *in Adult Age, and in Advanced Life, Considered in Their Physiological, Social, and Moral Relations*. Fourth edition. London: Churchill, 1865. www.bl.uk/collection-items/19th-century-medical-views-on-female-sexuality.

Brown, Isaac Baker. *On the Curability of Certain Forms of Insanity, Epilepsy, Catalepsy and Hysteria in Females*. London: Robert Hardwicke, 1866. archive.org/details/oncurabilitycer00browgoog/page/n6.

Chaucer, Geoffrey. *The Canterbury Tales*. Boston, Mass: Houghton Mifflin, 1957. quod.lib.umich.edu/c/cme/CT/1:1.4?rgn=div2;view=fulltext.

Donne, John. *The Complete English Poems*. Intro and Notes A. J. Smith. London: Penguin, 1971.

"Gay." Green's Dictionary of Slang. greensdictofslang.com/search/basic?q=gay.

"Gay." *Oxford English Dictionary*. www.oed.com/view/Entry/77207?rskey=OlSCVV&result=1#eid.

Gordon, A. G. "Diagnosis of Oscar Wilde." *The Lancet*, vol. 357, iss. 9263, 14 Apr. 2001, p. 1209. www.thelancet.com/action/showPdf?pii=S0140-6736%2800%2904359-2.

Harris, Frank. *Oscar Wilde: His Life and Confessions*. New York: Covici, Friede, 1930.

"Lucy Ricardo Tells Ricky Ricardo They're Having a Baby," *YouTube*, May 8, 2016, www.youtube.com/watch?v=bUpndu4rPEA.

Marvell, Andrew. *The Complete Poems,* edited by Elizabeth Story Donno. London: Penguin, 2005.

McKenna, Neal. *The Secret Life of Oscar Wilde*. London: Random House/Arrow, 2004.

"Private Lives of the Monarchs: Who Said the Victorians Were Prudish About Sex?" *The Smithsonian Channel*, n.d. www.smithsonianchannel.com/videos/who-said-the-victorians-were-prudish-about-sex/67243.

Sheehan, E. "Victorian Clitoridectomy: Isaac Baker Brown and His Harmless Operative Procedure." *Medical Anthropology Newsletter*, vol. 12, no. 4, Aug. 1981, pp. 9–15. www.ncbi.nlm.nih.gov/pubmed/12263443.

Weeks, Jeffrey. *The Languages of Sexuality*. London: Routledge, 2011.

Wilde, Oscar. *The Complete Letters of Oscar Wilde*, edited by Merlin Holland and Rupert Hart-Davis. New York: Henry Holt and Co., 2000.

Wilde, Oscar. *The Complete Works of Oscar Wilde*. Intro. Vyvyan Holland. New York: Harper & Row,1989.

Wilde's Social Comedies and the Well-Made Play

Anne Varty

Wilde structured his social comedies according to the rules of the "well-made play," the name given to the conventions of dramatic composition that dominated the stage throughout his lifetime and beyond. His intimate knowledge of what these rules were, and the expectations they raised for audiences, enabled him to bend them to his own ends. In this way he assured the popularity of his plays while at the same time smuggling subversive ideas into this most orthodox of forms.

The term "well-made play" may sound like a compliment, but it is, in fact, just a translation of the French, *la pièce bien faite*. It was a form that originated in France during the nineteenth century where its principal exponent was Victorien Sardou (1831–1908) who was himself a disciple of Eugène Scribe (1791–1861). Sardou was prolific and hugely popular, scripting comedies and tragedies that were swiftly translated into English. Sardou's work was performed across the English-speaking world, travelling to Britain and also to America; some of his plays, such as *La Tosca* (1887), were adapted as opera libretti by Puccini and other leading composers.

Even more dominant than translations and adaptations of Sardou's work was his method of composition. The well-made play was highly formulaic and therefore easy to copy. Driven by plot and populated by stock characters, the action takes place in four main movements that often correspond to Act divisions: Exposition, Complication, Crisis, and Resolution. The Exposition sets the scene, introduces the situation, and provides the audience with all the necessary information for the ensuing drama. Often in the Exposition we find minor characters discussing the protagonist before their appearance, or we may find the protagonist confiding in one of the stock characters, the "*confidant/e*", as a means of imparting the current situation to the audience. The Exposition establishes the social *status quo*, an ordered world that the audience expects to be tested in some way before its restoration at the end of the drama.

The Complication initiates disruption to the established order. A stranger may arrive, a false accusation may be made, and/or an incident from the past may become suddenly relevant. The plot often turns on the threat of marital infidelity. Dramatic suspense is built up throughout the Complication, and the use of props such as letters or personal accessories are important means of achieving heightened tension. This reaches its climax in the third Act, the Crisis, in which there is confrontation and an emotional or social clash. This was the most important element of the well-made play, an obligatory component (called in French the *scène à faire*) and nineteenth-century audiences would sometimes arrive at the theatre to watch only this scene. Finally, the Resolution, or *Dénouement* (literally, "unknotting") as it is termed in French, represents the dissipation of threat. The outsider is driven away (or dies, if it is a tragedy), the accusation is proven false, and/or the threat from the past is overpowered. One of the most important functions of the Resolution is to establish order and harmony by restoring the social *status quo* as presented in the Exposition; the worlds at the beginning and end of the play are balanced and mirroring.

The social norms of the world of the play are evident throughout, particularly when they are observed in the breach, and re-established in the Resolution by one of the key stock characters of the well-made play, known as the *raisonneur*. This is an authority figure, typically a professional man—a lawyer, priest, doctor, or teacher—who is respected in the community. The *raisonneur* embodies normative social values, uses these to solve the problems of the drama, and is not usually embroiled in the action himself.

This four-part patterning of stage drama was so prevalent that it acquired the semblance of representing real life. William Archer, an important theatre critic of the late Victorian period, wrote a book about his era's methods of dramatic composition, *Play-Making. A Manual of Craftsmanship*, in which he asserted, "in every crisis of real life (unless it be so short as to be mere incident) there is a rhythm of rise, progress, culmination, and solution" (106). But other critics were not so accepting. George Bernard Shaw was outspoken in his contempt for the well-made play: "the manufacture of well-made plays is not an art: it is an industry. It is not at all hard for a literary mechanic to acquire it" (541). Shaw attributed its late-Victorian flowering to the fact that a population made literate by the Education Acts of the 1870s needed easy entertainment, and he declared the well-made play to be nothing more than the "manufacture of a misunderstanding" (542). Shaw had been even more dismissive in 1895 when, as a critic, he was attempting to create taste for a more progressive type of drama that would include his own plays. On June 1, 1895, Shaw, theatre critic for the *Saturday Review*, reviewed two plays by Sardou that were running simultaneously in London (*Fedora* and *Gismonda*), not only with each other but also with the premiere of Shaw's own play, *Arms and the Man*. This was the moment Shaw chose to dismiss the well-made play as "Sardoodledom." Shaw's review was titled "Sardoodledom," and its contents made it clear that he coined the term to denote a bewildering excess of theatrical contrivance that was designed to please and pacify rather than to provoke and challenge.

Shaw's critique goes to the heart of the opportunity afforded by the well-made play that Wilde exploited. The form was popular because it was socially conservative. Society represented at the end of the drama is the same as that which prevailed at the start. The form allowed for no change, no progress, and no lasting challenge to established social or political views. Instead, the cultural establishment is endorsed and affirmed, having vanquished threat. Wilde's trick was to take the reactionary form and use it to cloak his progressive social vision. Both *Lady Windermere's Fan* (1892) and *An Ideal Husband* (1895) end with the restoration of a threatened marriage, but the terms on which those marriages are reconfigured do not resemble those with which they began. *A Woman of No Importance* (1893), more radically, ends with the complete rejection of the English cultural establishment by the leading characters.

Wilde's debts to the popular traditions of French theatre are uncontested. He wears their credentials as a badge of honor. He boasted about them to friends: in conversation with the famous actor

Marie Bancroft who thought she recognized a resemblance between *Lady Windermere's Fan* and a play on the contemporary Paris stage, Wilde declared, "taken bodily from it, dear lady. Why not?" (Bancroft and Bancroft 112). Alternatively, he paraded his admiration in his own dramatic dialogue. Jack and Algernon, discussing marriage at the start of *The Importance of Being Earnest*, banter:

> ALGERNON: You don't seem to realise that in married life three is company and two is none.
> JACK: That, my dear young friend, is the theory that the corrupt French Drama has been propounding for the last fifty years.
> ALGERNON: Yes, and that the happy English home has proved in half the time. (Wilde, 363)

Critics seized on Wilde's blatant capture of French theatrical fashion. A. B. Walkley, reviewing *Lady Windermere's Fan* for *The Speaker* on February 27, 1892, described it as a medley of "half a dozen familiar French plays," thereby invoking a culture shared by critic and audience alike.

Lady Windermere's Fan, Wilde's first and hugely successful social comedy is indeed a strong example of the structure of the well-made play. During the Exposition the audience is informed that Lady Windermere is preparing for her twenty-first birthday party, that her mother died twenty years ago, and that her husband is paying a great deal of attention and indeed money to a scandalous stranger, Mrs. Erlynne. The *confidante* role is played by Lady Berwick who, in a reversal of the conventional power relations between heroine and *confidante*, is possessed of rather more information about Lord Windermere's conduct than Lady Windermere herself. The Exposition ends with Lord Windermere's insistence that Mrs. Erlynne receive an invitation to the ball, and Lady Windermere's threat to strike Mrs. Erlynne with her fan if she dares to attend.

Act I has provided all the information the audience needs to follow the ensuing drama. It has shown discord in the Windermere marriage, and introduced Lady Windermere's character as a Puritan with a fixed moral compass. It sets up the suspense of Lady Windermere's threat against Mrs. Erlynne, creates mystery about her identity and the nature of her hold over Lord Windermere. Crucially, for Wilde's radicalizing purposes, it has pitted the moral relativism of Lord Windermere against the moral absolutism of Lady Windermere. The word "good" echoes through the closing dialogue between husband and wife as they dispute its meaning.

The Complication centers on Mrs. Erlynne's manipulation of Lord Windermere to "get back" into Society. It shows how she is ostracized and the way in which she overcomes it, while her successful re-entry is counterpointed by Lady Windermere's concurrent abandonment of her marriage. The heightened language of the Act's closing soliloquy in which Mrs. Erlynne reveals her identity as Lady Windermere's mother is justified by the extremity of the exclusion she has endured. The Crisis is set up, as the audience witnesses her passionate determination to prevent her daughter from following in her footsteps.

The Crisis, Act III, is set in Lord Darlington's rooms. It begins with a highly charged confrontation between Mrs. Erlynne and Lady Windermere. This is crisis enough, but Wilde develops it further by trapping the women in Lord Darlington's rooms. The incriminating clue of their presence, the fan, is left for the men to find. Wilde uses dramatic irony to build the tension of this scene as the action slows to a standstill with the witty exchange of homosocial epigram and suspense about the women's inevitable discovery becomes increasingly intense. Mrs. Erlynne is forced to make a second entrance, this time to create the diversion that will allow her daughter to escape unseen by all except the audience.

The setting for the Denouement, or Resolution, is the "*Same as in Act One*" (Wilde 454). The identity of location between Exposition and Resolution suggests the circuitous action of the well-made play and raises the expectation of a return to the original social order, with all characters restored to their correct and previously established place. And superficially this is exactly what the Resolution delivers: the Windermere marriage is saved, and Mrs. Erlynne returns to the Continent. But the terms on which the prior *status quo* re-emerges are far from conventional; they are dependent on a complex network of secrets rather than revelations, as well as an open dispute between husband and wife about the definition of a "good" woman. Dialogue between Lord and Lady Windermere at the end of the play literally mirrors that which had taken place during the Exposition, reversing the moral position first adopted by each character.

Wilde maintains suspense throughout the Denouement about whether any of the characters will reveal the secrets they hold in relation to one another. Power is finely balanced between them. Lord Windermere is fearful that Mrs. Erlynne will reveal herself as his wife's mother, a fear heightened by what he believes to be her shocking conduct in pursuing Lord Darlington to his rooms after the ball. Mrs. Erlynne fears that her daughter will confess to Lord Windermere that she deserted their marriage. Lady Windermere fears that her flight to Lord Darlington will be disclosed by Mrs. Erlynne. The vestiges of Lady Windermere's Puritanism torment her at the start of the Act: "Even if she doesn't tell, I must" (Wilde 455). But Mrs. Erlynne relieves her of its burden: "promise me that what passed last night will remain a secret between us" (Wilde 462). Yet right to the end, when Lord Augustus returns from his off-stage conversation with Mrs. Erlynne to announce that "she has explained every demmed thing," Lady Windermere responds "(*frightened*): Has Mrs. Erlynne. . .?" (Wilde 464). Mrs. Erlynne's evident silence about events leads directly to the socially regenerative triumph of the play as Lady Windermere's curtain line affirms the victory of moral relativism over absolutism: "you're marrying a very good woman!" (Wilde 464).

This transformation of ethical values, embodied by Lady Windermere's change of heart, represents a thoroughgoing, though playfully staged, assault on the conventions of the well-made play. It is achieved in part by Wilde's daring choice of which character to cast in the role of *raisonneur*. Rather than deploying a male authority figure to solve problems and dispense justice, Wilde gives this role to the female outsider, the disgraceful woman with a past. It is Mrs. Erlynne who controls the action from first to last. She rewards herself with the prize of respectability through the acquisition of a new husband, and she carries a stake in the future by winning her daughter's respect. She even confirms her ethical stance as the unmotherly mother, having found unbearable the outbreak of maternal sentiment that drove her to save her daughter's reputation.

Mrs. Erlynne's triumphs are symbolized on stage by her final ownership of the fan, which she commands Lord Augustus to carry for her. The circulation of this object throughout the drama is another nod by Wilde to the conventions of the well-made play. Sardou's first major success came in 1860 with a comedy called *A Scrap of Paper* (*Les Pattes de Mouche*) in which a potentially compromising letter is passed (unread) between characters, saved from flames by a gust of wind, used to wrap an insect specimen, and used as notepaper; its contents are eventually explained away to allow the new lovers to marry. The letter is the focus of suspense for the audience throughout *A Scrap of Paper*, as the playwright's game of hiding it in plain sight or devising ingenious means to pass it on teases with dramatic irony. Wilde's use of the fan in *Lady Windermere's Fan* is a more sophisticated use of the prop since the fan acquires a new symbolic value at every stage of its journey through the action. Moreover, unlike Sardou's letter, the movement of the fan is not brought about by a sequence of gratuitous tricks but is fully integrated in the plot. In another playful reference to the methods of the well-made play, Wilde uses the classic prop of a letter in the Complication to launch Mrs. Erlynne's intervention in her daughter's life. He spotlights this through both action and dialogue when Mrs. Erlynne drops the letter and Lord Windermere queries why she has a note in his wife's handwriting (Wilde 443–44). Wilde is deftly colluding with the audience about what can be expected of a well-made play.

While the plotting of *Lady Windermere's Fan* follows the conventions of the well-made play, with its arrangement of a drama in four movements, its speedy pace achieved by a patterning of tension and release, together with its use of props and stock characters, the way in which Wilde fulfils the requirements of the form is wittily subversive at every turn. The result is a drama in which the strictures of moral absolutism are shattered, the determinism of the past is resisted, women are given full social agency, and space is created for moral choice. This is far from an upholding of the safe cultural establishment and points instead to his radical politics for social regeneration.

Wilde continues to exploit the opportunities of the well-made play in his next social comedy, *A Woman of No Importance* (1893). Here he innovates in two particular ways: the first concerns the balance between action and dialogue and the second concerns the role of the *raisonneur*. His aim, once more, is to present a drama that affirms the need for social change rather than stasis. The trajectory of the progress represented can be marked by the mirroring phrases "a woman of no importance" and "a man of no importance." The first is said by Lord Illingworth referring to Mrs. Arbuthnot in the curtain line of the Exposition and the second by Mrs. Arbuthnot to denote Lord Illingworth in the curtain line of the Resolution, the last line of the play. Power has shifted from the man to the woman: the play represents a profound challenge to the values of patriarchy and exposes them as out of date.

Wilde retains the architecture of Exposition, Complication, Crisis, and Resolution but defies the way in which this traditional structure drives the plot with action, suspense, and confrontation. Instead, Wilde relies on carefully paced dialogue to move the drama forward throughout, alternating sharp stichomythic exchanges with longer meditative speeches. He allows only two major outbreaks of active confrontation in the course of the whole play: the first is the highly melodramatic climax to the Crisis as Gerald threatens to kill Lord Illingworth and the second is Mrs. Arbuthnot's striking of Lord Illingworth's cheek with his glove at the end of the Resolution. Shock, in both cases, is heightened by the extreme contrast between these physical clashes and the word-focused action that surrounds them. Wilde's instructions to Beerbohm Tree, the actor who played Lord Illingworth, reveal his ambition: "'above all you must forget that you ever played a duke in a melodrama by Henry Arthur Jones. . . . I think you had better forget that you ever acted at all'" (qtd. in Ellmann 359). Wilde's technique earned him the highest praise from William Archer who hailed the play's modernity in his review for the *World* on April 26, 1893, stating "there is no situation-hunting, no posturing . . . nothing insincere." Wilde's rejection of conventional theatricality brought the drama closer to the world it represented, making its critique of prevailing social values more directly pertinent.

This critique is further supported by his handling of the *raisonneur*. Unusually, the role is divided between two characters. Throughout the Exposition and Complication, and for most of the Crisis, it is Lord Illingworth who holds this position. He is a powerful patriarchal figure, he dominates the stage with his wit, and he puts forward a plan to perpetuate the hierarchical values he represents by offering Gerald employment. However, his authority is undermined when he assaults Hester. At this point his power and the role of *raisonneur* transfer to her, although she only becomes qualified for this role as a result of the way she changes in response to his assault. Previously, Hester had occupied the role of challenging outsider, the naïve American Puritan whose inflexible moral code was proving no match for the mannered decadence of her Old-World hosts. Following the attempted seduction, forgiveness replaces judgement as the North of Hester's moral compass. The demand by both Gerald and his father, that the only way out of their socially compromised position is for the parents to marry, is exposed as laughably old-fashioned. Hester offers a literal departure from these regressive normative values: "Leave him and come with me. . . . Other countries over the sea [are] . . . better, wiser, and less unjust lands" (Wilde 509). The Old World *raisonneur* gives way to the authority of the new.

An Ideal Husband is a structural reprise of *Lady Windermere's Fan*. The theme, too, had been anticipated when Mrs. Erlynne warns her daughter, "ideals are dangerous things. Realities are better. They wound, but they're better" (Wilde 461). An alternative anticipation of the theme is set up in *A Woman of No Importance* with Mrs. Allonby's assertion, "The Ideal Husband? There couldn't be such a thing. The institution is wrong" (Wilde 480). As in the earlier play, a marriage is threatened by the forces of the past, and it is reassembled through the agency of the *raisonneur* who modifies the Puritan wife's ethical absolutism. However, the journey from Exposition to Resolution in *An Ideal Husband* is faster-paced and more crowded with incident, plot, and counterplot than *Lady Windermere's Fan* and contains what the characters themselves call "terrible scenes" of emotional conflict.

To accommodate the multiple twists, Wilde trails the dark business of the Complication within the Exposition. He introduces the outsider, Mrs. Cheveley, early in the Exposition and by the time Act I closes the audience is fully apprised of Sir Robert Chiltern's youthful crime, and she has set the terms of her blackmail. Compressing the drama still further, as a means of increasing suspense, Wilde sets an exact time-limit by which Sir Robert must comply. Act II holds a double complication. How are Robert Chiltern's marriage and career to be saved? How will Mrs. Cheveley recover her lost diamond brooch? Not until the Crisis does it emerge that these two complications are in fact one, since her reunion with the brooch is also the means to saving both marriage and career.

Having compressed the time of the drama, Wilde next compresses the space in which it takes place. The obligatory Crisis, Act III, is set in Lord Goring's rooms. Wilde uses the same type of box set that he had deployed for the Crisis in *Lady Windermere's Fan*: a reception room with off-stage spaces in which visitors are hidden. The third Act of *An Ideal Husband* works as a micro-farce, with two unexpected visitors who do not meet (Lord Caversham and Sir Robert), mistaken identity (Lord Goring expects Lady Chiltern but receives, unwittingly, Mrs. Cheveley), a climax in which Mrs. Cheveley is branded a thief by reclaiming the brooch/bracelet, and a second climax in which she steals Lady Chiltern's potentially scandalous letter to Lord Goring.

The Resolution does not take a straightforward course towards the expected yet indeed finally delivered happy ending. There are reversals to the last, which take Sir Robert to the brink of retiring from public life and Lord Goring, falsely accused of philandering, to the brink of losing his fiancée. Finally, however, there is full disclosure as all misunderstanding is cleared up. Decisive in the move towards reconstituted harmony is Lord Goring's speech to Lady Chiltern in which he affirms traditional gender roles for men and women, assigning intellect and ambition to men, emotion and forgiveness to women. This may seem a contradictory way for Wilde to achieve a progressive social message through this play. However, just as at the happy ending of *Lady Windermere's Fan* was balanced on three secrets each tailored to one of the remaining characters, so too the happy ending of *An Ideal Husband* balances on individual ethical journeys. Sir Robert speaks against the Argentine Canal in Parliament, despite believing at the time that this would cost him his career and that his marriage was already ruined. His personal morality has therefore changed, and this private regeneration is seen to have public resonance. To save her marriage Lady Chiltern must also abandon her original moral position of puritanism. Lord Goring's speech to her is a means to this end, as he persuades her that in requiring her husband to give up his public office she is not only playing Mrs. Cheveley's cards, she is also just as culpable as the villainess in her moral inflexibility. The overriding progressive message of this play is the need for both personal and political regeneration. And, as with both *Lady Windermere's Fan* and *A Woman of No Importance*, it is moral relativism rather than moral absolutism that underwrites such change.

An Ideal Husband is Wilde's most commanding manipulation of the conventions of the well-made play, flaunting its excessive contrivance and reveling in the display of artifice. The drama turns not on one, but on two stolen letters: the letter that Sir Robert wrote twenty-two years earlier that proves his guilt in selling political secrets and on which Mrs. Cheveley's blackmail plot depends, and Lady Chiltern's letter that finds its way from Lord Goring to her husband via Mrs. Cheveley's second blackmail plot. The past connections between characters are also doubled. Not only did Lady Chiltern and Mrs. Cheveley attend school together (when their contrasting ethics and distinctive handwriting were formed), but Mrs. Cheveley was also Lord Goring's former lover. Wilde's playfulness with convention extends to swapping the gender of the traditional character with a past, making this a man rather than a woman, who is just as unapologetic for the choices he made as Mrs. Erlynne had been in *Lady Windermere's Fan*. This world of rampant doubles anticipates *The Importance of Being Earnest* (1895). So, too, does Wilde's treatment of the Dandy in *An Ideal Husband*: his boldest move in this redesign of convention is to cast the Dandy in the role of *raisonneur*. Rather than choosing an authority figure to assert normative culture, he selects a figure whose role is to criticise and subvert those values. In deploying Lord Goring as the *raisonneur*, Wilde destabilises the social values that the well-made play was expected to uphold; he also demonstrates that the Dandy's wit is not gratuitously iconoclastic but motivated by profound ethical vision.

The moral universe that Lord Goring creates is one in which judgment responds to circumstance, meeting it with compromise, pragmatism, and compassion. Mrs. Cheveley only has power because the moral universe she enters at the start of the play is not like this. It is, by contrast, absolute in its assignation of blame and guilt, unheeding of circumstance. Ironically, these are the very values that Lady Chiltern embodies throughout the Exposition and Complication, and about which she is probed first by her husband and then by Lord Goring. Equally ironically, the villainess is entirely correct when she states, "with our modern mania for morality, everyone has to pose as a paragon of purity . . . and what is the result? You all go over like ninepins" (Wilde 528). Wilde's enterprise in this play is to expose the weakness of ideals, whether they are ideal husbands, ideal wives, or ideal virtues. Mrs. Cheveley embodies the threat such ideals pose to society, and so does Lady Chiltern until she is enlightened by Lord Goring.

The play demonstrates that as static fixtures, ideals cannot respond to the exigencies of lived experience, they do not evolve with individuals, and they are unfit for the purpose of shaping a dynamic, thriving society. Wilde promotes instead a progressive morality for the renaissance of culture in which judgement takes account of context, present pressures, and its own future consequences.

This ambitious endeavour aligns with his manipulation of the well-made play, both in *An Ideal Husband* and in his two preceding social comedies. It is evident that, like Sir Robert Chiltern, he espoused the view that "every man of ambition has to fight his century with its own weapons" (Wilde 536). To disseminate his oppositional views to the widest possible public he deployed the era's most popular form of theatre. He took the conventions of the well-made play, an ideal theatrical form that traditionally served social stasis, and demonstrated how they could be adapted to promote a regenerative politics for the progressive needs of the age.

Works Cited

Archer, William. *Play-Making. A Manual of Craftsmanship.* 2nd ed. London: Chapman and Hall Ltd, 1913.

Bancroft, M. E., and Sir Squire Bancroft. *Empty Chairs.* London: John Murray, 1925.

Ellmann, Richard. *Oscar Wilde.* London: Hamish Hamilton, 1987.

Shaw, George Bernard. "Preface to an English translation of *Three Plays by Brieux*, 1911." *The Complete Prefaces. Volume I: 1889–1913*, edited by Dan H. Laurence and Daniel J. Leary. London: Allen Lane The Penguin P, 1993, pp. 531–65.

Wilde, Oscar. *The Complete Works of Oscar Wilde*, edited by Merlin Holland. Glasgow: HarperCollins, 1994.

The Importance of Artifice: Ritual and Language Play in *The Importance of Being Earnest*

Ruth Robbins

Recalling his first meeting with Oscar Wilde in his *Autobiographies*, the poet W. B. Yeats remembered his astonishment when he heard Wilde speak: "I never before heard a man talking with perfect sentences," he wrote; it was "as if he had written them all over night with labour and yet all spontaneous" (124). This amazement at Wilde's personal verbal dexterity is repeated by many of those who knew him. It should come as no surprise, therefore, that the language he uses in his plays shares that same precision and articulacy, since despite his apparent indolence, he often did write his dialogue overnight with great labor. This essay is largely about Wilde's language use in his most famous play. But along the way it is also concerned with the ways in which language and behaviour—what people say in a drama and what they do—have similar effects to each other, and that part of that effect is to mislead. I am making use of a number of different theories that help to illuminate what Wilde was up to when he made his original audiences laugh, and when he made them think, even in a play that was certainly understood at the time of its first production as a farce, that is, a play that "inspires hilarity mixed with panic . . . in its audience" as it is led through "an increasingly rapid and improbable series of ludicrous confusions" as its plot unfolds (Baldick 82). A farce, in other words, is a play that is not meant to be taken seriously. Its purpose is to provoke laughter, its characters and plots are "stock," that is, purely conventional, and its humor is often broad or bawdy, its action often physical horseplay. It is not quite where one might expect to find a serious philosophical position being outlined. Before we turn to the details of Wilde's play, however, there are some important things to say about the context in which it was written and first produced in England in the middle years of the 1890s.

Kerry Powell's very important book on Wilde's relationship to the dramatic traditions in which he both wrote and against which he reacted (*Oscar Wilde and the Theatre of the 1890s*) demonstrates at length that Wilde, who as working journalist was a frequent reviewer of plays from the mid-1880s onwards, was profoundly influenced—sometimes to the point of outright plagiarism—by the plays that he had seen. These included the commercial theatrical extravaganzas of the West End of London (where the elite classes went to be entertained) as well as more experimental dramas, viewed in private clubs by a more bohemian audience. As a frequent traveller to Paris, Wilde was also very familiar with French drama, again both experimental and commercial. It is commonplace of criticism of nineteenth-century English drama that it was formulaic, derivative of French models, reliant on stereotyped gestures and characters, and politically conservative, not least because all plays for public performance had to be licensed by the Lord Chamberlain's office (an ancient provision to prevent dramatic sedition that dated from the time of King Henry VIII in the sixteenth century and remained in force in the United Kingdom until the late 1960s). Wilde had fallen foul of the judgement of this office in 1891, when he had sought a licence for his play *Salomé*, and had his request denied. Censorship in the theater meant that difficult themes had to be treated carefully within carefully calibrated limits of social propriety. If Wilde wanted to make serious points, to some degree he had to do so in disguise. All the modern comedies he wrote in the 1890s, ending with *The Importance of Being Earnest*, sneak their uncomfortable themes in, under a cloak of comedic convention.

We know a great deal about what Wilde thought about the theater of his period because he wrote about it often, sometimes in short reviews, but also in an extended essay on how Shakespeare should best be played entitled "The Truth of Masks," a title that is very suggestive when it comes to thinking about Wilde's own theatrical practice. We also see him making use of his novel, *The Picture of Dorian Gray*, to make some trenchant comments on popular theater in the less salubrious environs of London's East End, an area that was, in the 1890s, notorious for its poverty, violence, and crime. In the novel, Dorian, seeking illicit adventure in the East End, happens upon a theater and is curious to see *Romeo and Juliet* played in such a context. The theater building horrifies him. It is a vulgar attempt to ape the luxurious décor of a West End playhouse: "It was a tawdry affair, all Cupids and cornucopias, like a third-rate wedding cake," he comments (Wilde Gray 44). The audience is impoverished and inhabits only the cheap seats in the pit. "Women went about with oranges and ginger-beer, and there was a terrible consumption of nuts" (Wilde Gray, 44). Additionally, the cast is not all it should be. The romantic hero, Romeo "was a stout elderly gentleman with corked eyebrows" and the players and audience do not obey the rules of serious theater: "Mercutio . . . was played by the low comedian, who had introduced gags of his own and was on most friendly terms" with the audience in the cheapest seats (Wilde Gray 45). The play offends Dorian's upper-class sense of taste and decorum. The things he notices tell us what he sees as exceptional in relation to his normal experiences in the West End, and he takes exception to them. His observation of the public consumption of food and drink while the play proceeds, for instance, tells us that this is not how one behaves in a proper theater. It is against the rules to break the illusion of the theatrical space by direct addresses to the audience. It is even more against the rules to introduce your own jokes in competition with the hallowed words of Shakespeare and to invite the audience to join in. And while most Victorian theaters were lavish in their decorations, this palace of performance fails the taste test by overdoing everything and doing it all too cheaply.

From Dorian's outrage, alongside other evidence, we can reconstruct what serious or respectable theater was meant to be like in the 1890s. It was a space in which to be entertained and even instructed, but that entertainment took place amid rigid conventions of decorum. The West End players maintained a strict cordon sanitaire between the action on the stage and the audience beyond the so-called fourth wall of the rooms in which that action occurred. Theater produced an illusion of a real world, just like this one, beyond the orchestra pit, on which the audience was permitted to spy and eavesdrop. Writing of Wilde's first social comedy, *Lady*

Windermere's Fan, Katharine Worth observes that the careful staging of rooms that looked like home and the "elaborate costumes worn on . . . stage reflected the clothes of the audience with a precision that made for a rather uncanny mirror-image effect" (6). The audience, in other words, was meant to be looking at a version of itself, watching its own problems and concerns being played out for its edification or amusement with either serious or comic consequences, depending on the play in question. The people on the stage were also speaking the language that the audience itself spoke—at least in when that audience was articulate and witty. By the time that Wilde produced *The Importance of Being Earnest*, he had already shown himself to be an adept player of the social game of theater that this description implies. His name on the playbill guaranteed an amusing evening— the other plays all have their resident wit to keep the dialogue light— which might also prove instructive in its discussion of the current obsession with the relationship between the sexes, which is the theme of the three more serious social comedies, *Lady Windermere's Fan*, *A Woman of No Importance*, and *An Ideal Husband*. Theater, in other words, was a social contract, or even a ritual. *The Importance of Being Earnest* by way of contrast, only appears to play by those rules. It offers instead of a comforting illusion a minor revolution dressed up as a joke.

The Shallow Mask of Manners: Exploded Rituals

This section of the chapter is informed by the discipline of performance studies. Although performance is related to formal forms of theater (performances obviously take place there), it is not precisely the same thing, having its origins at least as much in sociology and anthropology, fields of study that are concerned with human behaviors in both formal and informal settings, as in theater studies. In the words of Francesca Coppa, performance, in the sense of "performance studies" is:

> behaviour on display, but this display is not limited to theatrical productions or ritual events . . . behaviour . . . is a language that has rules and is structured by a grammar, and, as with any other language,

comprehension depends on recognition, which is to say re-cognition, or knowing something again when we see it. (73)

At its simplest, we recognize (re-know, re-see, re-understand) certain common social gestures as standing in for an emotion that they represent. A person weeping is sad, or laughing is happy. We know both that these gestures are "real"—it is difficult to do either weeping or laughing involuntarily. We also know that there are moments when to do one or the other is highly inappropriate: there are rules, like the grammar of a language that make laughter at a funeral or weeping in a supermarket extremely inappropriate. The gestures themselves might not always be under our conscious control, but we know where and when to do them, having learned the rules as part of our socialization, just as with our use of language, we may not always speak perfectly, but we know when we have broken the rules. The move that performance studies makes is to demonstrate that performance is not confined to overtly theatrical spaces. As Marvin Carlson puts it, "The recognition that our lives are structured according to repeated and socially sanctioned modes of behavior raises the possibility that all human activity could potentially be considered as 'performance'" (72). This position was first elucidated by the sociologist Erving Goffman in his book *The Presentation of Self in Everyday Life*. Goffman suggests that we are all acting, to some degree, all the time, and the success of our performance depends partly on our own prowess in playing the part, and partly on the willingness of those with whom we interact to participate in the performance:

> When an individual plays a part he implicitly requests his observers to take seriously the impression that is fostered before them. They are asked to believe that the character they see actually possesses the attributes he appears to possess, that the task he performs will have the consequences that are implicitly claimed for it, and that, in general, matters are what they appear to be. (61)

In other words the performance of the self in everyday life is part of a social contract. Our behavior is observed and interpreted. Those who observe us (mostly) agree that the performance they are seeing is truthful and appropriate.

But what happens when the social contract is deliberately broken? On the opening night of *Lady Windermere's Fan,* Oscar Wilde addressed his audience, as was typical of the period on an opening night. So far, so conventional. But Wilde's address to his audience (what he said) and his demeanor (he spoke to them while lounging and smoking) were not in line with the expectations of social decorum in the period. He told the crowd:

> "Ladies and gentlemen: I have enjoyed this evening *immensely.* The actors have given us a *charming* rendering of a *delightful* play, and your appreciation has been *most* intelligent. I congratulate you on the *great* success of your performance, which persuades me that you think almost as highly of the play as I do myself." (qtd. in Ellmann 346)

The ritual contract between audience and play was broken when he addressed them as bit-part players in the drama that he had constructed. He also broke the rules that suggest that he should have performed the part of becoming modest, and should not have been smoking cigarettes before the ladies in the auditorium. The audience appears to have been amused, but some of the reviews of his curtain speech were scathing about his manner and his manners.

The western world is not used to thinking about its everyday social behaviors as rituals. Ritual appears to belong to the heightened spaces of religious observance, or to the apparently primitive spaces of other cultures. Turning the mirror back to the audience in the case of the *Lady Windermere's Fan* curtain speech exposes that norms of behaviour are merely conventions, artificial forms that oil the social wheels. The relevance of this episode to *The Importance of Being Earnest* is that the play is constructed around two ritual tea tables that lead to two proposals with other (much more serious) rituals—a baptism and a funeral—invoked for purely comic purposes. Wilde's play shows us that rituals are part of the social fabric of the period. The modes of behavior and the modes of speech demanded by the social norms of the period were carefully regulated and defined. As

Anne Varty has pointed out, "The Victorians had strict codes for how social visits were to be made, cards left, and for how tea was to be served and consumed. There were numerous handbooks on etiquette and the problem pages of ladies' papers were crowded with questions about how to deal with social niceties" (197). Knowing how to behave was one of the keys to social cachet. Tea amongst the upper classes was an extremely formalized affair. Standards of correct behavior and habits of verbal reticence and rectitude kept the social surface smooth. There were things one could not do or say in such a setting.

The tea tables in *Earnest*, however, are not so well regulated. In the play's first act when Jack Worthing joins his friend Algernon Moncrieff for tea, he does so uninvited, and he and Algy indulge in slapstick horseplay in their battle over the lost cigarette case. The two men reach an accommodation about that over explanations of their behavior and Jack's alias as Ernest, which means that Algy agrees to manipulate the situation so that Jack and Gwendolen might be alone, against the rules of chaperonage that argued that unmarried men and women should never be unaccompanied. When Lady Bracknell and Gwendolen finally arrive there are multiple examples of the rules of polite society and polite conversation being twisted to breaking point, signalled from the very first exchange between Lady Bracknell and her nephew:

> LADY BRACKNELL: Good afternoon, dear Algernon, I hope you are behaving very well.
> ALGERNON: I am feeling very well, Aunt Augusta.
> LADY BRACKNELL: That's not quite the same thing. In fact the two things rarely go together. (*Sees Jack and bows to him with icy coldness.*) (Wilde Earnest 260)

Normal forms of greeting in this period included questions about one's state of health. Lady Bracknell is the first one in this encounter to break the rules by twisting the normal question from "Are you well" to "Are you behaving well?" Algy answers the question he should have been asked by the normal rules. Her response is cutting—both to her nephew, and then in the stage direction, to her nephew's guest, to whom she is, during the course of the apparently civilized space of the tea table, astonishingly rude. The comedy comes from the breaking of the convention, supplemented by crescendos of verbal sparring. These make audiences laugh, but if the characters were more sensitive, Lady Bracknell's sallies would be perceived not as funny but as cruel. The catty commentary on the recently widowed Lady Harbury whose hair has apparently "turned quite gold from grief" and who "seems . . . to be living entirely for pleasure now" (Wilde Earnest 261) sets a tone that is at odds with the apparently civilized upper-class setting. The ritual masks vituperation, rather than enacting sincere good manners.

The idea of ritual is nonetheless attractive to Gwendolen who wishes the social forms to be maintained. While Algy has manoeuvred her mother into another room leaving the two love birds alone, Gwendolen and Jack move from a discussion of the weather (the most conventional subject in British conversation) to a disquisition on nominative determinism—the importance of the name Ernest—to a proposal of marriage, in double quick time. However, Gwendolen insists, with comic effect, that the appropriate conventions of formal proposals are maintained. Although they both know that the proposal will be accepted, Gwendolen still insists that Jack do it properly according to accepted forms and norms.

> GWENDOLEN: Yes, Mr Worthing, what have you got to say to me?
> JACK: You know what I have got to say to you.
> GWENDOLEN: Yes, but you don't say it.
> JACK: Gwendolen, will you marry me? (*Goes on his knees.*)
> GWENDOLEN: Of course I will, darling. How long you have been about it! I am afraid you have had very little experience in how to propose. (Wilde Earnest 263–64)

The rules of the romantic game are insisted on. It is not a proposal until the man has been on his knees to beg for the lady's hand. At the same time, though, the romance of the situation is severely undercut by Gwendolen's comment that Jack is an inexperienced proposer. A romantic young lady would of course, greatly prefer her lover to love her and her alone, and to be inexperienced.

This semi-romantic interlude is interrupted by the re-entry of Lady Bracknell and Algy, which leads to a further ritual—the question of whether or not Jack might be an eligible bachelor. Normally the hard-headed financial questions about the viability of this projected upper-class marriage and the discussion of Jack's character as a potential husband would not be addressed to the suitor himself. Roundabout inquiries behind the scenes would be required, but they would not be so overt. Lady Bracknell's questions to Jack expose him as an idle, smoking, loafing know-nothing, none of which failings makes any difference to his attractiveness as a husband. Indeed, in a reversal of the norms of the society that is being mocked, Lady Bracknell approves of his "occupation" of smoking, his non-engagement in politics (Liberal Unionism is a kind of contradiction in terms), and of his "delicate bloom of ignorance" (Wilde Earnest 265). She also approves very heartily indeed of his very comfortable financial affairs. All seems set fair until the discovery that Jack has no respectable ancestors of either sex to bring to the marriage settlement, and that he is, in fact, a foundling child.

By another set of ritual conventions, those of genre, the foundling is a stock character of melodrama, the exaggerated theatrical form that was central to much Victorian experience and, indeed, to major novels of the nineteenth century (*Oliver Twist* is probably the most famous example). The foundling raises the spectre of illegitimacy, of the fallen woman and of the unfortunate offspring of an illicit sexual relationship. The bastard child could have no place and no name in the best echelons of Victorian high society, as Lady Bracknell's riposte to Jack's revelation makes clear.

> Mr Worthing, I confess I feel somewhat bewildered by what you have just told me. To be born, or at any rate bred, in a hand-bag . . . seems to me to display a contempt for the ordinary decencies of family life that reminds one of the worst excesses of the French Revolution. . . . As for the particular locality in which the hand-bag was found, a cloak-room at a railway station might serve to conceal a social indiscretion . . . but it could hardly be regarded as an assured basis for a recognized position in good society. (Wilde Earnest 267)

Whatever other qualities he may or may not have, Jack's unknown and possibly dubious parentage is an insuperable barrier for Lady Bracknell. Her speech is both funny and desperately cruel. But it is also in absolute breech of good manners. The self-styled arbiter of what good society might accept is hyperbolic and impolite in her dismissal of Jack's claims. The ritual has been ruptured.

The second tea table is similarly disruptive of social norms. When Jack worries to Algy that his chosen beloved might turn out like her mother, Algy has no comfort to offer him ("all women become like their mothers," he tells him [Wilde Earnest 268]). The evidence of the second tea table in Act 2 makes it clear that Jack is right to be concerned. The microaggressions that Cecily serves up alongside over-sugared tea and a hefty hunk of cake when no sugar, and bread and butter, have been requested are the feminine equivalent of Jack Algy's horseplay over the cigarette case in the first Act. But both men will also meet their verbal matches if the spoken exchanges between Gwendolen and Cecily are anything to go by. The encounter between the two women starts well, with them inviting each other to use their Christian names—something that may seem very simple to our contemporary eyes, but which was a mark of significant intimacy between friends in the more formal world of Victorian social meetings. If Gwendolen is taken aback by her perception of Cecily's youth and good looks ("I wish that you were fully forty-two and more than usually plain for you age" [Wilde Earnest, 387]), it is only at the point that they both realize that they are engaged to be married to the (of course non-existent) Ernest Worthing that hostilities break out and each girl discards what Cecily calls "the shallow mask of manners" (Wilde Earnest 388). They are forced into a temporary ceasefire by the arrival of the tea table and the servants who bring it to them; as the stage direction puts it *"The presence of the servant exercises a restraining influence, under which both girls chafe"* (Wilde Earnest 389). But they each manage verbal sallies against the other when the servants have departed of which Lady Bracknell herself might have been proud. It is only when Jack and Algy enter the scene and they come to the realization that neither of them is engaged to the man they thought they were that hostilities cease, and in a swift reversal, they embrace each other and call each other "sister." Another such reversal would come as no surprise. The shallow mask of manners is extremely shallow indeed.

One other ritual that we see in Act 2 is Jack's performance of mourning for his allegedly deceased brother. To make sense of this scene, it is important to realize that the Victorians had an "elaborately codified behavior" in relation to death and mourning. Mourning rituals included carefully graded costume (full black for a year of full mourning, shades of violet and grey worn for up to three years after the deceased had departed), spectacular funeral rites, and cloistered segregation from society for those who had been bereaved. If the comprehension of performance depends on "recognition . . . [on] knowing something again when we see it" (Coppa 73), then no one in Wilde's original audience could have mistaken the message of Jack's costume and inhibited motion of distress: "*Enter Jack slowly . . . He is dressed in the deepest mourning, with crape hatband and black gloves*" (Wilde Earnest 277). That everyone would know what this must mean—a death in the family—is signalled by the fact that the signs of his mourning are immediately legible to the play's two most foolish characters, Miss Prism and Canon Chasuble. Part of Wilde's point, however, is that those who focus merely on surface signs are likely to be fooled and to be fools as well. While the two older folk respond (mostly) appropriately to the ritualized performance of sadness, Cecily takes one look at her uncle and exclaims: "Uncle Jack! Oh, I am pleased to see you back. But what horrid clothes you have got on. Do go and change them . . . Do look happy! You look as if you had toothache" (Wilde Earnest 279). Cecily's apparent misreading of the signs is in fact a true reading, for after all, she is about to announce that Jack's supposedly dead brother is in the dining room seeking reconciliation. As Anne Varty puts it, "Not only does Jack's display of grief relate to a figment, and therefore emphasises the theatricality of Victorian mourning practice, but the audience knows that within minutes, his ruse will be tumbled by the entrance of another masquerader" (199).

It's not just Ernest and Bunbury who are about to be exploded, so are the conventions of proper demeanor.

When I See a Spade . . . Language at Play

The Importance of Being Earnest is a play whose name is a pun, a word with two meanings, in this case the moral quality of seriousness and a proper name. This matters because a word with two meanings points out that words themselves, and by extension the communications that they carry, might just be unstable. Words have the capacity to be another place in which the social contracts of good behavior might break down. If performance itself is like a language, with rules and grammars and conventions, and if performance is unstable and uncertain, as Jack's playacting of distress has turned out to be, the analogy suggests that words are also problematic and may not obviously speak the truths that speakers and listeners presume they do. This section of the chapter is drawing on theories of language and literature that have come to be known as structuralist approaches. A brief explanation of this term is in order before we turn to see how it might apply to what Wilde was doing in his play.

Structuralist theories of language derive ultimately from the Swiss linguist Ferdinand de Saussure, who taught philosophies of language in Geneva early in the twentieth century. His *General Course in Linguistics* was published in 1915, posthumously collated from notes his students had taken on his lectures delivered between 1906 and 1911. The ideas he propounded came to be known as structuralist ideas because his focus was not on self-expression or emotion, nor on the history of language, but on the rules by which language operates as a structure—no matter what language is being discussed. He distinguished between two dimensions of language, which he named *langue* and *parole*. *Langue* was used to refer to the total system of a given language—its grammar, vocabulary, its rules; *parole* referred to the individual instance of speech or writing. Terence Hawkes gives the following helpful definition: "The distinction between *langue* and *parole* is more or less that which pertains between the abstract language-system which in English we simply call 'language,' and the individual utterances made by speakers of the language in concrete every-day situations, which we call 'speech'" (20). For Saussure, the aim of linguistics was to map the *langue* or system of language. But the only evidence we have for that system is the individual utterances that make it up. *Langue* has no existence without *Parole*. There must be rules—and we know that there are. There are millions of words in the English language, and billions of ways of combining them into speech or writing. Despite the almost infinite possibilities, you would all know if I broke the linguistic rules by introducing untenable grammatical structures, or threw in some nonsense words or some foreign phrases. We all know that the rules exist, even if we cannot always say exactly what they are. Saussure also quickly came to the conclusion that he could not map any entire language, even if he could work out what most of its structures might be because the permutations are too huge for this to be viable. Therefore, the only thing to do, he suggested, was to look at the patterns that exist between the larger structure of the language as whole and the individual utterance—to consider the relationship between the language system and what I can say when I use it.

Saussurean linguistics is all about *relationships between structures, be they large or small.* Saussure's thought suggested that the logical conclusion of the obvious point that there is no natural relationship between a word and the thing or abstract idea it conveys is that meaning must be relational—that is related to conventions and rules that we have internalized as we learned to speak and write within a given language community. Without those rules all utterances would be purely arbitrary. If I use the word *dog*, you know conceptually that it is different from other animals I might have mentioned—*cat, hamster, giraffe.* You also recognise its visual difference on the page and its aural difference in speech from other words that are a bit like it: *dog* is not the same as *fog, hog, bog, log.* The complex computations of your language abilities enable you to pick the right concept and the right sound/image; but it is from difference not intrinsic qualities that a word, and thence a sentence, and thence an entire text, get their meanings.

To return to *Earnest*, a punning word is one that oscillates between two or more meanings. Only time—the time it takes to get to the end of the sentence, or even to the end of the play—will tell which meaning is the focus at a given point in time. The joy of the pun is that it often yokes together two meanings that are incompatible or incongruous. Given that the Oxford English Dictionary tells us that *earnest* means in its first definition—"Seriousness; serious intention, as opposed to jest or play"—there is a neat irony in the fact that a serious word is being used for comic purposes. In the context of a system like a genre (which might be an equivalent to *langue*) like farce, where fun and frivolity are the point, it may not matter too much that seriousness has become silly. It could, though, matter a great deal.

The play opens with Algy offstage, playing an unidentified tune on the piano. When he enters the scene he announces that "I don't play accurately—anyone can play accurately—but I play with wonderful expression" (Wilde Earnest 253). Virtually the first words of the play tell us that accuracy is not a virtue according to one of its main protagonists. Truthfulness, regarded by most of us as an important virtue, is not highly valued in the topsy-turvy moral universe of Wilde's play. As we have already seen, Algy is happy to lie to his aunt about the unavailability of cucumbers in the market that day; in fact his whole life of pleasure is based on bare-faced prevarications. His invalid friend, Bunbury, used as an excuse to escape dinner at his aunt's that evening, is a fiction, a word that has no reference to the real world, which exemplifies one of Saussure's key contributions to linguistic thought—that the meaning of individual words is arbitrary and conventional. And when he adopts the name Ernest in order to woo Cecily he further enacts the separation of word from designated thing or person.

Algy is far from being alone in his manipulation of words to mean what he wants them to mean. In the wrangle over the cigarette case Jack is equally willing to lie that the case is a gift from his short Aunt Cecily who lives in Tunbridge Wells to put Algy off the scent of his well-endowed ward. As manipulators go, though, Jack—who is really Ernest (and earnest perhaps) is less adept at making others believe his factual inexactitudes. The men have certainly met their match in the women as well. Cecily announces to Algy-as-Ernest that she has written evidence—her diary and love letters—of his proposal on Valentine's Day the previous year. She has constructed their engagement out of a tissue of words:

> CECILY: Worn out by your entire ignorance of my existence, I determined to end the matter one way of the other, and after a long struggle with myself, I accepted you under this dear old tree here. The next day I bought this little ring in your name . . . And this is the box in which I keep all your dear letters . . .
> ALGERNON: My letters! But my own sweet Cecily, I have never written you any letters.
> CECILY: You need hardly remind me of that, Ernest. I remember only too well that I was forced to write your letters for you. I wrote always three times a week and sometimes oftener. (Wilde Earnest 283–84)

This is the evidence to which Cecily turns when she sets out to prove that Ernest is hers. But it is also clear evidence that she is as much of a fantasist and liar as her prospective husband. Moreover, Gwendolen herself also points out the fictiveness of her own diary, drawn out for the same purpose of proving her claim to Ernest, commenting that she never goes anywhere without it because "One should always have something sensational to read in the train" (Wilde Earnest 288). The reference is here is to a popular fictional form—the sensation novel, which was also often known as a railway novel. Sensation fictions were sensational in the sense that their plots were concerned with crime and sexual irregularity. If Gwendolen's diary is similarly "larger than life," its value as a truthful record of her life is not secure.

The successful manipulation of words—to score a point off a rival, to escape from an unpleasant duty, to put down a social inferior—is the mark of a hero or heroine in this play. Verbal wit that has no necessary relationship with reality is the only "virtue" consistently rewarded. As Gwendolen puts it in response to Jack and Algy's excuses for their deceptions, recycling an epigram Wilde had used before, "In matters of grave importance, style not sincerity, is the vital thing" (295). It does not appear to matter that she and

Cecily do not believe what they have just been told, because of the "wonderful beauty of the answer" (295). Those who are less articulate and more trusting of the truthfulness of words like Chasuble and Miss Prism, are marked down as the butts of the joke, fumbling their way through elaborate metaphors in circumlocutions that disguise rather than express their passion for each other. Nonetheless, even the heroes and heroines of this drama speak of the things that are meant to be most sacred, like their love for their chosen spouses, in phrases that mirror each other so closely that it is clear that Wilde is suggesting that even grand passions are stereotyped emotions in this intensely artificial world. Katharine Worth has commented that Wilde's dialogue is "strongly musical, markedly accented, dominated by musical devices such as repetition and variation on a theme" (21); the speeches Gwendolen and Cecily give to each other, and those of the menfolk to their chosen girls, make the point about repetition very effectively. The musicality of the speeches reaches its apotheosis when the couples speak to each in unison as they resolve their difficulties about the ownership of the name of Ernest and of the young man to whom it is supposed to belong. To those metaphors of musical repetition and unison I would add the crescendo of Lady Bracknell's various speeches where she puts Jack firmly in his place ('Until yesterday I had no idea that there were any families or persons whose origin was a terminus' [298]). Just as the elaborate codes of behavior around taking tea, or proposing, or mourning, are all—like Bunbury—exploded as shams and facades, so, too, are the elaborate conventions of polite conversation, which is stylized to the point that no sincere emotion can be expressed in these words by these people in this setting, and with the conventions that surround them. When, at the end of the play, Jack laments the fact that he has inadvertently been telling the truth all his life, Gwendolen is able to reassure him that she can forgive him this lapse, "For I feel that you are sure to change" (Wilde Earnest 307). Lying is the only triumphant value as the curtain falls.

To some degree this might not seem to matter at all. The world of the play is a game world of make-believe. No one could mistake it for the reality in which we actually live, could they? For Wilde's earliest audiences, the world they were looking at was a very close approximation to the one they inhabited. As Russell Jackson has pointed out, the actor-manager George Alexander paid his wife to stage-manage the set so that it would be detailed: "I loved to make things look real," she wrote (162.). The setting in drawing rooms and rose gardens is their idealized setting—where they would have lived if they had the choice; the costumes were just like the clothes they were wearing and the routines of taking tea for the purpose participation in the marriage market were rituals in which they participated. The game is one that they were also playing. Underneath the triviality and surface and fun, *The Importance of Being Earnest* makes some important points. It attacks the shallow values of the society it mirrors—but the attack is disguised by the mask not of manners but of laughter. In a telling exchange that brings down the curtain on Act 1, Jack berates Algy for never taking anything seriously:

> JACK: You never talk anything but nonsense.
> ALGERNON: Nobody ever does. (Wilde Earnest 271)

The logical conclusion of the play's message that neither words nor forms of behavior have firm, fixed meanings is that an alternative basis for social interaction is required. And that is actually a revolutionary idea that might just have led to "acts of violence in Grosvenor Square" (Wilde Earnest 265).

Works Cited

Baldick, Chris. *The Concise Oxford Dictionary of Literary Terms*. Oxford: Oxford U P, 1990.

Carlson, Marvin. "What Is Performance?" *The Presentation of the Self in Everyday Life*. Reprinted in Henry Bial, edited by *The Performance Studies Reader*, 2nd Edition. London: Routledge, 2004, pp. 70–75.

Coppa, Francesca. "Performance Theory and Performativity". *Palgrave Advances: Oscar Wilde Studies*, edited by Frederick S. Roden. Basingstoke: Palgrave,2004, pp. 72–95.

Ellmann, Richard. *Oscar Wilde*. Harmondsworth: Penguin, 1988.

Goffman, Erving. "Performances: Belief in the Part One Is Playing". *The Presentation of the Self in Everyday Life* (1959). Reprinted in Henry Bial, edited by *The Performance Studies Reader*, 2nd Edition. London: Routledge, 2004. pp. 61–65.

Hawkes, Terence. *Structuralism and Semiotics*. 2nd Edition. London: Methuen, 1983.

Jackson, Russell. *The Importance of Being Earnest. The Cambridge Companion to Oscar Wilde*, edited by Peter Raby. Cambridge: Cambridge U P, 1997, pp. 161–80.

Powell, Kerry. *Oscar Wilde and the Theatre of the 1890s*, Cambridge: Cambridge U P, 1990.

Varty, Anne. *A Preface to Oscar Wilde*. London: Pearson Education, 1998.

Wilde, Oscar. *The Importance of Being Earnest and Other Plays*, edited by Peter Raby. Oxford: Oxford World's Classics, 1995.

_____. *The Picture of Dorian Gray*, edited by Joseph Bristow. Oxford: Oxford World's Classics, 2006.

Worth, Katharine. *Oscar Wilde*. London: Macmillan, 1983.

Yeats, W.B. *Autobiographies. Collected Works of W. B. Yeats*, edited by William H. O'Donnell and Douglas N. Archibald. New York: Scribner 1999.

Beyond the Romantic Imagination: Oscar Wilde's Aesthetics_____

Julie-Ann Robson

Oscar Wilde is best known as the author of *The Importance of Being Earnest, The Picture of Dorian Gray* and perhaps *Salomé*, but also as a nineteenth-century dandy and aesthete whose face is instantly recognizable to a twenty-first-century audience. On both sides of the Atlantic in the late nineteenth century, Wilde was the epitome of art for art's sake, and when he travelled across America he did so as a Professor of Aesthetics. Aesthetics—a word that has come to mean the philosophical study of art—had its origins in Ancient Greece, where philosophers like Plato and Aristotle questioned the links between art and knowledge, and art and truth. The word was coined in the eighteenth century by A. G. Baumgarten and is derived from the Ancient Greek *aisthêsis*, meaning sensation, perception, and to *aisthêton*: the object of perception.

In the current context, though, it might be best to define aesthetics with a quote from Water Pater—a prominent voice in Victorian aesthetics and a significant "influencer" in the circles in which Wilde moved, who would write in the "Preface" to his remarkable *The Renaissance: Studies in Art and Poetry* (1873): "To define beauty, not in the most abstract, but in the most concrete terms possible, to find, not a universal formula for it, but the formula which expresses most adequately this or that special manifestation of it, is the aim of the true student of aesthetics" (vii).

The Critical Background to Wildean Aesthetics
Wilde's interest in art began at an early age, and in his place of birth, Ireland. His letters and notebooks are scattered with references to art and aesthetics, and he published poetry during his years at Trinity College in Dublin. His early years were filled with opportunities to experience literature and art, with his parents entertaining Dublin's literati at regular salons held at their home in Merrion

---

Square—the heart of Dublin's establishment. Both his parents were writers—his mother was an acclaimed Irish nationalist, poet, and revolutionary in her youth—but it was at Trinity College (1871–1874), and later at Oxford (1874–1879) that his aesthetic ideas began to take shape. Wilde would have been familiar with Edmund Burke's *A Philosophical Inquiry into the Origin of Our Ideas of the Sublime and Beautiful* (1757), published when Burke, too, was a student at Trinity College; in his second year at Trinity Wilde's tutor published a translation of Immanuel Kant's *The Aesthetic and Analytic* (1872) and would also publish *Kant's Critical Philosophy for English Readers* (in two volumes, 1874). Trinity offered a course on aesthetics, and the young Oscar's first published poems appeared in the University's magazines. At Oxford he attended the lectures of (among others) the University's first Professor of Fine Art, John Ruskin, and would become familiar with the ideas of Walter Pater, whose "Conclusion" to *Studies in the History of the Renaissance*—that Wilde would later call his "'golden book'" (qtd. in Ellmann 80)—caused a scandal. Pater's "Conclusion"—together with his description of the *Mona Lisa* (*La Gioconda*), which brought a very small Renaissance painting into public consciousness in a way that has never left her—is probably more famous than almost any philosophical writing on art (apart from the Greeks). Of the *Mona Lisa* Pater would write:

> She is older than the rocks among which she sits; like the vampire, she has been dead many times, and learned the secrets of the grave; and has been a diver in deep seas, and keeps their fallen day about her; and trafficked for strange webs with Eastern merchants; and, as Leda, was the mother of Helen of Troy, and, as Saint Anne, the mother of Mary; and all this has been to her but as the sound of lyres and flutes, and lives only in the delicacy with which it has moulded the changing lineaments, and tinged the eyelids and the hands. (125)

Pater's description of the painting created the mystery with which she is now shrouded, and gives us a hint not only at the direction Wilde would take in his aesthetic, but the influence Pater had on his readership. Wilde's fellow Irishman, the poet W.B. Yeats—eleven years Wilde's junior who did not, like Wilde, attend Oxford or move in Pater's circle—would concede Pater's influence, writing "we consciously looked to Pater for our philosophy" (201).

Ruskin and Pater were intellectual rivals, in that the two had very different ideas on the relationship between the work of art and the individual. These two prominent thinkers—both at Oxford when the young Wilde was a student—together with Matthew Arnold, Professor of Poetry at Oxford a little less than a generation earlier, were probably the most influential writers to undertake philosophical studies of art and culture in the Victorian era, and Wilde's own theories on art are—in part—a conversation with, and a movement beyond, these key intellectuals.

Matthew Arnold was a poet and cultural critic whose influential essays had a significant impact on nineteenth-century British thought. He saw the society around him failing; arguing that with industrialism, materialism, and puritanism, ideas were narrowing in ways that cast aside intellectual growth—what he terms "sweetness and light" (Arnold Culture and Anarchy 4). In *Culture and Anarchy* (1869) he urges a reassessment of the idea of "culture" itself. The essay argues that the aim of culture should be the study of perfection: and that the aim of culture should be to learn "the best which has been thought and said in the world" (Arnold Culture and Anarchy viii). Without this he feared—and not without reason, given the waves of revolution that rumbled across Europe throughout the nineteenth century—culture had the potential to descend into anarchy.

John Ruskin, author of *The Seven Lamps of Architecture* (1849) and *The Stones of Venice* (1851–1853), was an artist, critic, and commentator on the role of art in society. He was also an idealist whose admiration of medieval architecture, which he argued not only required the collaboration of the community, but reflected nature and its relation to God, helped formulate his ideas. His socialist leanings led him to reject the modern cult of manufacture and the cruelty of industrialization, with its factories, cotton gins, slavery, child labor, and mass production, preferring medievalism's craftsmanship and the artist's more intimate connection with the work of art—a philosophy taken up by William Morris and the Arts and Crafts

Movement. Like Morris, for whom the relationship between the work of art and the artist was bound to a kind of social and ethical covenant, Ruskin regarded the connection between the work of art and society as an intensely moral one. When Oscar Wilde toured the United States in 1882, he drew—perhaps a little too heavily—on the ideas of Morris and Ruskin for his lectures on "The House Beautiful" and "The Decorative Arts." He would write, for example,

> In asking you to build and decorate your houses more beautifully, I do not ask you to spend large sums, as art does not depend in the slightest degree upon extravagance or luxury, but rather that the procuring of articles which, however cheaply purchased and unpretending, are beautiful and fitted to impart pleasure to the observer as they did to the maker. (Wilde The House Beautiful 913)

Ruskin was an idealist; a pious man who believed the value of the work of art should be judged first by its "thought and moral purpose," second its "technical skill," and third—curiously, when reflecting from a twenty-first century digital world—its "bodily industry":

> All art which is worth its room in this world, all art which is not a piece of blundering refuse, occupying the foot or two of earth which, if unencumbered by it, would have grown corn or violets, or some better thing, is *art which proceeds from an individual mind, working through instruments which assist, but do not supersede, the muscular action of the human hand, upon the materials which most tenderly receive, and most securely retain, the impressions of such human labor*. (Ruskin Stones of Venice Vol. I 189–90, emphasis in original)

This relationship between artist, artwork, idea, and moral purpose is crucial to Ruskin and is why he condemned mass production. For Ruskin the maker needs to have real intellectual, physical, cultural, and spiritual engagement with the thing being created. Mass production is, for Ruskin, immoral. So, too, in Ruskin's idealized world is the depiction of sensuality without moral intent. His description of "Beggar Boys"—a painting by the Italian artist Murillo (1617–1682)—reveals his disgust that an artist would portray the act of eating for pleasure's sake. Murillo, Ruskin says, "might have shown hunger in other ways. . . But he did not care to do this. He delighted merely in the disgusting manner of eating, the food filling the cheek; the boy is not hungry, else he would not turn round to talk and grin as he eats" (Ruskin The Stones of Venice Vol. II 193).

Walter Pater, on the other hand, was a materialist for whom the object—the work of art—is a means through which to experience sensation. As can be seen from his description of the *Mona Lisa*, his impulse is to explore his "impression" of the work of art, at the same time revealing the darker recesses of his mind, and to relish the work of art without recourse to moral purpose. In response to Matthew Arnold, he would write in the Preface to his *Renaissance,*

> "To see the object as in itself it really is," has been justly said to be the aim of all true criticism whatever; and in aesthetic criticism the first step towards seeing one's object as it really is, is to know one's own impression as it really is, to discriminate it, to realise it distinctly. . . . What is this song or picture, this engaging personality presented in life or in a book, to ME? What effect does it really produce on me? Does it give me pleasure? And if so, what sort or degree of pleasure? How is my nature modified by its presence, and under its influence? (Pater viii)

In this ego-centered search for aesthetic pleasure, Pater argues, the purpose of philosophy and the culture of speculation is to "rouse, to startle it into sharp and eager observation" (236). The "Conclusion" to his *Renaissance*—which was removed from subsequent editions because it was deemed too dangerous an influence on young minds—called for an abandonment of selfhood in return for a series of heightened experiences:

> Every moment some form grows perfect in hand or face; some tone on the hills or the sea is choicer than the rest; some mood of passion or insight or intellectual excitement is irresistibly real and attractive for us,—for that moment only. Not the fruit of experience, but experience itself, is the end. A counted number of pulses only is

given to us of a variegated, dramatic life. How may we see in them all that is to be seen in them by the finest senses? How shall we pass most swiftly from point to point, and be present always at the focus where the greatest number of vital forces unite in their purest energy?

To burn always with this hard, gemlike flame, to maintain this ecstasy, is success in life. (Pater 236)

In *The Picture of Dorian Gray* (1890–91) this concentration on momentary perfection, experience, and heightened sensation is echoed, particularly in Dorian's exploration of the senses in Chapter 11:

But it appeared to Dorian Gray that the true nature of the senses had never been understood, and that they had remained savage and animal merely because the world had sought to starve them into submission or to kill them by pain, instead of aiming at making them elements of a new spirituality, of which a fine instinct for beauty was to be the dominant characteristic. As he looked back upon man moving through history, he was haunted by a feeling of loss. So much had been surrendered! And to such little purpose! . . .

He used to wonder at the shallow psychology of those who conceive the ego in man as a thing simple, permanent, reliable, and of one essence. To him, man was a being with myriad lives and myriad sensations, a complex multiform creature that bore within itself strange legacies of thought and passion, and whose very flesh was tainted with the monstrous maladies of the dead. (Wilde The Picture of Dorian Gray 99, 107)

The works of Arnold, Ruskin, and Pater were seminal not only in terms of Victorian culture. They were critical to Wilde's aesthetic development, and these divergent yet prevailing philosophical approaches—present as they were at Oxford throughout Wilde's formative undergraduate years—had permeated almost every corner of British intellectual culture and provided fertile ground in which the seeds of Wilde's own aesthetic could germinate.

Beyond Oxford: Launching a Cosmopolitan Aesthetic Career

By 1877 Wilde was venturing beyond the "dreaming spires" (Arnold Thyrsis 542) of Oxford. His interest ranged from the Pre-Raphaelite Movement and the poet Algernon Swinburne, expanding to the French writers Gautier and Baudelaire—whose works came to epitomize *l'art pour l'art* in France and beyond—and on to the Symbolist movement. It's important to realize that these artists—painters, poets, and playwrights—were also intellectuals and essayists, engaging in debates and writing treatises on the nature of art and the role of the artist. Wilde was beginning to craft a career in the *zeitgeist*, emerging as both artist and critic. And while his affection and respect for Ruskin is real—in 1888 he wrote "from you I learned nothing but what was good" (Wilde to E.W. Godwin [April 1855] 257)—he could not long hold with Ruskin's moralistic views on art. In an early critical essay "The English Renaissance of Art" he talks of Ruskin's "faultless and fervent eloquence" (Wilde, The English Renaissance of Art) , but dismisses the artist's social obligation.

As part of his process of crafting a career, Wilde drew significant attention to himself through his poetry, his dress, his wit, and his critical observations on art, and quite possibly walked down London's Piccadilly with a sunflower (or a lily) in his hand—a performative declaration of his status as "an aesthetic young man." This image of Wilde as aesthete was picked up by the satirical magazine *Punch*, and together with other proponents of aestheticism, was lampooned not only in cartoons, but also in Gilbert and Sullivan's comic opera, *Patience*. Offered the opportunity to promote the operetta's American tour, Wilde jumped at the chance, repurposing his "English Renaissance" essay—shortened, revised, and lightened for his American audiences—for a tour that lasted a year, during which time he reinvented himself and his aesthetic.

The European dissemination of the idea of *l'art pour l'art*—which translates as "Art for Art's Sake"—can arguably be attributed to the French writer Théophile Gautier (1811–1872), a poet, dramatist, novelist, and essayist first espoused the idea as part of an artistic manifesto in the "Preface" to his novel *Mademoiselle de Maupin* (1835). Unlike the art theories developed by his British counterparts, Gautier and his fellow countryman Baudelaire (1821–1867), author of *Les fleurs du mal* (*Flowers of Evil*, 1857), did not impose on art the need to be anything but itself. Gautier wrote in the preface to his novel, "There is nothing truly beautiful but that which can never be of any use whatsoever; everything useful is ugly, for it is the expression of some need, and man's needs are ignoble and disgusting like his own poor and infirm nature" (Gautier 82).

Returning from the United States, Wilde would assert his aesthetic break with *L'Envoi*: a preface to Rendell Rodd's collected poems, *Rose Leaf and Apple Leaf*: declaring "the rule of art is not the rule of morals" (Wilde L'Envoi 6). He would claim this little-read essay signifies his "departure from Ruskin and the Pre-Raphaelites, and marks an era in the aesthetic movement" (Wilde to J.M. Stoddart [?19 Feb. 1882] 140). On his return to London (via Paris) Wilde refined his aesthetic skills in public. James Abbott McNeill Whistler (1834–1903) is perhaps nowadays best known for a remarkable painting of his mother, "Arrangement in Black and Grey," and some significant society portraits. But Whistler was a cosmopolitan artist and raconteur who had a disastrous run-in with Ruskin, (who claimed that Whistler was "flinging a pot of paint in the public's face" (qtd. in Ellmann 78) with his painting *Nocturne in Black and Gold—The Falling Rocket*). Whistler took up the ideas of Gautier and Baudelaire, claiming them as his own in his lecture "Mr Whistler's Ten O'clock" (1885), capitalizing on the publicity provided by Gilbert and Sullivan's operetta and *Punch*'s satire of the Aesthetic Movement, with intelligence and wit. Wilde would engage Whistler in a well-matched public duel of amusing repartee, and although Wilde and Whistler had a falling out—Wilde's fairy-tale "The Remarkable Rocket" is quite possibly based on Whistler, and the artist in *Dorian Gray* may also reference him—Wilde would go on to eclipse his former mentor and develop an aesthetic theory based on many of the ideas the intellectual thrust and parry had honed.

From Art for Art's Sake to Lying and the Invention of a New Aesthetic

In *L'Envoi*, Wilde identified himself as a neo-Romantic in the style of Gautier, and it must be remembered that Wilde was no mere *poseur*—he was intellectually brilliant, with a strong Classical education. He won the Berkeley Medal for Greek at Trinity College in Dublin, and graduated from Oxford with double first in Classical Moderations and *Literae Humaniores* (Greats). He had a deep grounding in philosophical thought on matters of literature, art, culture, and ethics. The depth of his reading can be found in his poetry, fiction, and drama, but is most rigorous—if insouciant—in his mature critical writings, particularly in "The Critic as Artist" and "The Decay of Lying," both of which were published in 1891 in his collection *Intentions*.

The art for art's sake movement to which Wilde secured himself—and for which he would become the leading proponent in England—had its roots in Romanticism, and, in philosophical terms, in the works of Immanuel Kant. "Kant's aesthetics had, via Hegel, Goethe, Schiller, etc., been proclaimed in France by Mme de Staël and [Benjamin] Constant, the latter using the term *"l'art pour l'art"* in connection with Kant as early as 1804" (Tennant 126n.). Kant's *Critique of Judgment* is arguably the most important dissertation on aesthetics since the Greeks, and his work was certainly familiar to Wilde from his association with Mahaffy. *The Critique of Judgment* explores the nature of aesthetic judgment, and the way in which we respond to the work of art, which, says Kant, is a matter of taste: "The judgement of taste is . . . not a judgement of cognition, and is consequently not logical but aesthetical, by which we understand that whose determining ground can be *no other than subjective*" (I. Kant 55). He claims that aesthetic judgment is not passive, outlining a role for the imagination in aesthetic judgment. In this sense Kant had a profound effect on the Romantic tradition (and thus art for art's sake), allowing a wholehearted rejection of enlightenment views of a mechanistic universe, and sanctioning a worldview that locates individual imagination at its center.

This distinction between objective "truth" and subjective imagination—between reason and taste—is central to Kant's view of aesthetic judgement. In his Oxford Notebooks, Wilde would reduce this with aphoristic brevity: "Knowledge to Kant was the thinking of our sensations" (Wilde *Oscar Wilde's Oxford Notebooks* 128). However, it should be noted that for Kant and the Romantics who followed in his wake, the importance of the imagination is not merely subjective, but universal: the Romantics insist that the subjective "I" is in a sense humanity as a whole. However, as we have seen with Pater, the post-Romantic sensibility points away from universality, placing the individual at the center of experience—and specifically, the experience of the work of art.

In his critical writings, Wilde describes the aesthetic critic as one for whom the Romantic notion of the "I" is individualized—even anarchic—although it retains a vestige of universality, in that individual experience exists in collaborative isolation. In an eloquent botanical metaphor, he writes in "The Soul of Man Under Socialism" (which despite its name is a deep exploration of the politics of Individualism) that "A red rose is not selfish because it wants to be a red rose. It would be horribly selfish if it wanted all the other flowers in the garden to be both red and roses" (Wilde *The Soul of Man Under Socialism* 1195). Individualism, then, in its most perfect form allows an "infinite variety of type" (Wilde *The Soul of Man Under Socialism* 1195), rather than Kantian subjective universalism or the Romantic's everyman.

Wilde's critical writings, then, deal with this complex relationship between art and the individual or subjective imagination. His key ideas on this relationship are documented in two Socratic-style dialogues: "The Decay of Lying" and "The Critic as Artist." "The Decay of Lying"—a dialogue between Cyril and Vivian[1]—examines this relationship between art, Realism, nature, life, and truth; "The Critic as Artist"—a dialogue between Ernest and Gilbert—scrutinizes the role of criticism as a creative imaginative act, rather than simply a documenting of the subjective experience of observation.

The use of the dialogues as a form is not surprising, in that Socrates—as revealed in Chapter 10 of *The Republic* (a dialogue chronicled by his pupil Plato *circa* 380 BCE)—denies artists citizenship in his ideal Republic. The reasons, to put it concisely, are that drama evokes emotions in the audience that fly against reason; and that art is a mere copy—a mimetic representation—of an ideal truth and is therefore deceitful. Given Wilde's penchant for paradox, it's hardly surprising that he takes up the Socratic form of the dialogue to set out the architecture of an aesthetic that has "lying" as a key premise, and to do so through conversations between young idle men engaged in seemingly frivolous conversations. Moreover, whereas Socrates had banned the artists from the Republic for creating mere copies—and thus for misleading the Polis with lies—Wilde inverts this hierarchy, asserting the imagination—lying (or copies)—over the natural and the real. What's more, for Wilde "mind" is pivotal, and nature only comes into existence through mind: "Nature is no great mother who has borne us. She is our creation. It is in our brain that she quickens to life. Indeed things are because we see them, and what we see, and how we see it, depends on the Arts that have influenced us" (Wilde The Decay of Lying 1086).

And while this takes us back to the individual subjective response to the object, Wilde goes beyond Arnold's aim to "see the object as in itself it really is" (Arnold Poetry and Criticism of Matthew Arnold 239), and Pater's call to "know one's own impression as it really is" (viii). For Wilde, "the primary aim of the critic is to see the object as in itself it really is not" (Wilde The Critic as Artist 1128). To understand this seemingly absurd claim, it's important to examine the fundamental argument of both dialogues, and to note that—although Wilde had spoken of the "imagination" in his earlier essays and would appropriate it as a keystone to his aesthetic—with "The Decay of Lying" he works to destabilize the idea of the imagination. He does so, as Richard Ellmann his biographer points out, because for Wilde the word imagination had "grown stale and innocuous, though he is, of course, upholding imagination against reason and observation. Imagination was also a word that sounded too natural and involuntary for Wilde. Lying is better because it is no outpouring of the self, but a conscious effort to mislead" (285).

By reconceptualizing imagination as lying, the individual's relationship to the object is no longer stable—it is subject to mood, influence, creativity, and willful misreading: one does not merely see the object, one is in a creative engagement with it, and the consequences of such an engagement are subjective and capricious. One is, after all, seeing the object *as it is not*. Life, Truth, and Nature take on subordinate roles, and Arnold's call for objective truth is replaced with the assertion of a subjective and wilful lie. "Art takes life as part of her rough material, recreates it, and refashions it in fresh forms, is absolutely indifferent to fact, invents, imagines, dreams, and keeps between herself and reality the impenetrable barrier of beautiful style, of decorative or ideal treatment" (Wilde The Decay of Lying 1078).

Lying, then recreates nature through form, erects an "impenetrable barrier," and separates the chaos of life from the ideal of art. This is why Wilde takes particular exception with the contemporary style of "Realism." Realism, a form that spanned both sides of the Channel and crossed the Atlantic, aims at a faithful artistic representation of the local, the ordinary, the banal, the ugly, and often the poor and middle classes. Of its chief proponent Emile Zola's characters Wilde would write "They have their dreary vices, and their drearier virtues. The record of their lives is absolutely without interest. Who cares what happens to them?" (Wilde The Decay of Lying 1075) If the Romantic imagination aimed for the universal, Realism attempted an objective, sometimes journalistic observation of life—including the prosaic and the bathetic—and to reveal the arbitrariness of life. Wilde urges a turning away from reality to art, because, he says,

> She is not to be judged by any external standard of resemblance. . .
> She can bid the almond-tree blossom in winter, and send the snow
> upon the ripe cornfield. At her word the frost lays its silver finger
> upon the burning mouth of June, and the winged lions creep out from
> the hollows of the Lydian Hills. . . She has hawk-faced gods that

worship her, and the centaurs gallop at her side. (Wilde The Decay of Lying 1082)

And in "The Critic as Artist" Wilde continues this trajectory in which he wilfully aims to see the object as it is not. This time, though, he is placing an additional barrier between Nature and Art. If the artist uses Nature and Life as her rough materials, the Critic uses art:

> the great artists, from Homer and Æschylus, down to Shakespeare and Keats, did not go directly to life for their subject-matter, but sought for it in myth, and legend, and ancient tale, so the critic deals with materials that others have, as it were, purified for him, and to which imaginative form and colour have been already added. . . the highest Criticism, being the purest form of personal impression, is in its way more creative than creation, as it has least reference to any standard external to itself, and is, in fact, its own reason for existing, and, as the Greeks would put it, in itself, and to itself, an end. (Wilde The Critic as Artist 1125).

Writing in 1885, five years before "The Critic as Artist," he argued that "The true artist is known by the use he makes of what he annexes, and he annexes everything" (Wilde "Olivia at the Lyceum" 955). He claimed that between Victor Hugo and Shakespeare all original subject matter had been taken up and that "In a very ugly and sensible age, the arts borrow, not from life, but from each other" (Wilde Pen, Pencil and Poison 1100). Nature and life provide little that is beautiful or original: "Nature is a foolish place to look for inspiration in, but a charming one in which to forget one ever had any" (Wilde to E.W. Godwin [April 1855] 275). Art, on the contrary, has been purified by aesthetic sensibility—it is something to which form and style have been added.

Harold Bloom—himself a scholar of Wilde—in his seminal book *The Anxiety of Influence* (1973) argued that appropriation "always proceeds by a misreading of the prior [writer], an act of creative correction that is actually and necessarily a misinterpretation. . . [it is] wilful revisionism without which modern [writing] as such could not exist" (30). Wilde seized this form of revisionism—or lying—with both hands. Using another botanical metaphor, he declares "when I see a monstrous tulip with *four* petals in someone else's garden, I am impelled to grow a monstrous tulip with *five* wonderful petals" (qtd. in Ellmann 320). To put this in more tangible terms, "lying" means taking a work of art as a subjective starting point for another work of art, thus taking literally Pater's aim to define "beauty. . . in the most concrete terms possible" (vii). This is perhaps most tellingly captured in a rather scathing review of *Salomé* published in 1893:

> Mr. Wilde has many masters and the influence of each master asserts itself in his pages as strips of different colours assert themselves in stuffs from the East. . . Now it is the voice of Gautier, painting pictures in words of princesses in jewels and flowers and unguents. Anon it is Maeterlinck who speaks—Maeterlinck the Lord of the Low countries—with his iterations and reiterations, his questions and conundrums. . . But the voices that breathe the breath of life into Salomé are dominated by one voice, the voice of Flaubert. If Flaubert had not written Salammbô, if Flaubert had not written Hérodias, Salomé might boast an originality to which it cannot now lay claim. (Unnamed reviewer in Beckson 93)

The unnamed reviewer is lost to time, but the observations—damning though they are—reveal that Wilde did indeed apply the theories he put forward in *Intentions*. Moreover, he reinvented the biblical fragment of the death of Jokanaan (John the Baptist) and in doing so created a myth. Part of the play's originality is that it is Salomé, not her mother, who asks for the head of the prophet—a pure invention from Wilde that has gone down as the legend of Salomé, Princess of Judea. Like Pater's *La Gioconda*, this story has attained a mythical status as work of art: its reinvention paradoxically attaining a truth of its own.

In a more nuanced and discerning review—this time of *Intentions*—Arthur Symonds, wrote

> Mr Wilde is always suggestive; he is interesting even when he is provoking. At his best, to our thinking, when he is most himself—

an artist in epigram—he can be admirable even when his eloquence reminds us of the eloquent writing of others. He is conscious of the charm of graceful echoes, and is always original in his quotations. (Symonds in Beckson 96)

Wilde's aesthetic theory—his philosophical study of art—is, of course, much more complex in its engagement with philosophical debates on the relationship between art and truth, art and life, and art and ethics than is possible to cover here: his analysis of aesthetic debates harkens back to Socrates, who cast artists from his ideal Republic, and to Aristotle, who let them back in. But the individual's engagement with the object, traced here through debates from Arnold to Wilde, are a crucial part of the development of his aesthetic, his conceptualization of subjectivity, individualism, identity, and of his writing. To summarize the key arguments and concepts covered here in Wilde's own words, "Lying, the telling of beautiful untrue things, is the proper aim of Art" (Wilde The Decay of Lying 1091–92), and "criticism is that which reveals in the work of Art what the artist had not put there" (Wilde The Critic as Artist 1154). To arrive at these aphoristic encapsulations of his aesthetic, though, there has been much philosophical ground to cover.

Note

1. Wilde's own children were called Cyril and Vyvyan. After Wilde's trial, the children's surnames were changed from Wilde to Holland. Cyril (1885–1914) was a pilot, who died in WWI; Vyvyan (1886–1967) would become a writer and father to Merlin Holland (b. 1945).

Works Cited

Anonymous. "Review of Salomé in the *Pall Mall Gazette* (27 Feb. 1893) reprinted." Beckson, Karl. *Oscar Wilde: The Critical Heritage*. London and New York: Kegan & Paul, 1970.

Arnold, Matthew. *Culture and Anarchy*. London: John Murray, 1961.

_____. *Poetry and Criticism of Matthew Arnold*, edited by A Dwight Culler. Boston: Houghton Mifflin Company, 1961.

_____. "Thyrsis." Cunningham, edited by Valentine. *The Victorians: An Anthology of Poetry and Poetics*. Oxford: Blackwell, 2000.

Bloom, Harold. *The Anxiety of Influence: A Theory of Poetry*. 2nd Edition. Oxford U P, 1997.

Ellmann, Richard. *Oscar Wilde*. New York: Random House, 1988.

Gautier, Théophile. *Madamoiselle De Maupin*, translated and edited by Fredrick C. de Sumichrast. C.T. Brainard Publishing, 1900.

Kant, Immanuel. *Kant's Critical Philosophy for English Readers in Two Volumes*, translated by J.P. Mahaffy, 2 vols. London: Macmillan and Company, 1889.

_____. *The Critique of Judgement*, edited and translated by J. H. Bernard. London: Macmillan, 1914.

Pater, Walter. *The Renaissance: Studies in Art and Poetry*. London: Macmillan, 1902.

Rodd, Renndell. *Rose Leaf and Apple Leaf: L'Envoi*, Introduction by Oscar Wilde, Portland, Maine: Thomas B. Mosher, 1906.

Ruskin, John. *Stones of Venice*. vol. I. The Foundations, 1851. London: Smith, Elder & Co.

_____. *The Stones of Venice*. vol. II. The Sea-stories, 1853. London: Smith, Elder & Co.

_____. *The Stones of Venice*. vol. III. The Fall, 1853, London: Smith, Elder & Co.

Symonds, Arthur. "Review of 'Intentions' in *The Speaker* (4 July 1891)." *Oscar Wilde: The Critical Heritage*, edited by Karl Beckson. London and New York: Kegan Paul, 1970.

Tennant, P.E. *Théophile Gautier*. London: Althone P, 1975.

von Goethe, Johann Wolfgang. "Introduction to the 'Proplyäea." *Goethe on Art,* translated and edited by John Gage, Berkeley & Los Angeles: Cambridge U P, 1980, p. 6.

Wilde, Oscar. "'Olivia at the Lyceum.'" *The Complete Works of Oscar Wilde*. Glasgow: Harper Collins, 1999.

_____. *Oscar Wilde's Oxford Notebooks: A Portrait of a Mind in the Making*, edited by Phillip E. Smith II and Michael S. Helfand. New York and Oxford: Oxford U P, 1989.

_____. "Pen, Pencil and Poison." *The Complete Works of Oscar Wilde*. Glasgow: Harper Collins, 1999.

_____. "The Critic as Artist." *The Complete Works of Oscar Wilde.* Glasgow: Harper Collins, 1999.

_____. "The Decay of Lying." *The Complete Works of Oscar Wilde.* Glasgow: Harper Collins, n.d. 1999.

_____. "The English Renaissance of Art." 2015. *eBooks@Adelaide.* The University of Adelaide. June 2019. ebooks.adelaide.edu.au/w/wilde/oscar/english-renaissance-of-art/.

_____. "The House Beautiful." Wilde, Oscar. *The Complete Works of Oscar Wilde.* Glasgow: Harper Collins, 1999.

_____. "The Picture of Dorian Gray." *The Complete Works of Oscar Wilde.* Glasgow: Harper Collins, 2000.

_____. "The Soul of Man under Socialism." *The Complete Works of Oscar Wilde.* Glasgow: Harper Collins, 1999, pp. 1174–97.

_____. "Wilde to E.W. Godwin [April 1855]." *The Complete Letters of Oscar Wilde,* edited by Merlin Holland and Rupert Hart-Davis. New York: Henry Holt and Co., 2000.

_____. "Wilde to John Ruskin" [June 1888], *The Complete Letters of Oscar Wilde,* edited by Merlin Holland and Rupert Hart-Davis. New York: Henry Holt and Co., 2000,p. 348.

_____. "Wilde to J.M. Stoddart [19 Feb. 1882]." *The Complete Letters of Oscar Wilde.* New York: Henry Holt and Co., 2000.

Yeats, W. B. *Autobiography of William Butler Yeats.* New York: Doubleday and Co., 1958.

"I Believe in Willie Hughes": *The Portrait of Mr W. H.*

Sharon Bickle and Marie Heneghan

Oscar Wilde's *The Portrait of Mr W. H.* positions itself at the site of one of literary history's great mysteries: the identity of the young man of William Shakespeare's sonnets and the source of its ambiguous dedication to the "onlie begetter of these insuing sonnets Mr W. H." This first appeared in *Blackwood's Magazine* in July 1889, although the extended story was not published until after Wilde's death. Framing the narrator's obsessive pursuit of the young man is the title's portrait of Willie Hughes, which is presented from the very start in the context of a discussion of literary forgeries. Throughout the story the portrait is described as forged rather than faked—which leaves ambiguously open the prospect of a "real" portrait. In fact, the portrait is a doubled lie: the name of Shakespeare's boy-actor, Willie Hughes, is created from the fabric of the sonnets themselves, while the portrait is revealed as the work of a print shop in Holborn. Nevertheless, the forgery exists not to conceal the lie of Willie Hughes, but rather to reveal a truth: as Erskine declares, to show "how firm and flawless his faith in the whole thing was" (Wilde WH 19). In this way, the novella sets up a familiar Wildean paradox that plays with the interrelationship between truth and lies, reality and artifice.

This chapter seeks to contextualize this unusual and often overlooked text within Wilde's *oeuvre*. While it is often the question of the forgery that draws the attention of critics like Nicholas Frankel, who calls the novella a "Liar's Manifesto" (43), here we want to focus not on the forgery itself and its central lie, or even its relationship to Art, but the way it spotlights the factitious passions of the "inexpert" reader and the way this then authorizes Shakespeare's, and ultimately Wilde's, male-centered desire. Frankel comments:

From the point of view of the reader or viewer whose belief and enjoyment are subsequently exposed as inauthentic, the value of forgery lies not in the corrections it makes to the discipline of criticism but in the enthusiasm it engenders, however briefly, for something never previously incarnated in material form. (45)

When the narrator finishes gathering his evidence, he makes his case to Erskine in a letter that "covered sheets of paper with passionate reiteration of the arguments and proofs . . . I put into the letter all my enthusiasm. I put into the letter all my faith" (Wilde WH 79). We want to suggest that this dangerous obsession, inspired by Cyril Graham's fervor and, in turn, passed on to Erskine, reveals something more often associated with twentieth-century culture than the nineteenth century: the excessive devotion of the fan. It is worth pausing to note that the text's detailed exegesis of the sonnets is presented as inexpert rather than scholarly criticism—although Wilde as a graduate of Oxford was certainly capable of the latter, and the analysis of the sonnets falls not far outside some contemporary professional theories of the sequence. As fiction, what the text emphasises is not the evidence itself but the "strange fascination" (Wilde WH 5) of the characters. The pleasures the text revels in are illicit desires.

Oscar Wilde and Nineteenth-Century Celebrity

Sharon Marcus argues that in the nineteenth century, celebrity was structured by theatricality and Wilde, who before emerging as a dramatist was best known for his often-caricatured celebrity, "deftly used photography, advertising, the mass press and international travel to gain public recognition" (1003). Marcus argues that celebrity relied on a combination of bodily presence and representation such that "performers script themselves and that authors put themselves on display" (1018), overtly constructing and performing their own celebrity identity. Celebrity was therefore closely related to theatrical presence in which "an actor performs in front of an audience that listens and watches but neither overtly acknowledges the other" (Marcus 1003). In this, both audience and actor participate in a visual play of identity that intensifies the theatricality of the experience and is not dissimilar to how forgery operates in the novella, in that the open awareness of forgery seems rather to intensify the portrait's effect as evidence for the truth of Willie Hughes rather than dismiss it. There are other overtly theatrical elements to the novella, for example, it contains five chapters, like the five acts of a Shakespearean drama, it contains almost melodramatic death scenes, and the forged portrait includes "the two masks of Tragedy and Comedy that hung somewhat formally from the marble pedestal" (Wilde WH 4).

What's in a Name? Shakespeare's Queer Sonnets

Shakespeare's sonnet cycle or sequence is comprised of 154 poems that were probably written in the 1590s, but not published together until 1609, and which are structurally divided into two sub-sequences addressed to a beautiful young man (1–126) and to a dark lady (127–54). In spite of the fact that most critics of the sonnets assert, as Joel Fineman does, "there is very little autobiography that can be plausibly derived out of the sonnets" (335), many also rehearse the most common theories of Mr W. H. including William Herbert, Lord Pembroke, and Henry Wriothesley, Earl of Southampton. The obsessive pursuit of the young man by the novella's narrator thus replicates critical practices that often underpin biographical debates around the young man as well as the Anti-Stratfordians who question Shakespeare's own authorship.

Typically, sonnet cycles follow what is known as a Courtly Love tradition of a male speaker and a female beloved, but what makes Shakespeare's sonnets queer lies in his depiction of the relationship with the young man, sometimes described as flattery to his patron, literary experiment (Burrow 100), or idealized passion (Culler 316). And yet the sonnets undeniably present an eroticized love relationship between men. Lisa Moore argues that the normative assertion of the masculinity of the sonnet's speaker that became prevalent in the Romantic period is a reaction to "the open secret of sonnet history, the famed Renaissance sonnet sequences of love between men" (828). Moore claims even this male homosexual tradition overwrites the "DNA" of the sonnet that lies in its Sapphic origins of love between women and depicts a central relationship between lover and beloved which "images masculinity in terms that sometime mirror femininity, ventriloquize eroticism between women, or voice female masculinity": in other words, that the tension between the lovers in the sonnet sequence is a mark of its lesbian origins (828). This suggests that Shakespeare's sequence does not queer a heteronormative tradition but is rather a return to its original state.

The novella is structured into five chapters or acts: the first presents the portrait and clearly identifies it as a forgery; the second chapter is devoted to a close reading of Shakespeare's famous sonnet sequence, which finds evidence for Willie Hughes as its object; the third provides a more general history of the Shakespearean boy-actor; the fourth deals with the dark lady sonnets that, rather than initiating a separate relationship for the speaker, form part of a love triangle the focus of which continues to be the young man; and the fifth provides the *denouemont* with a list of deaths of which even Shakespeare could be proud.

The novella shifts the primary interest of the sonnets to Willie Hughes whose name is derived directly from the sonnets:

> The Christian name he found of course in the punning sonnets 135 and 143; the surname was, according to him hidden in the seventh line of Sonnet 29, where Mr W. H. is described as "*A man in hew, all* Hews *in his controlling.*" (Wilde WH 14, emphasis in original)

Just as Shakespeare assures his young man an immortality based in poetry, "So long lives this, and this gives life to thee" (18.14), so do Wilde's words give life to Willie Hughes. More than that, the shift of attention from the young man to Willie Hughes also grants Shakespeare's desire a specific embodiment in the boy-actor. While Wilde's characters reproduce many of the practices informing scholarly searches for the identity of the young man, the desire to identify the young man is also a search for Shakespeare's desire; a desire mirrored in Graham's, Erskine's, the narrator's, and even Wilde's own desire.

Shakespeare's Fanboys

We often own our fandom with apology—the narrator calls his passion "a perfectly silly enthusiasm" (Wilde WH 82)—and are embarrassed by a manufactured, even delusory, familiarity with the objects of our esteem based on feelings rather than rationality. Ecstasy is an intensity of emotion that we distrust and, at its extremes, the fervor of the fan is seen as unhealthy or dysfunctional: a form of madness. Critic Jolie Jensen contrasts the passion of the scholar with that of the fan, and questions whether it is only a "cultural hierarchy" (20) that divides the two. Jensen, like other critics of fan culture, situates the fan in twentieth-century ideas of mass media, although the *OED* dates the first usage of the term to as early as 1682, closer to Shakespeare's time than our own. In the 1890s, the word "fan" was more likely to be understood in terms of American baseball, but it is worth noting that the intensity of emotion it describes is also characteristic of Walter Pater's ideas about the function of Art associated with the literary movement Wilde is most associated with: Decadence.

Reflections of Desire: Wildean Portraits

There are several similarities between *The Portrait of Mr W. H.* and Wilde's novel, *The Picture of Dorian Gray*. As in *Dorian Gray*, the painting exerts its effect on a trio of men: the narrator-Erskine-Graham and Dorian-Basil-Lord Henry. The early descriptions of both works of art are also remarkably similar: *The Portrait of Mr W. H.* is referred to as a

> full-length portrait of a young man in late sixteenth-century costume, standing by a table, with his right hand resting on an open book. He seemed about seventeen years of age, and was of quite extraordinary personal beauty. (Wilde WH 302)

In *Dorian Gray*, the description of the painting truncates this as "the full-length portrait of a young man of extraordinary personal beauty" (Wilde DG 18). In both cases the creation of the portraits are reflections of desire. Basil Hallward says:

I have put into it some expression of all this curious artistic idolatry, of which, of course, I have not cared to speak to him. He knows nothing about it. He shall never know anything about it. But the world might guess it; and I will not bare my soul to their shallow, prying eyes. My heart shall never be put under their microscope. (Wilde DG 14)

Early in the novella, the narrator notes that influence "is simply a transference of personality, a mode of giving away what is most precious to one's self" (Wilde WH 79). This, too, echoes Lord Harry's assertion in *Dorian Gray* that "to influence a person is to give him one's own soul" (Wilde 58). At the close of the novella, the narrator—now a confirmed skeptic—looks at the portrait, and wonders: "Had I been influenced by the beauty of the forged portrait, charmed by that Shelley-like face into faith and credence?" (Wilde WH 81). The word "influence" itself takes on a particular meaning across these texts specifically relating to the transits of desire from artist to art to viewer.

In their attention to the intense sensations produced by their experiences of art, these texts evoke Walter Pater's often cited invocation about the aim of life "to burn always with this hard gem-like flame, to maintain this ecstasy" (329). The narrator catalogues his intense experience of the Sonnets in terms of "senses that quickened, passions that came to birth, spiritual ecstasies of contemplation, ardours of fiery-coloured love" (Wilde WH 78). However, while Decadent theories of *L'Art pour L'Art* emphasize Pater's controversial privileging of intensity over virtue or morality, both of these texts culminate in fairytale-esque endings in which the exponents of the portraits and their expression of desire die. Dorian Gray murders Basil and ultimately kills himself by thrusting a knife into the portrait that reflects his own monstrosity, and the narrator of the novella survives only by a very timely disavowal of the portrait's influence as the "Willie Hughes theory" (Wilde WH 88).

If, in the ending that returns the world to the *status quo, The Portrait of Mr W. H.* seems incongruously moral to sit within the confines of Literary Decadence, the shift of focus from the literary in the sonnets to the visual in the portrait accords very well with Marcus's notion of nineteenth-century celebrity as structured by theatricality. In Wilde's novella, the sonnets themselves and even the histories of the Shakespearean boy-actor and the Dark Lady are not sufficient proofs in themselves: it is rather the visual "evidence" of the forged portrait that is needed to call Willie Hughes into being. Marcus comments that it was the star's presence and the representations that functioned as its substitute that were particularly important to nineteenth-century celebrity: "the images of stage actors that circulated . . . did not efface the theatrical aura but supplemented it" (1004). The creation of an aura that both convinces and confirms the idea of Willie Hughes relies ultimately not on the sonnets themselves but instead on the visual presence of the portrait.

The Dangers of Addiction: A Celebrity of Impudence
Returning briefly to Jensen's idea of the excessive devotion of the fan as representing an intensity of emotion that we distrust and that may be unhealthy or even a form of madness, it is clear in the novella that the pursuit of Willie Hughes is not one likely to assure longevity. Cyril Graham shoots himself before the action of the novella commences. Graham is perhaps a fitting "patient zero" for the infection represented by Willie Hughes because, as Erskine notes Cyril was "effeminate" (Wilde WH 6); he was "very languid in his manner, and not a little vain of his good looks" (Wilde WH 7) and "was always cast for the girls' parts" (Wilde WH 8). Erskine, for whom Graham commissions the forgery and who receives the portrait after Graham's death is described as Graham's foil but nevertheless still quite effeminately as "a rather awkward, weakly lad" (Wilde WH 7). Erskine attempts in his suicide note to reproduce the influence of Graham's declaration of the truth of Willie Hughes, now "*stained with the blood of two lives*" (Wilde WH 85, emphasis in original). Erskine's suicide is itself called into question by his doctor who reveals he has died from consumption. The story of Willie Hughes affects, or perhaps infects, each of the characters in the novella: passing from Cyril Graham to Erskine to the narrator and then back to Erskine, leaving two of the three who come in contact with his haunting presence dead.

In charting his journey of discovery, the narrator is possessed by Willie Hughes, and time ceases to have meaning for him. He says:

> As from opal dawns to sunsets of withered rose I read and reread them in garden or chamber, it seemed to me that I was deciphering the story of a life that had once been mine, unrolling the record of a romance that, without my knowing it, had coloured the very texture of my nature, had dyed it with strange and subtle dyes. (Wilde WH 76)

While the narrator presents his experience as revelatory, there is nevertheless something disquietingly Gothic in its withered roses and the strange and subtle dyes with which it alters his nature. Indeed, the narrator admits that "the soul, the secret soul, was the only reality" (Wilde WH 78).

The narrator escapes the fate of the other proponents of Willie Hughes only by an explicit disavowal. At the end of the novella, the narrator states:

> This curious work of art hangs now in my library, where it is very much admired by my artistic friends, one of whom has etched it for me. They have decided that it is not a Clouet, but an Ouvry. I have never cared to tell them its true history, but sometimes, when I look at it, I think there is really a great deal to be said for the Willie Hughes theory of Shakespeare's Sonnets. (Wilde WH 88)

Like Wilde's own admiration for young men and in prosecution of which this text would be cited in Wilde's trial, the portrait that marks Shakespeare's passion hangs in plain sight at the end of the novella—a purloined letter. This enables the narrator to display it to his "artistic friends" (Wilde WH 88). The narrator, having lost his capacity for belief in Willie Hughes although the last sentence leaves open the potential for relapse, nevertheless provides a detailed account of the materiality of his portrait: the portrait hangs, it has a "true history"; it is etched, it has an authorizing hand (Clouet or Ouvry). Now history not story, the portrait has mass, it has its own genealogy, and if questions about authenticity have ceased to trouble the narrator this underlying question about the complex sexualities it embodies may linger.

Mirroring the traditional division between fame as an authentic and earned form of value and celebrity as its spurious and transient shadow, Marcus divides nineteenth-century celebrity into exemplarity and impudence. What characterizes the impudent, according to Marcus, is "the impudent shamelessly chose their differences and elected to exhibit that choice" (1011). The celebrity of impudence is characterized by Wilde's very public persona, his dress, his famous *bon mots*, his adoption of the green carnation. Shakespeare, it might be justifiably presumed, is authentically famous rather than superficially a celebrity, yet this, too, conveniently leaps over the problems of the original sonnets: in this sense, Shakespeare sits awkwardly within a discourse of exemplarity. Frankel notes, forgery in the novella functions as an instigator to propel further knowledge: it is "a fiction that contains or suggests an essential truth" (57), although what that truth is remains ambiguous. In focusing on the strange fascinations produced by the forged portrait, however, it is belief rather than evidence that propels the sonnets' dangerous knowledge. In this way, the portrait of Willie Hughes produces an unauthorized portrait that authorizes Shakespeare's male-centered desires. If Wilde is using Shakespeare impudently, he also produces an impudent Shakespeare. Indeed, Wilde's impudence is doubled by Shakespeare's in a way that confuses timelines and doubles Wilde's own desires.

Queer Time

> [P]art of the creativity of queer lies in its ability to imagine seemingly impossible futures and tangle seemingly fixed time lines. If it is queer to cross ages, it is also peculiarly queer, perhaps, to get lost in the process of crossing. (Thomas 327)

Time is a central concern throughout Shakespeare's sonnets, but particularly in the first seventeen in which the speaker urges the young man to marry and procreate. In Sonnet 5, the speaker warns the young man of the inevitable effects of time:

For never-resting Time leads summer on
To hideous winter, and confounds him there,
Sap checked with frost and lusty leaves quite gone,
Beauty o'er-snowed and bareness everywhere. (5.5–8)

In this second quatrain, time stalks the young man, leading him on into a winter that appears as a trap to confound him. The loss of sexual desire (lust) and the bareness that characterises a beauty that has become o'er-snowed links the span of a human life to the progress of the seasons from Summer's prime to Winter's aged hideousness. The solution to the unstoppable progress of time and its ravages offered by the speaker is procreation, as he urges the young man in the couplet of Sonnet 12, "And nothing 'gainst Time's scythe can make defence/Save breed to brave him when he takes thee hence" (12.13–14). But are children really a form of personal immortality? (In Sonnet 18, the speaker suggests that poetry—Shakespeare's poetry—is a more reliable form of eternal life.) In Shakespeare's Sonnets, the young man is held in thrall to time in at least two different forms: Nature's cycles, a trap that cannot be undone, and submitting himself to another type of time-based tyranny, procreative time.

Time works quite differently in Wilde's novella. Cyril Graham not only uses the portrait as key evidence to convince Erskine of the existence of Willie Hughes, but he retrospectively introduces the portrait itself as Shakespeare's own primary inspiration for the sonnets: "what was I to say? It is quite clear from Sonnet XLVII that Shakespeare had a portrait of Mr W. H. in his possession" (Wilde WH 310). As a nineteenth-century forgery, however, it is not possible for the portrait of Mr W. H. to be anterior to Shakespeare's own sonnets: Wilde is twisting time.

One way to interpret Wilde's twisting of time in the novella is a rejection of Nature and an embrace of artifice. Literature is not required to emulate the linear nature of time; indeed, many literary texts begin at the end of the story and end at the beginning. Frankel points to K. K. Ruthven's argument that one feature that forgery and literature share is "remoteness from a discourse of truth" (46).

To believe in Willie Hughes is thus to reject Nature's time and the heterosexual normativity of cycles of procreative time: to engage with Queer time.

If it is confusing to cross and re-cross the temporality of Shakespeare's time with Wilde's own, nevertheless, as Kate Thomas declares "it is time to pay attention to that queer sense of being out of sync" (330). What then is the value of being "out of sync" to Wilde? To choose to read the figure in the forged portrait as the Mr W. H. of the sonnets is to choose to read Willie Hughes as the destination to which both Shakespeare's text and Wilde's own travel toward. The connection that Wilde forges to Shakespeare and to his boy-actor is not just "out of time" but also "outside of time"; life and death in the novella do not follow Shakespeare's cycles of the seasons, nor yet the cycles of procreative time, but rather rise and fall artificially with cycles of enchantment and disenchantment associated with Willie Hughes himself.

Literary history is also often thought of in terms of genealogy, a passing from one great writer to the next. Thomas describes Dorian Gray's love for Sybil Vane as the embodiment of Shakespeare's women as a folding of time: kinky time (335). Wilde's queer immortality in his atemporal creation of Willie Hughes is also a self-canonizing gesture in that it passes Shakespeare's legacy directly to Wilde with little concern for the intervening generations of authors and scholars. The peremptory appropriation of legacy returns us to what Marcus earlier identified as the celebrity of impudence: a shameless assertion of difference. It is just this sort of impudent re-folding or re-writing of history that Wilde engages in *The Portrait of Mr W. H.*

This is not to suggest that Wilde is engaging in a de-historicizing of Shakespeare, releasing him from the implications of homosexual desire in either Shakespeare's time or Wilde's own. Rather, if anything, Wilde raises the awareness of the dangers of male-oriented desire. Suicide is always close in the text for those marked by desire for Willie Hughes and is inherently linked to the notion that belief in the portrait means giving your life to "the cause" (Wilde WH 85).

Conclusion

It seems whatever the varied threads of *The Portrait of Mr W. H.* we follow, the text continually leads the reader back to the idea of disorientation and illusion, yet nevertheless in disorientation lies a form of truth, the disavowal of which results in survival but only in a compromised reality. In this chapter, we have focused not on the portrait itself as a forgery or on the idea of the lie, but rather on the idea of inexpert enthusiasm: fan obsession as a false, even dangerous, familiarity founded, according to Sharon Marcus, in nineteenth-century theatricality, the creation of an aura of celebrity. A narrative possibly best described as fan fiction and founded in discourses of illness and addiction. Yet, if surviving Willie Hughes makes it possible to display his face and his form openly upon the wall, the cost it requires is the concealment of the portrait's "true history" and a sense of loss and yearning for the desires he represents. It is only by dying for the lie that the true passions of the novella can be revealed. What are these true passions? To be consumed by the inexpert view of Willie Hughes is to call forth Shakespeare himself as an improperly desiring body in a timeline that is temporally disrupted and chaotic. In taking Shakespeare outside of time into queer time, Wilde is able to fold time and forge connection between desiring bodies and desiring objects, while coyly asserting but never specifically identifying why it is that there is "really a great deal to be said for the Willie Hughes theory of Shakespeare's sonnets" (WH 88).

Works Cited

Culler, Jonathan. *Theory of the Lyric*. Cambridge: Harvard U P, 2015.

Burrow, Colin. "Shakespeare the Poet." *New Cambridge Companion to Shakespeare,* edited by Margreta de Grazia and Stanley Wells. London: Cambridge U P, 2010, pp. 91–104.

Fineman, Joel. *Shakespeare's Perjured Eye: The Invention of Poetic Subjectivity in the Sonnets*. Berkeley: U of California P, 1986.

Frankel, Nicholas. *Masking the Text: Essays on Literature and Mediation in the 1890s*. Rivendale P, 2009.

Jensen, Jolie. "Fandom as Pathology: The Consequences of Characterisation." *Adoring Audience: Fan Culture and Popular Media*, edited by Lisa Lewis. London: Routledge, 1992, pp. 9–29.

Marcus, Sharon. "Salomé!! Sarah Bernhardt, Oscar Wilde, and the Drama of Celebrity," *PMLA*, vol. 126, no.4, 2011, pp. 999–1021.

Moore, Lisa. "A Lesbian History or the Sonnet." *Critical Inquiry*, vol. 43, no. 4, 2017, pp. 813–38.

Pater, Walter. "The Critic as Artist," Oscar Wilde, *The Picture of Dorian Gray*, edited by Michael Patrick Gillespie, 2nd edition. New York: W. W. Norton and Co., 2007, pp. 326–29.

Shakespeare, William. *Complete Sonnets and Poems.* Ed. Stanley Wells. Oxford: Oxford U P, 2002.

Thomas, Kate. "'What Time We Kiss': Michael Field's Queer Temporalities." *GLQ: A Journal of Lesbian and Gay Studies*, vol. 13, no. 2–3, 2007, pp. 327–51.

Wilde, Oscar. *The Picture of Dorian Gray.* 2nd ed, edited by Michael Patrick Gillespie. New York: W. W. Norton and Co., 2007.

_____. *The Portrait of Mr W. H.* London: Hesperus P, 2003.

The Importance of Being Green: *Pen, Pencil and Poison* as a Study in Close Reading and Color De-coding

Chris Foss

By the time Oscar Wilde triumphantly left Oxford in 1878 with its Newdigate Prize for poetry and a rare double first in his final exams, he already was famous. Relatively early on this flamboyant young aesthete from Ireland had caused a stir there with his now-classic remark, "I find it harder and harder every day to live up to my blue china." He had played to the crowds in London by wearing his renowned red/bronze/brown cello coat to the grand opening of the Grosvenor Gallery, and after moving there legend has it he walked down Piccadilly with a white lily in hand.

Wilde is indisputably one of the most colorful figures in literature, not surprising perhaps for someone who once wrote that "a colour-sense is more important, in the development of the individual, than a sense of right and wrong" ("Critic" 1058). Given his Irish heritage, it might seem fitting enough to suggest green as the most significant pigment on his palette, a claim convincingly supported by his largely overlooked prose piece "Pen, Pencil and Poison: A Study in Green." This short essay, republished and newly minted with its green subtitle during Wilde's golden year of 1891, offers an intriguing inventory of the various inflections of green that comprise the full range of spectral coordinates for this secondary color's primary place in Wilde's life and work. As such, it serves as a superb case study for how attention to minor works not only may open up rewarding reads less traveled but also provide crucial context for fuller appreciation of the more famous masterpieces.

In May 1891 Wilde published *Intentions*, a collection of essays known for its pair of tour de force critical dialogues, "The Critic as Artist" and "The Decay of Lying." "Pen, Pencil and Poison," one of the other works included, comes nowhere near to matching the sheer brilliance of its justifiably more celebrated companion pieces, but it nonetheless offers a uniquely tinted window into Wilde's affinity for the color green. The essay pays tribute to Thomas Griffiths Wainewright—a now-obscure minor poet, painter, and man of letters from the first half of the century, known more as a convicted forger and suspected poisoner than as an artist. The secret to unpacking Wilde's impressionistic rendering of his subject depends upon his subtle application of the various shades of green at play in the piece, shadings that invoke not only his Irish nationalism but also his homophile desire and his own particular version of aestheticism. His little-known commentary on Wainewright reveals how these hues are inextricably intertwined—intertwined with each other and intertwined with *fin-de-siècle* decadence and its dangerous liaisons with sin and crime. Accordingly, "Pen, Pencil and Poison" serves as a superb springboard from which to (re)consider major works such as *The Picture of Dorian Gray* in order to glean a more nuanced understanding of his multivalent sense of the importance of being green.

When "Pen, Pencil and Poison" was originally published in January 1889, its subtitle was merely "A Study." Why, then, might Wilde have changed it to "A Study in Green" for *Intentions*? What might he have intended to highlight by calling attention to the color, especially as there are only two brief referencings of green in the whole essay? The first and most significant of these instances comes a few pages in, when he asserts of Wainewright, "He had that curious love of green, which in individuals is always the sign of a subtle artistic temperament, and in nations is said to denote a laxity, if not a decadence of morals" (Wilde, "Pen" 996).[1] Wilde opened the essay with a discussion of the artistic temperament, and in the paragraph immediately following the initial green reference, Wilde specifically links this temperament to aestheticism when he claims, of Wainewright, "he was one of the first to recognise what is, indeed, the very keynote of aesthetic eclecticism, I mean the true harmony of all really beautiful things . . ." (996). He characterizes his Wainewright as "a true virtuoso, a subtle connoisseur" (996) in large part because "as an art-critic he concerned himself primarily with the complex impressions produced by a work of art" (997)—

for, as Wilde continues, "certainly the first step in aesthetic criticism is to realise one's own impressions" (997).

In his essay, Wilde borrows heavily from W. Carew Hazlitt's 1880 *Essays and Criticisms by Thomas Griffiths Wainewright*. However, as Josephine M. Guy asserts, Wilde does not simply regurgitate lifted lines from Hazlitt, but rather "rewrit[es] Hazlitt in order to affiliate Wainewright more closely to some salient characteristics of late 19th-century aestheticism" (415). To Guy, Wilde reinforces this affiliation through frequent echoes of and allusions to Walter Pater; indeed, for her, "Wainewright seems intended as a disguised . . . portrait of Pater" (418). The parallels are quite striking at times, including that Pater himself loved the color green, but Wilde's Wainewright even more so seems a thinly disguised self-portrait. Wilde leaves plenty of clues that he is writing himself into this ostensibly biographical sketch. For example, he observes, "there was something in [Wainewright] of Balzac's Lucien de Rubempré . . . and [of Stendhal's] Julien Sorel" (995), two of his own favorite literary characters when he was young. He also claims that in "everything connected with the stage," Wainewright "strongly upheld the necessity for archaeological accuracy in costume and scene painting" (1001), the selfsame position Wilde championed throughout the 1880s (including in "The Truth of Masks," *Intentions'* other lesser-known essay).

Above all, however, it is when he talks about Wainwright's appearance and personality that Wilde seems engaged in shameless self-promotion under the guise of a curiosity piece. Wilde, for instance, remarks upon "the influence of the strange fascination that [Wainewright] exercised on every one who knew him" (995), one of his own universally acknowledged qualities, agreed upon even by those who disliked him. He also takes care to report how Wainewright "determined to startle the town as a dandy," how Wainewright's appearance "gave him the dangerous and delightful distinction of being different from others" (995), and how Wainewright's dress was "regarded by Hazlitt as being the signs of a new manner in literature" (995). Thus, for Wilde, "the highest praise we can give to [Wainewright] is that he tried to revive style as a conscious tradition" (998). Perhaps most tellingly, Wilde judged Wainewright's personality as the true marker of his success: "it is only the Philistine who seeks to estimate a personality by the vulgar test of production. This young dandy sought to be somebody, rather than to do something. He recognised that Life itself is an art, and has its modes of style no less than the arts that seek to express it" (995). Not only that, but he further asserts Wainewright very self-consciously pursued this agenda, as he "saw that it was quite easy by continued reiteration to make the public interested in his own personality" (1002). In all of these passages, Wilde reiterates things either others have said of him or he has claimed of himself.

Vivian, the Wildean spokescritic in "The Decay of Lying," would approve; as he tells Cyril, "The only portraits in which one believes are portraits where there is very little of the sitter and a very great deal of the artist" (Wilde 989). If Wainewright's "curious love of green" thus may stand in for Wilde's own aestheticism, it equally is suggestive where his sexuality is concerned. Guy posits that the updated subtitle hinges on "the connection between the colour green and decadent sexuality," a sexuality with "distinct homoerotic suggestions" (411). Wilde in fact claimed to have invented the green carnation (*Complete Letters* 617), a purported esoteric symbol for homophile desire, and *The Green Carnation* subsequently served as the title of Robert Hichens's 1894 satirical novel on Decadence, with main characters modeled on Wilde and Lord Alfred Douglas (Wilde's great love, whose father precipitated Wilde's imprisonment for crimes of gross indecency). Given this reputed association of the color green with decadent homophilia, "Pen, Pencil and Poison" (as a "Study in Green") appears as not just a celebration of Wildean aestheticism but further a coded defense of the homophile desire that for Wilde was inextricably intertwined with said aestheticism.

Indeed, in what Guy describes as a "private joke" (448), at the essay's end Wilde mentions three writers who have penned "charming studies of the great criminals of the Italian Renaissance," the success of which he attributes to their ability to treat their subjects "in that fine spirit of disinterested curiosity" (1008). All three (John Addington Symonds, Vernon Lee, and Agnes Mary Frances Robinson) had established ties to homophilic circles. Wainewright, the subject of Wilde's own charming study of a cultured criminal, is linked to these three through their shared association with curiosity/curious love. He had begun this final paragraph by insisting Wainewright was "far too close to our own time for us to be able to form any purely artistic judgment about him" because it "is impossible not to feel a strong prejudice against a man who might have poisoned Lord Tennyson, or Mr. Gladstone . . ." (1008). However, in going on to assert, "Nobody with the true historical sense ever dreams of blaming Nero, or scolding Tiberius, or censuring Caesar Borgia" (1008), Wilde encourages readers to agree to the same "spirit of disinterested curiosity" informing our view of these historical subjects also should be applied to Wainewright's case. Given his linkage of *curious* with *green*, and *green* with *homophile desire*, Wilde further implicitly asserts that history will not blame/scold/censure the life and work of present-day and/or future "criminals" such as himself—and, what is more, that it may require a particular sort of temperament (one affiliated with the alternative sexualities of Lee, Robinson, and Symonds) to fully realize the necessary aforementioned spirit of disinterested curiosity.

Wilde plausibly, then, intended his study in green as a subtle justification of his own particular version of aestheticism and of the homophile orientation so powerfully informing it. But this "curious love of green" that "in individuals always [is] the sign of a subtle artistic temperament" also has a more collective dimension—namely, that "in nations [it] is said to denote a laxity, if not a decadence of morals." Thus, the above two interrelated shadings arguably are tinted by his nationalist colors as well, by the green he always figuratively was wearing as the proud son of two Irish patriots. Until the 1990s there was very little consideration of Wilde as an Irish writer; he typically was viewed as more Anglo than Irish, having left behind all pretence of claim to the latter with the brogue he abandoned at Oxford. While it is true he rarely explicitly addresses the Irish Question or his identity as an Irishman in his published writings, contemporary scholarship has firmly established how essential Wilde's Irishness was to his self-identity, as well as to his aesthetics, his politics, and even his sexual orientation.

Wilde was, after all, the son of two famous Anglo-Irish parents with profound nationalist sympathies. His mother, Speranza, whose own reputation as a writer was first won through her involvement with the Young Ireland movement in the 1840s, was particularly influential in this regard. Wilde was a founding member of the William Butler Yeats's Irish Literary Society in London, and both Yeats and his fellow Anglo-Irish literary giant George Bernard Shaw never saw Wilde as anything but an Irish writer. Perhaps most famously, Yeats praised Wilde's "'extravagant Celtic crusade against Anglo-Saxon stupidity'" (qtd. in Pine 337) while Shaw insisted, "'though by culture Wilde was a citizen of all civilized capitals, he was at root a *very Irish Irishman*, and as such a foreigner everywhere but in Ireland'" (qtd. in Pine 11). Wilde did in fact publish short journalistic pieces against unionist writings by A.C. Swinburne and J.A. Froude, describing Ireland as "heroically struggling against the injustice of centuries" and characterizing England's occupation of Ireland as "one of the great tragedies of modern Europe," respectively (qtd. in Beckson 165). He was an open supporter of nationalist Irish politicians Charles Parnell and Michael Davitt, as well as of their Home Rule and Land League movements. In fact, in the very month "Pen, Pencil and Poison" originally appeared, Wilde published a review of the prison poems of English writer Wilfrid Scawen Blunt, who had been jailed in Ireland for his opposition to the British government and its policies there. According to Wilde, Blunt's jail experience had "converted a clever rhymer into an earnest and deep-thinking poet" because "an unjust imprisonment for a noble cause strengthens as well as deepens the nature" ("Poetry and Prison" 151). Aubrey de Vere has asserted, "'Sympathy for the criminal, rather than the law, is an [sic] hereditary disease [in Ireland]'" (qtd. in Pine 333), and the virtually simultaneous appearance of the Blunt review and "Pen, Pencil and Poison" suggests Wilde had, in fact, inherited this disease; together, they help illuminate how Wilde's attraction to the figure of the artist-criminal is as much a part of his nationality and his politics as a part of his sexuality and his aesthetics.

This figure of the artist-criminal is a useful segue to Wilde's second green reference in "Pen, Pencil and Poison." It is important to recall he uses the adjective *subtle* not only to describe the sort of artistic temperament that accompanies Wainewright's "curious love of green" but also to characterize Wainewright's criminal talents as well. According to Wilde, Wainewright was "a forger of no mean or ordinary capabilities, and as a subtle and secret poisoner almost without rival in this or any age" (993). This association of art and crime is fleshed out in the paragraph where the second green reference occurs, only three paragraphs from the end of the essay, as Wilde begins his concluding argument. Having just rehearsed the supposed details of Wainewright's career as a forger and a poisoner, Wilde opens this paragraph by noting, "His crimes seem to have had an important effect upon his art"—namely, "They gave a strong personality to his style" (1007). As evidence building toward the paragraph's clincher sentence, "One can fancy an intense personality being created out of sin," Wilde first cites a note to John Forster's *Life of Dickens* that mentions a painting by Wainewright in which the artist "had contrived to put the expression of his own wickedness into the portrait of a nice, kind-hearted girl" (1007). He then offers a fictional analogue from Émile Zola's *Thérèse Roquin*, where a young murderer "takes to art, and paints greenish impressionist portraits of perfectly respectable people, all of which bear a curious resemblance to his victim" (1007). Here, then, Wilde applies green—which he already has established as a sign of an artistic temperament—as a marker of a wicked personality.

This second reference to green, then, reinforces the color's intense association with crime and sin, with lax and/or decadent morals—and, by extension, not merely with a suspect aesthetic temperament, but also with unlawful homophilic desire and lawless Irish rebellion. All three may be shaded as dangerous, debauched, and duplicitous. For Wilde, however, such greening should be cultivated, even celebrated, not repressed, or disciplined, or eradicated. He wants his study of Wainewright, in general, and the two painter anecdotes, in particular, to allow that the result of the admixture of aesthetics and crime/sin is not a corruption but rather a strengthening of the artistic temperament. For Wilde, then, ultimately, "There is no essential incongruity between crime and culture" (1008). By the time he has finished with his own greenish painting of his dandified predecessor, one strong impression it provides is how an explication of the two brief, seemingly insignificant references to the color green reveals the curious extent to which such small details may make crucial contributions to an assessment and appreciation of the big picture.

Furthermore, "Pen, Pencil and Poison" also serves as an instructive case study for how attention to minor works may help illuminate in intriguing ways the more familiar major works. For example, Wilde's portrait of Wainewright in green is a fascinating text for contextualizing his presentation of similar ideas in his controversial novel *The Picture of Dorian Gray*. Indeed, Wilde's essay seems an even more fitting introductory document to his famous fiction than the official 1891 Preface itself. In the wake of the furor over the initial appearance of what for many was a dangerous decadent book, Wilde insisted, "there is a terrible moral in *Dorian Gray*—a moral which the prurient will not be able to find in it, but which will be revealed to all whose minds are healthy" (*Complete Letters* 430–31). "Pen, Pencil and Poison" helps one grasp how, even if one may read *Dorian* as a book that has a terrible moral, there nonetheless are many ways in which one simultaneously may read it as a book that endorses the very aesthetics and sexual orientation (if not politics) aligned with crime/sin in Wilde's essay on Wainewright.

Such a possibility is apparent from the story's outset as Basil describes the "subtle influence" of Dorian upon both his soul and his art, an influence that leads to his "curious artistic idolatry" of his young friend (Wilde, *Picture* 24).[2] Just as Wainewright represented for Hazlitt "a new manner of literature," so Dorian represents for Basil a new era of "importance in the world's history" (24). Basil explains, "[Dorian's] personality has suggested to me an entirely new manner in art, an entirely new mode of style," adding, "I find him in the curves of certain lines, in the loveliness and subtleties of certain colours" (24). Lord Henry sees a similar potential in Dorian, telling him, "You might be [a new Hedonism's] visible symbol" (32), though he believes this only is possible under his own auspices, for he sees himself as precisely the sort of "complex personality" who may "assume[] the office of art" and reveal the mysteries of life to Dorian (55). Interestingly, Lord Henry employs the adjectives *subtle* and *curious* in relation to both *colour* and *poison* while pondering his own powers to "vivisect" Dorian's life and bring about Dorian's (self) development via what he characterizes as his "experimental method" (56). "To note the curious hard logic of passion, and the emotional coloured life of the intellect," one learns, is exceedingly delightful to Lord Henry (55), but he also clearly understands there is a danger to the experimentation, the vivisection through which he may observe and contemplate such things—a danger to Dorian, as one sees all too clearly, if not to Lord Henry himself. He acknowledges, "It was true that as one watched life in its curious crucible of pain and pleasure, one could not wear over one's face a mask of glass, nor keep the sulphurous fumes from troubling the brain. . . . There were poisons so subtle that to know their properties one had to sicken of them" (55). "And yet," Lord Henry concludes, "what a great reward one received" (55). Significantly, one may trace this mixing of mask, poison, and sickness in with curiosity, subtlety, and temperament back to "Pen, Pencil and Poison."

This mixing is echoed when Dorian first reads Lord Henry's "yellow book" (101). Dorian becomes completely "absorbed" with this fictional "psychological study," filled as it is with "metaphors as monstrous as orchids, and as subtle in colour" (101). One may see this moment as the point of no return for Dorian's downward spiral toward his own terrible death. Dorian himself admits, after all, he might have ended differently if he had turned to Basil instead of Lord Henry; Basil's homophilic love for him, he confesses, is the one thing that "could have saved him" (97). This "noble and intellectual" love (the love of Michael Angelo, Montaigne, Winckelmann, and Shakespeare) "would have helped him to resist Lord Henry's influence, and the still more poisonous influences that came from his own temperament" (97). At the same time, however, the role of Lord Henry and his yellow book (with its monstrous yet subtly colored metaphors) is far from unambiguously negative.

Lord Henry, after all, is the novel's strongest advocate of ideas associated with positive expressions of Wilde's aestheticism and homophilia elsewhere (ideas he seems to heartily endorse within these other contexts). For instance, in his dismissive conversation about marriage with Basil, Lord Henry extols the virtues of "certain temperaments" that cannot be "spoiled" by marriage, even though "the real drawback to marriage is that it makes one unselfish. And unselfish people are colourless. They lack individuality" (66). This sort of temperament—marked as it is by selfishness, color/fulness, and individualism—is very much in line with the green temperament celebrated in "Pen, Pencil and Poison."

As a result of Lord Henry's influence (and that of his yellow book), Dorian himself comes to view his own development along similar lines. For this Dorian, "Life itself was the first, the greatest, of the arts," and thus "Fashion, by which what is really fantastic becomes for a moment universal, and Dandyism, which, in its own way, is an attempt to assert the absolute modernity of beauty, had, of course, their fascination for him" (103). Through Fashion and Dandyism, just like Wainewright, Dorian "sought to elaborate some new scheme of life that would have its reasoned philosophy and its ordered principles and find in the spiritualising of the senses its highest realisation" (104). In order to embody this new scheme, to realize this world "that had been refashioned anew in the darkness for our pleasure," Dorian "would often adopt certain modes of thought . . . alien to his nature, abandon himself to their subtle influences, and then, having . . . caught their colour and satisfied his intellectual curiosity, leave them with that curious indifference that is not incompatible with a real ardour of temperament . . ." (105). Because Dorian has come to see the self as a "complex multiform creature" with "myriad lives and myriad sensations," he posits that insincerity, far from being a "terrible thing," is instead "merely a method by which we can multiply our personalities" (112).

Dorian's belief about insincerity is reminiscent of Wilde's own commentary on Wainewright's use of masks/disguises as a means of intensifying his personality. Wilde references a "series of articles on artistic subjects" Wainewright, each "under a series of fanciful pseudonyms," through which "he began to contribute to the literature of his day" (995). According to Wilde, Wainewright's recourse to pseudonymic personalities such as Janus Weathercock and Egomet Bonmot played a crucial role in allowing him "to have made his mark" in such "an incredibly short time" (995). For Wilde, "the grotesque masks under which he [chose] to hide his seriousness or to reveal his levity" are significant precisely because "these disguises intensified his personality" (995). After all, "A mask tells us more than a face" (995). As delineated above, in "Pen, Pencil and Poison" he ultimately links such dissembling to sin and crime, both of which he explicitly asserts intensify personality. The same connection is evident in *The Picture of Dorian Gray* as he inflects Dorian's development throughout with the suggestion of sin and crime. Lord Henry, in explaining to Dorian how this New Hedonism's form of individualism should be his "higher aim" (69), tells him, "I represent to you all the sins you have never had the courage to commit" (70). Lord Henry is as artful a poisoner, in his own way, as Wainewright himself; it is his "subtle poisonous theories," after all, that "stirred within [Dorian] the passion for impossible things" (79) and influence Dorian's decision (after the death of Sibyl Vane) to allow Basil's picture to be the "visible symbol of the degradation of sin" (81) rather than the "visible emblem of conscience" (79).

The yellow book he receives from Lord Henry merely reinforces for him all of his friend's poisonous theories. "The Renaissance knew of strange manners of poisoning" (115), Wilde's narrator tells us, subtly invoking the end of "Pen, Pencil and Poison" where aesthetic temperament and homophilic desire are implicitly associated with the ability to form a purely artistic judgment of morally complicated individuals such as Nero, Tiberius, and Caesar Borgia (or, Dorian). "Dorian Gray," Wilde writes, "had been poisoned by a book. There were moments when he looked on evil simply as a mode through which he could realise his conception of the beautiful" (115). While this poisoning seems to ensure he will continue down the path that leads him to murder his friend and potential savior Basil, for many readers there is a strong sense that things might have ended up very differently, and thus that Dorian's life and Lord Henry's philosophy should not be summarily rejected as wholly, or even necessarily evil. Indeed, there is much that seems to ask to be regarded as attractive about them, especially when contextualized in relation to expressions of similar ideas in other Wilde works.

Wilde once wrote, in a letter responding to a review of the *Lippincott's* version, "The real moral of [*Dorian Gray*] is that all excess, as well as all renunciation, brings its punishment" (*Complete Letters* 435). Immediately after implying that Dorian's excess brings its own punishment upon itself, however, he defends Dorian's character against the charge he is "cool, calculating, [and] conscienceless" by insisting he instead is "extremely impulsive, absurdly romantic, and is haunted all through his life by an exaggerated sense of conscience which mars his pleasures for him . . ." (*Complete Letters* 436). Wilde typically employs ambiguity and oxymoron to allow for multiple responses to Dorian's character, including the perverse, if not inverse, understanding of his poisoning as something as appealing as it is dangerous. For instance, in a later letter Wilde responds to a query about any actual real-life equivalent for Lord Henry's yellow book with the playful answer, "The book that poisoned, or made perfect, Dorian Gray does not exist; it is a fancy of mine merely" (*Complete Letters* 585). He then continues on to remark, "I am glad you like that strangely coloured book of mine: it contains much of me in it. Basil Hallward is what I think I am: Lord Henry what the world thinks me: Dorian what I would like to be—in other ages, perhaps" (*Complete Letters* 585).

Wilde here cycles back to comments from his conclusion to the other earlier letter, where he presented a similar conflation of the poisonous and the perfect in order to assert his novel's cultivated, complex treatment of its vision:

> the aesthetic movement produced certain colours, subtle in their loveliness and fascinating in their almost mystical tone. They were, and are, our reaction against the crude primaries of a doubtless more respectable but certainly less cultivated age. My story is an essay on decorative arts. It reacts against the crude brutality of plain realism. It is poisonous if you like, but you cannot deny that it is also perfect, and perfection is what we artists aim at. (*Complete Letters* 436)

As such, "A Study in Green" would seem to have been as fitting a subtitle for Dorian as for "Pen, Pencil and Poison"—though, since the Old Irish word for green, *glas*, also could stand in for gray in some contexts, perhaps it already was implied. Regardless, Wilde's preference for subtle and fascinating secondary colors over and against crude and respectable primaries is amply if also ambiguously rendered in both the essay's greenish portrait and the novel's grayish picture.

In one of his chapters, Pine discusses what he sees as "three interrelated aspects of the manner in which Wilde lived both openly and covertly within English society—as an Irishman, in social contradistinction; as an artist, in aesthetic revolt; and as a homosexual, proposing the restoration of Greek attitudes to, and practices of, love" (316). Surprisingly, Pine never mentions "Pen, Pencil and Poison" in this discussion, but it is precisely these three interrelated aspects of Wilde's life and work that are suggestively put in play by his greenish impressionist painting of Wainewright. Wilde's "Study in Green"—or, perhaps more properly, his self-study in green—is, in fact, the ideal text for suggesting how these three interrelated aspects come together, not only in the essay itself but also across various other important works by Wilde, including *The Picture of Dorian Gray*. "Pen, Pencil and Poison" may seem an insignificant minor text not worth much more than a cursory glance, but, in fact, its colorful window into Wilde's life and work reveals, on the contrary, how one might realize for the first time in one's life the vital importance of being Green.

Notes

1. All subsequent citations of "Pen, Pencil and Poison" will provide only the page number.
2. All subsequent citations of *The Picture of Dorian Gray* will provide only the page number.

Works Cited

Beckson, Karl. *The Oscar Wilde Encyclopedia (Ams Studies in the Nineteenth Century)*. New York: AMS, 1998.

Guy, Josephine M., editor. *The Complete Works of Oscar Wilde: Historical Criticism, Intentions, the Soul of Man*, vol. 4, Oxford: Oxford U P, 2007.

Pine, Richard. *The Thief of Reason: Oscar Wilde and Modern Ireland*. Dublin: Gill & Macmillan, 1995.

Wilde, Oscar. *Complete Letters of Oscar Wilde*, edited by Merlin Holland and Rupert Hart-Davis. New York: Holt, 2000.

_____. "The Critic as Artist." *Complete Works of Oscar Wilde (Collins Classics)*. London: Collins, 2001, pp. 1009–59.

_____. "The Decay of Lying." *Complete Works of Oscar Wilde (Collins Classics)*. London: Collins, 2001, pp. 970–92.

_____. "Pen, Pencil and Poison." *Complete Works of Oscar Wilde (Collins Classics)*. London: Collins, 2001, pp. 993–1008.

_____. *The Picture of Dorian Gray. Complete Works of Oscar Wilde (Collins Classics)*. London: Collins, 2001, pp. 17–167.

_____. "Poetry and Prison." *The Complete Works of Oscar Wilde*, vol. 7, edited by John Stokes and Mark W. Turner. Oxford: Oxford U P, 2007, pp. 149–52.

"Two Men of Note": Oscar Wilde and Sherlock Holmes

Rebecca Nesvet

> Here dwell together still two men of note
> Who never lived and so can never die:
> How very near they seem, yet how remote
> That age before the world all went awry.
> Vincent Starrett, "221B"
>
> *Autolycus in Limbo* (1943)

In August 1889, J. M. Stoddart, managing editor of Philadelphia-based *Lippincott's Magazine,* visited London to recruit British writers. Stoddart arranged a dinner party at the Langham Hotel in Regent Street. He invited two distinguished guests: Oscar Wilde and Irish nationalist politician Thomas Patrick Gill, M.P., as well as a young physician moonlighting as a writer. Dr. Arthur Conan Doyle, eye specialist, had hurried from his home in Portsmouth just to attend Stoddart's soirée. At the table, Doyle was grateful for the celebrated Wilde's generosity and *sprezzatura.* As Doyle recalled in his autobiography *Memories and Adventures* (1924), Wilde praised Doyle's recently published historical romance novel *Micah Clarke* (1889) to Stoddart and Gill, making Doyle feel less like "a complete outsider" (*Memories* 94).

If *Micah Clarke* truly pleased Wilde, he more than compensated Doyle for its composition by inspiring him for the next forty years. The night at the Langham Hotel, Doyle reminisces in the *Memories,* was "a golden evening for me" (94). Stoddart, impressed by both Wilde and Doyle, offered each of them the opportunity to write a novella for *Lippincott's.* In response to this invitation, Doyle wrote *The Sign of Four,* which was published in the February 1890 issue of *Lippincott's,* while Wilde composed *The Picture of Dorian Gray,* printed in July. Into *The Sign of Four,* Doyle interpolated gleanings from his golden evening. Captain Morstan, the father of heroine Mary Morstan, vanishes from the Langham Hotel and recognizable aspects of Wilde's conversation and taste in fashion and home decoration distinguish the amiable aesthete Thaddeus Sholto. Wilde also informs Doyle's subsequent fifty-six Sherlock Holmes stories and two novels, which are, with his first two Holmes novels, collectively known as "the canon." As this essay will show, aestheticism as popularized by Wilde fascinated Doyle, who drew upon it to invent his enduring character Sherlock Holmes. Doyle represents Holmes as a Wildean aesthete, makes the acid criticism of social hypocrisy in which Wilde specialized the focus of Holmes's energies, and subtly argues for the acceptance of a queer model of domesticity; a radical proposition in the 1890s and for some time after. In the twentieth century, the prominent Chicago writer Vincent Starrett detected Sherlock's aestheticism and queerness, repeatedly interpreting Holmes and Watson's relationship in clearly homoerotic terms. In critical and creative writing, Starrett identifies Sherlock Holmes as a queer icon, an identity that has to some extent endured at least as a plausible possibility. This chain of influence reveals that some of Wilde's most controversial ideas, although condemned in his lifetime, shape the enduring characterization of one of British popular fiction's most successful recurring characters. Without Wilde, the "two gentlemen" of 221B Baker Street might never have been imagined.

Aestheticism, the artistic movement that maintained that art should be beautiful and should serve no utilitarian, didactic, or moral purpose, arose in the late nineteenth century. Academics such as the Oxford University dons Walter Pater and John Ruskin championed it and personally mentored Wilde when he was a student at Magdalen College, Oxford, welcoming him as a young leader of the movement. In 1882, Wilde completed a lecture tour of the United States and Canada, speaking about aestheticism to audiences who knew it mainly as parodied in William S. Gilbert and Arthur Sullivan's operetta *Patience* (1881). By this point, aestheticism involved an attempted revolution in fashion. Its leaders considered Victorian men's clothing to be especially uninspired and ugly in comparison with the fashions of the early modern era. Wilde wore aesthetic dress while lecturing, posing for a series of now-iconic photographs by the New York City celebrity snapper Napoleon Sarony, and in William Frith's painting *A Private View at the Royal Academy* (1881).

Doyle must have been aware of aestheticism from the beginning of his literary career, for he claims that even before his magical dinner at the Langham Hotel, he recognized Wilde as its main proponent (*Memories and Adventures* 95). In 1886, when Doyle wrote *A Study in Scarlet,* he made his consulting detective protagonist an aesthete. In creating Holmes, Doyle "domesticated the detective's aesthetic propensities, making them palatable to a vast, popular audience" (Barolsky 92). Holmes is "obsessive" and "consumed by his art," the detection of crime, in unsettling ways. He acknowledges certain murders as masterpieces and admires the corresponding criminal geniuses even as he tracks them down. He is a collector—of books, cigar ashes, his priceless Stradivarius violin, and, of course, as Doyle's *Casebooks of Sherlock Holmes* (1927) demonstrates, of files on his own cases. Holmes categorizes murder as an art not unlike painting. "There's the scarlet thread of murder running through the colourless skein of life," he tells Watson, "and our duty is to unravel it and isolate it and expose every inch of it. And now for lunch and then for Norman Neruda" (Doyle *A Study in Scarlet* 28). Holmes's mind free-associates from the "duty" to display murder as if it is a painting, to the decadent pleasures of dining out and classical music.

Holmes's chosen vocation reinforces his self-fashioning in aesthetic terms. As he explains to Watson in *A Study in Scarlet,* Holmes is a specialist. As such, he stands out in a world of generalists. There are entire bodies of knowledge that, contrary to social expectation, he does not know, but he is a meticulous connoisseur of other bodies of knowledge more germane to his crime-solving. According to Regenia Gagnier's study of Wilde's aestheticism, "[s]pecialization, with its seemingly independent realms of activity, and the possibilities for social mobility in Britain at the end of the nineteenth century," was a key aesthetic practice, because it "made the notion of an aestheticized, or free, life not only possible but fashionable" (14). In Holmes's specialization, he resembles Wilde. In 1878, Oxford University denied Wilde, then an undergraduate, a scholarship to pursue postgraduate study. Undaunted, he recorded his occupation on a public register as "Professor of Aesthetics" (Gagnier 11). He might have as accurately qualified it *"Consulting* Professor of Aesthetics."

Paul Barolsky, arguing that Doyle deliberately characterizes Holmes as a "domesticated aesthete," points out that Holmes's attention to "details" also constitutes aestheticism (96). This is most evident in Holmes's debt to one of Wilde's most important literary models for the characterization of Dorian Gray: the protagonist of the scandalous "yellow book" that Dorian Gray avidly reads, Joris-Karl Huysmans's 1884 novel *A Rebours,* usually translated as *Against the Grain.* In Huysmans's masterpiece, the thirty-year-old aesthete Jean, Duc des Esseintes strongly anticipates Holmes in his cynicism. Finding humanity too coarse and stupid, he despairs that he will never find anyone as intelligent as himself. He resolves this problem by fleeing to a carefully curated home on the top floor of a building in the Parisian suburbs, the sort of remove from the urban center that, in the 1880s, Baker Street occupied. Des Esseintes envisions his retreat as "a refined solitude, a comfortable desert, a motionless ark in which to seek refuge from the unending deluge of human stupidity" (Huysmans 36). This is a good description of 221B Baker Street when the clients have gone home. Furthermore, both des Esseintes and Holmes are aesthetic connoisseurs. Des Esseintes collects books, more as objects than as texts. He "examined them, re-arranged them on the shelves, anxious to learn if the hot weather and the rains had damaged the bindings and injured the rare paper" (Huysmans 222). He also collects and classifies perfumes, "long skilled in the science of smell" (Huysmans 180). Holmes pursues the same pastime, in a way. He studies cigar ash and identifies it by brand. Given the distinctive smell of cigars, this activity probably involves paying attention to the ash's lingering odors.

There are closer parallels between Holmes and Wilde's aesthete-protagonist Dorian Gray. Both practice aestheticism by appreciating flowers. "Sherlock Holmes of all people pauses in the midst of solving the mystery of a stolen naval treaty to meditate on the importance of roses," Sheldon Goldfarb observes in his reading of "The Adventure of the Naval Treaty" (1893), noting that "this digression is meant to suggest the importance of embellishments" (Goldfarb), which is a key ethic of aestheticism. Dorian Gray and Sherlock Holmes also both aesthetically research the histories of famous, seemingly cursed jewels. Holmes chooses his cases for their capacity to intrigue him, and several of those that do intrigue him involve jewel theft, including the cases related in *The Sign of Four* and "The Mazarin Stone." He sometimes finds himself accidentally in possession of famous jewels, the history of which he usually knows in advance. This is the situation in Doyle's "The Six Napoleons" and "The Blue Carbuncle." In speaking of the jewels, Doyle invests them with rich character. In fact, he sometimes goes a step further than Dorian does, by personifying the jewels. "Let me introduce you to the Black Pearl of the Borgias!" Holmes declares at the end of "The Six Napoleons" (Doyle *Original Illustrated* 563).

Doyle's depiction of Holmes as an aesthete implicitly associates the famous detective with revolutionary social critique, particularly pertaining to class, sexuality, gender roles, and marriage. During Wilde's 1895 prosecution for "gross indecency" with men, the aesthete was implicitly understood to be a homosexual man who inhabits "a secret, private realm of art and sexuality impervious to middle-class conformity" and foments "an engaged protest against . . . the whole middle-class drive to conform," which incorporates "a social revolution in domestic options" (Gagnier 11). Doyle's fiction advances this type of aestheticism even before 1895. "Art is not to be taught in the academies," Wilde rails in a vicious review, "A Note in Black and White on Mr. Whistler's Lecture," published in the *Pall Mall Gazette* on February 28, 1885. "The real schools should be the streets." Holmes would surely have approved of this revolt against classism, given his cultivation of the espionage talents of young Cockney Wiggins and the street-dwelling Baker Street Irregulars, and the fact that after taking down each client's story in the comfort of No. 221B, he drags Watson out into the street to do the class-transcending creative work of crime solving.

Doyle's representation of aesthetic sexuality is also arguably revolutionary, thanks in part to Wilde. In *The Sign of Four,* the only character to escape the curse of the Great Agra Treasure is the aesthete Thaddeus Sholto, who has treasure enough in the form of his suburban aesthetic retreat. That novella ends with Watson accepting companionate marriage on very similar terms, when he claims that the real treasure is not the lost jewels but Mary Morstan, suddenly no longer an heiress. Contrast Thaddeus's outlook with that of the facetiously named "Noble Bachelor," a straight collector of pictures and artifacts and a modern Bluebeard, with several murdered wives on his account. Holmes finds common ground with a fellow social rebel in "The Adventure of the Copper Beeches" (1892), in which the heroine is an unmarried young woman who seeks work as a governess. Refusing to pursue economic subsistence via marriage instead, Violet Hunter obtains a position by cutting off her hair. As in Victorian culture long hair was understood as a signifier of femininity, Hunter acknowledges to Holmes that she is willing to lose her femininity in order to gain economic independence. At the *fin de siècle,* this would have constituted a radically queer value-system. Holmes's investigation of the disturbing behavior of her upper-class, married employer, the father of her pupil, ultimately saves her life and that of her employer's imprisoned daughter, and the story ends with Hunter, still unmarried by choice, happily managing her own school. Holmes's art of detection facilitates this resolution.

Other Sherlock Holmes tales pointedly explore the struggles of many 1890s homosexual men by drawing attention to a crime that largely targeted this demographic. With the 1886 passage of the Labouchère Amendment, or "Blackmailer's Charter," which criminalized "gross indecency"—the crime of which Oscar Wilde was convicted—blackmail skyrocketed. In the first Sherlock Holmes story that Doyle wrote for the *Strand* magazine, "A Scandal in Bohemia" (1890), the King of Bohemia comes to Sherlock Holmes in Baker Street, needing the now-famous consulting detective to exfiltrate compromising photographs of himself and the adventuress Irene Adler from her possession. Certain that his intended queen would call off their marriage were she to know of these photographs, the King is terrified that Adler will blackmail him. Adler is a woman, but she often cross-dresses, including in public. She wears men's clothes by default and finds it liberating, as she indicates by calling these outfits her "walking clothes" (Doyle *Original Illustrated* 25). When, thus dressed, she spies on Holmes, he and Watson both believe they have glimpsed a young man. Therefore, the King of Bohemia—a place-name suggestive of London's Bohemia, or countercultural underworld—fears being blackmailed by a person the public sees as a beautiful young man. Other Sherlock Holmes stories demonize blackmail by representing its victims as married women who, for minor romantic transgressions, have fallen afoul of unreasonable expectations of female purity. These tales include "The Dancing Men," "The Second Stain," and "Charles Augustus Milverton." Christopher Clausen theorizes that, in the last of those stories, Doyle's fascination with blackmail is a protest against "the hypocritical cult of innocent Victorian femininity" (Clausen 93), but Victorian homophobia would have discouraged Doyle from accurately depicting blackmailers' far more typical extortion of homosexual men. In "Charles Augustus Milverton," Doyle takes a great risk by carefully leaving open the possibility that one of the victims of Milverton's blackmail is a man. Doyle does not divulge the specific extortionable transgression that ended one Colonel Dorking's engagement to the Honourable Miss Miles, nor whose transgression it was. In simply stating that Milverton's blackmail exposed information that caused the end of this engagement, Doyle echoes Oscar Wilde's euphemistic depictions of Dorian Gray's homosexual activity and its social consequences. "There was that wretched boy in the Guards who committed suicide," Basil accuses Dorian. "You were his great friend . . . What about the Duke of Perth? What sort of life has he got now? What gentleman would associate with him?" (Wilde *Dorian* 182). In a possible allusion to this passage, the 1992 Granada Television adaptation of "Charles Augustus Milverton" represents Dorking as the lover of a young man who performs as a drag queen in the music halls. Exposed by Milverton, Granada's Dorking commits suicide. This adaptation correctly recognizes Doyle's critique of Victorian homophobia's facilitation of white-collar crime and legalized manslaughter.

After 1895, Doyle continued to participate in the aesthetic revolt against bourgeois Victorian values by making Sherlock Holmes's specialist investigations "subject the English class system to as penetrating a scrutiny as it ever received from Jane Austen" (Clausen 73). In the *Strand* tales collected in *The Return of Sherlock Holmes* (1905), the detective sometimes allows people to appeal to him to provide extralegal justice that the court system is unlikely to allow them and proves willing to comply (Clausen 75). One of the most striking *Return* stories, "The Adventure of the Abbey Grange," concerns a young Australian-born woman and her faithful serving woman who claim that a gang of robbers murdered her alcoholic husband and badly beat her. Holmes correctly induces that this is a lie. In fact, he surmises, the lady is a survivor of marital violence. A man in love with her has murdered her intoxicated, raging husband to stop him from killing her. Holmes recognizes that this murder has structural causes, and so he and Watson let the murderer go. In so doing, they deliver a vigilante verdict that indicts Victorian marriage law's facilitation of domestic violence, class hegemony, and sexual hypocrisy (Cranfield 91). This indictment makes Holmes's jurisprudence as much a protest of Victorian convention as is Wilde's art.

A particularly aesthetic element of Holmes's existence is his cohabitation with Watson, the homoerotic possibilities of which some readers have noted. An early proponent of this interpretive tradition is Vincent Starrett (1886–1974), a journalist for several Chicago newspapers, pulp novelist, poet, and founder of an early and lasting Sherlockian society, the Chicago-based Baker Street Irregulars. Starrett appears to have been a closeted homosexual or bisexual writer, intensely searching for LGBT representation both on the page and among the literati of two continents. His autobiography features an obvious crush on a high school classmate, a young man with whom he planned international travels that, in the end, they never undertook (Starrett *Born in a Bookshop*, 53–5). He documents H. L. Mencken's censorship of his story about a transgender woman's suicide and his seeking out of the bisexual poet Richard Le Gallienne, whom he treasures as one of the last living members of Wilde's coterie. Starrett corresponded with Le Gallienne for years and dedicated a poetry chapbook to him (*Born in a Bookshop*, 158, 235–6). Furthermore, some of Starrett's poetry appears to depict a struggle to come out to himself, expressed in decidedly Wildean terms. For instance, "Masquerade" (1943) asserts:

> I know his family and his mates
> But what they see is not at allThe man my fancy celebrates. . .
>
> (Starrett, *Autolycus in Limbo* 79)

Seemingly alluding to the self-outed Dorian Gray's destruction of the soul-mirror painting and himself, Starrett concludes:

> The other me I dare not know
> Lest he be gruesome or absurd
> I broke my mirror long ago
> When in its shadows something stirred.
>
> (*Autolycus in Limbo* 79)

Starrett's monograph *The Private Life of Sherlock Holmes* (1933), a decadent prose homage to Holmes masquerading as a work of literary criticism, offers what now sounds like very deliberate innuendo about the famous duo. "It was late in the year 1880, or perhaps early in 1881," Starrett claims, "that Holmes and Watson met and discovered their common need of the moment" (Starrett *Private Life* 13). Their need is not for each other, nor for other men, but for "a comfortable suite of rooms at a figure that would suit their pocket-books" (Starrett *Private Life* 9). Starrett employs this rhetorical move throughout his book. In another example, "Watson, returning from a professional visit, passed the rooms in Baker Street . . . saw the spare figure of his friend" and was "filled with the *irresistible desire* to look in on him" only (Starrett *Private Life* 20). With the prose *volta* "to look in on him," *Watson's* "desire" is neutralized, yet, like many other crimson threads that run through bourgeois life, remains detectable.

As *The Private Life of Sherlock Holmes* continues, Starrett makes his case for Holmes's queerness far less equivocally. As in a seasoned companionate marriage, "the relationship between the collaborators was ideal, after the years had taught them to know each other" (Starrett *Private Life* 72). The flat has "two bedrooms," Starrett concedes, but he suggests that only one room is mindfully designed and regularly occupied. "[A]bout the doctor's, we have the scantiest possible information. He comes from it, he goes into it; and there the record ends," while "[o]f Holmes's private chamber there is a clear description" (Starrett *Private Life* 74). Starrett also rather boldly endeavors to make the reader imagine Holmes as a sexual being, primarily by asking readers to imagine him as a corporeal body, not just an overactive brain. Holmes's room, Starrett notes, contains "a dressing gown," and "[w]ithin the dressing gown is Sherlock Holmes," implicitly otherwise unclothed (*Private Life* 74). Finally, Starrett suggests that Holmes really does have a controversial "private life" not divulged by the knowing and perhaps complicit Dr. Watson. "And who is Sherlock Holmes?" Starrett asks. "What is the story behind that drawn blind in London? . . . From him you may expect something much too subtle to be advertised" (Starrett *Private Life* 76). What the subtle "private" quality is, Starrett does not say, but he claims that "queer folk came to the rooms of Sherlock Holmes in Baker Street, and always they came when they were in trouble" (*Private Life* 25–6). Should we read Starrett's "queer" in the modern sense? I think so. According to the Oxford English Dictionary, writers employed the adjective "queer" as a synonym for "homosexual" since at least the 1910s, with one example derived from Christopher Isherwood's acclaimed and popular *Goodbye to Berlin* (1939), a book that the bibliophile Starrett almost certainly would have known. The use of "queer" to indicate homosexual men has continued since at least 1914. It is, therefore, unlikely that Starrett employs the term without intending at least some readers to view Holmes as a savior of homosexual and otherwise culturally alienated people. That Starrett wishes the reader to consider Holmes himself a closeted gay man appears more likely given the similarity of his monograph's title to that of that the Broadway sensation of

             Critical Insights

1930, produced only three years prior to the book's publication, the social satire *Private Lives: An Intimate Comedy,* by the semi-closeted British playwright Noël Coward.

Holmes and Watson appear to be a homosexual couple in Starrett's poem "221B," which he composed in 1942 and published in his chapbook *Autolycus in Limbo* (1943). The poem's first lines, which provide this essay with its epigraph, reiterate that Starrett cherishes No. 221B, Baker Street as the idyllic home of "two men of note" who "dwell together still." Later in the same poem, Starrett claims that the lesson that Holmes and Watson teach their twentieth-century readers is that "only those things the heart believes are true" (Poem No. 32).[1] Unable to prove by deductive reasoning that Holmes and Watson live together as lovers, he nevertheless knows it by heart, as I think many readers over the generations have done, and have needed to do. In 1942, the second year of United States participation in the Second World War, Starrett finds the idea of Holmes and Watson at home at 221B reassuring: "Though the world explode, these two survive / And it is always eighteen ninety-five." Intriguingly, this date points the reader towards Wilde. No collection of canonical Sherlock Holmes tales nor any of the canonical novels appeared in 1895, but that is the year of what Starrett calls "the fiery ordeal of Oscar Wilde," in which Britain tried Wilde for "a flagrant offense against the public morals" (*Books Alive* 79). In the same passage, Starrett protests the prison censorship of Wilde's reading material, and observes that in 1897, the playwright emerged from prison "a living corpse" (*Books Alive* 79). To return to "221B," if it is always 1895, and not yet April, then Wilde remains safe, as do the many homosexual men who fled to France by steamer on the evening of his conviction, and the entire generation of such men traumatized by the cultural memory of the Wilde trials. This, Starrett insists, is the fantasy that Doyle offers the fans of Sherlock Holmes.

More recently, some writers have protested that Holmes and Watson are both straight and conventional, without supporting this proposition with the careful reconstruction of historical context that distinguishes Gagnier's study. One such commentator is the octogenarian British crime novelist June Thomson, whose later works include several Sherlock Holmes spinoffs with titles such as *The Secret Journals of Sherlock Holmes* (1993), *The Secret Chronicles of Sherlock Holmes* (1994), and *The Secret Documents of Sherlock Holmes* (1999). In 1995, Thomson conjured a critical monograph, *Holmes and Watson,* seemingly out of an intense drive to deny that there is any homoeroticism in their shared domestic life. Thomson claims that Holmes "[a]lmost certainly remained celibate all his life," and was "not asexual" (she cannot bring herself to say "homosexual"), was partial "to one woman in particular [Adler] and, had events not prevented it, might have married her or at least had an affair with her" (17). Doyle certainly never states in "A Scandal in Bohemia" or any other canonical adventure that Holmes ever wished either to marry or to seduce Adler. Thomson's analysis of Watson reveals a virulent homophobic agenda. In her interpretation, Watson "marri[ed] twice, the first time very happily," so his "attitude to women was normal" (Thomson 24). Steven Moffat, co-creator with Mark Gatiss of the recent British Broadcasting Corporation series *Sherlock,* agrees with Thomson on the subject of Holmes's sexuality, though not with her overt homophobia. In an interview in the newspaper *The Guardian,* Moffat claims:

> There's no indication in the [Doyle's] original stories that he [Holmes] was asexual or gay. He actually says he declines the attention of women because he doesn't want the distraction. What does that tell you about him? Straightforward deduction. He wouldn't be living with a man if he thought men were interesting. (Jeffries)

This response to mass audience speculation demonstrates the enduring appeal, albeit perhaps to a small constituency of readers, of Starrett and Gagnier's conception of Sherlock Holmes as a domesticated aesthete, engaging in an artistic revolution against Victorian conformity from the flat that he shares joyously with a fellow man. For the seeds of this revolutionary yet popular idea, we must thank Doyle's dining companion of one night in August 1889, Oscar Wilde.

Note

1. The 1943 only edition of Starrett's *Autolycus in Limbo* is unpaginated, but the poems are numbered.

Works Cited

Barolsky, Paul. "The Case of the Domesticated Aesthete." *Critical Essays on Sir Arthur Conan Doyle,* edited by Harold Orel. New York: GK Hall, 1992, pp. 92–102.

Clausen, Christopher V. "Sherlock Holmes, Order, and the Late Victorian Mind." *Critical Essays on Sir Arthur Conan Doyle,* edited by Harold Orel. New York: GK Hall, 1992, pp. 66–92.

Cranfield, Jonathan. *Twentieth-Century Victorian: Arthur Conan Doyle and the Strand Magazine, 1891–1930.* Edinburgh: Edinburgh U P, 2016.

Doyle, Arthur Conan, Sir. *A Study in Scarlet: The First Book about Sherlock Holmes.* Mineola: Dover, 2003.

_____. *The Complete Sherlock Holmes.* New York: Castle, 1976.

_____. *Memories and Adventures.* 1930. London: Hodder and Stoughton, 1924.

Gagnier, Regina. *Idylls of the Marketplace: Oscar Wilde and the Victorian Public.* Stanford: Stanford U P, 1986.

Goldfarb, Sheldon. "Re: Victorian Gardens and Greenhouses." [Listserv Post] *Victoria-L.* 19, June 2019.

Huysmans, Joris-Karl. *Against the Grain.* Translated by John Howard. New York: Lieber and Lewis, 1922.

Moffat, Steven. "There Is a Clue Everybody's Missed: *Sherlock* Writer Steven Moffat Interviewed." Interview by Stuart Jeffries, *The Guardian*, 20 Jan. 2012, www.theguardian.com/tv-and-radio/2012/jan/20/steven-moffat-sherlock-doctor-who.

"Queer, adj.1." *OED Online*, Oxford U P, June 2019, www.oed.com/view/Entry/156236.

Starrett, Vincent. "221B." *Autolycus in Limbo,* New York: E.P. Dutton, 1943, p. 32.

_____. *Books Alive: A Profane Chronicle of Literary Endeavor and Literary Misdemeanor.* New York: Random House, 1940.

_____. *Born in a Bookshop: Chapters from the Chicago Renascence.* Norman: U of Oklahoma P, 1965.

_____. *The Private Life of Sherlock Holmes.* New York: Macmillan, 1933.

Thomson, June. *Holmes and Watson: A Study in Friendship.* London: Constable, 1995.

Wilde, Oscar. *The Picture of Dorian Gray*, edited by Norman Page. Peterborough, Ontario: Broadview, 1998.

Oscar Wilde's Mysticism in *De Profundis*_____

Oswaldo Gallo-Serratos

Among the reasons that explain why Catholicism has survived persecutions, religious wars, schismatic movements, and secularization processes, perhaps the most important is a certain sense of belonging to a community that does not solely imply living members but every person that has been a member of the Church, living and dead, baptized—certainly a discussion that goes beyond the purpose of this paper. The Communion of Saints, the doctrine that supports this kind of relationship by stating the spiritual links between all Christians, embraces both local communities and the entire Church. What is unique about Roman Catholicism is the fact that it developed such a cultural permeability that made it able not only to evangelize but also to absorb some elements of its converted societies.

The following passage shows how this permeability, during the Victorian era, made many homosexual men such as Oscar Wilde feel attracted to the Roman Catholic Church by means of a sort of sublimation of a same-sex desire. Thus, despite the fact that neither then nor now does the Church allow what it considers a sin, Catholicism was conceived by many Victorian homosexuals as a suitable realm where their desire could be tolerated and indeed not even noticed:

> Catholicism in particular is famous for giving countless gay and proto-gay children the shock of the possibility of adults who don't marry, of men in dresses, of passionate theatre, of introspective investment, of lives filled with what could, ideally without diminution, be called the work of the fetish. . . And presiding over all are the images of Jesus. These have, indeed, a unique position in modern culture as images of the unclothed or unclothable male body, often in extremis and/or in ecstasy, prescriptively mean to be gazed at and adored. (Sedgwick 140)

In his great account of Victorian religious culture, Frederick S. Roden points out that the Catholic identity at the end of the nineteenth century "was not a collapse of the possibilities in the spiritual life for men and women of same-sex desire. Rather, while religious life was once the haven of retreat from same-sex desire in the world, by the end of the century it had become a site of recognition of that desire which could be enjoyed rather than denied" (Roden SSD 126). In order to understand to what extent this relationship between same-sex desire and Roman Catholicism influenced Oscar Wilde's *De Profundis*, it is necessary to start from his first approaches to the Catholic Church and particularly to the figure of Cardinal Newman, a pivotal reference of his classic letter-essay.

The Scarlet Woman

To a certain extent, Wilde's approaches to Catholicism can be explained by the homophile environment that arose within English Catholicism. It was not a mere coincidence that a young Victorian man with homoerotic tendencies felt attracted to the Catholic Church: since its inception in the 1830s, the English Catholic revival known as the Oxford Movement was accused of stimulating an unmanly lifestyle (Hilliard 185–86; Faber 216–17). For a Church such as the Anglican—where most of its clergy were married—the option for a celibate ministerial life was, at least, suspicious. Some unmarried clergy remained within the Anglican Church, while others embraced Roman Catholicism.

We are able to find through his letters from 1876 that Wilde felt thoroughly enticed by the Roman Church, whom he referred as "the Scarlet Woman" (*CL* 41), an apocalyptic allusion commonly employed pejoratively by Protestants referring to its seductive corruption, along with other sexual epithets such as "the whore of Babylon." Several reasons may explain why Wilde was dallying with a Catholic lifestyle when he was a young scholar at Oxford; some may argue that it was simply a trivial engagement based on the aesthetics of an institution whose liturgy was full of iridescent vestments, silver smoky thuribles, Latin prayers and hymns, holy relics, processions, jeweled objects, and golden tabernacles that fascinated the mind of the future's most famous British aesthete. However, given the fact that he was not the only artist with a Roman Catholic infatuation—a list would include Aubrey Beardsley, Lionel Johnson, Ernest Dowson, Frederick Rolfe, and John Gray, the model of Dorian Gray, who later became a Catholic priest—it is plausible to consider it a case of rebellion against the scientist spirit of his age.

During the second half of the nineteenth century, in the middle of a spiritual crisis created by the collapse of traditional beliefs in the infallibility of the Scriptures over topics like Creation, certain Christian thinkers and theologians evolved a school of thought, later known as Modernism, which contended that religious knowledge may be, and even must be, filtered through scientific knowledge. In doing so, the spiritual realm was subordinated to the scientific one, drawing an apparently irreconcilable gap. Against this background, some theologians such as John Henry Newman (1801–1890) and Edward Bouverie Pusey (1800–1880) faced the daunting challenge of developing an ecclesiological and doctrinal theory on the nature of the Anglican Church, specifically regarding its historical origin, through publishing tracts. Thus, the *Tractarians*, or the Oxford Movement, as they were rapidly called, rescued the memory of Patristic theology, and the works of St. Augustine, St. Athanasius, St. John Chrysostom, and other Church Fathers spread again in Anglican circles. The aim of the Tractarians was both to defend the autonomy of religious knowledge against the prevailing commitment to rationalism in the moment, and to definitively show that the foundation of Anglicanism was anchored in the early Christian Church, from whose Catholic—if not Roman—branch they descended.

At the time Wilde was at Oxford, the memory of Newman, by then a converted Roman Catholic priest and later cardinal, inspired him up to the point of spending entire months in the study of his theology, as he wrote to his friend William Ward:

> I am going to edit an unfinished work of my father's, the *Life of Gabriel Beranger, Artist*, for next Christmas, so between this and Newman I will have no time for any reading for scholarship. About Newman I think that his higher emotions revolted against Rome but

that he was swept on by Logic to accept it as the only rational form of Christianity. His life is a terrible tragedy. I fear he is a very unhappy man. I bought a lot of his books before leaving Oxford. (*CL* 25)

The true motivation behind Wilde's interest in Catholic theology, and in particular in Newman's works, is uncertain at some level. Wilde actually wanted to pay him a visit, following the example of one of his colleagues, who "wrote to Newman about several things: and received the most charming letters back and invitations to come and see him: I am awfully keen for an interview, not of course to argue but merely to be in the presence of that divine man. . . But perhaps my courage will fail, as I could hardly resist Newman I am afraid" (*CL* 41). This last line may explain why the meeting never took place—if so, there's no evidence.[1] It is hard not to remember, with this passage, that famous grumble from St Augustine: "O Master! Make me chaste–but not yet"! (Augustine 7, 17) Newman was widely known as a very prolific apologist whose charm enchanted an entire generation: "*Credo in Newmannum*" ("I believe in Newman") was the basic proposition under which a considerable number of young Anglicans followed his steps towards Rome or at least to what are known as Anglo-Catholic communities: parishes in the Anglican tradition that incorporate in their religious style traditional Catholic practices such as Eucharistic adoration, confession, a Tridentine-like Mass, and the most relevant—clerical celibacy.

James Eli Adams provides an account of Wilde's interest in Newman and Anglo-Catholicism:

> The Tractarians offered the model of an elite brotherhood that defined itself through the possession of arcane (and presumably unorthodox) wisdom or values. That same structure helps to explain the popularity of later Tractarianism, or "ritualism," among gay men. . . . It was not just theology that led Wilde to repeatedly request the works of Newman for his reading material in prison: the structure of Tractarian reserve parallels in remarkable detail Wilde's preoccupation with the double life, another extremely exacting mode of masculine discipline. (117–19)

Newman's conversion is worth mentioning insofar as he embodied all the prejudices against Catholic converts from Anglicanism, particularly regarding his "effeminate" personality[2] in a cultural context where manliness meant to be married and to endorse the stereotypical figure of a family man. As a matter of fact, not a few men of his circle had homoerotic tendencies; the next-generation Jesuit poet Gerard Manley Hopkins was one of the most remarkable ones. There is no reason to think that Newman tried to beguile them into converting to the Catholic Church; quite the contrary: it seems that they wanted to keep contact with him because, unknowingly, they looked for shelter. In a society where homoerotic tendencies were persecuted, the Catholic ideal of virginity and the clerical structure based on homosocial groups allowed them to sublimate desires and psychosexual repressions.

What is worth mentioning is that, like other authors, Wilde felt attracted to the Roman Catholic Church because of the homosocial and even subtly homoerotic environment it cultivated in Great Britain.[3] Yet in the twentieth century, writers such as Evelyn Waugh wrote about the Oxford of the 1920s: "Beware of the Anglo-Catholics—they're all sodomites with unpleasant accents" (35). This relationship between homosexual desire and religion is the focal point of David's Hilliard's article "Unenglish and Unmanly: Anglo-Catholicism and Homosexuality," where he states that

> For many homosexual men in the late nineteenth and early twentieth centuries, Anglo-Catholicism provided a set of institutions and religious practices through which they could express their sense of difference in an oblique and symbolical way. A large number of religious and social rebels were similarly attracted to Anglo-Catholicism at this time. Some were drawn by the Anglo-Catholic idea of the church as a divinely constituted religious society and by its emphasis on tradition, dogma, and visible beauty in worship. Others, of radical temperament, found in Anglo-Catholicism a religion freed from the respectability and the puritanism of the churches in which they had grown up. (182)

Whatever interest Wilde may have had in Catholicism, whether purely aesthetic, erotic or religious, his entire literary work proves that it was genuine, even though theological discussions vanished from his letters after the 1870s. Newman made a great impression on Wilde: "In what a fine 'temper' Newman always wrote! The temper of the scholar. But how subtle was his simple mind!" (*CL* 452) he wrote in 1890, some days after the Cardinal passed away. Newman appeared anew five years later, when Wilde was in Reading Gaol; Arthur Clifton's account of Wilde in prison shows his reading. Newman's influence on Wilde's letter-essay is pivotal, as Jan B. Gordon suggests:

> Rupert Hart-Davis' discovery of the list of books sent to Oscar Wilde at Wandsworth Prison in July, 1895, reveals therein a preference for the confessional mode: St. Augustine's *Confessions* [. . .], Pascal's *Provincial Letters*, Pater's *The Renaissance* [. . .], and finally, Newman's *Apologia Pro Vita Sua*. A year later, Arthur Clifton wrote [. . .] that the convict had been spending his time "reading Pater and Newman lately, one book a week" [CL 665]. Both of these records of Wilde's reading habits following his incarceration would suggest that his most notorious letter, the *De Profundis*, written between January and March of 1897, while disguised as a sincere *cri de coeur*, exhibits certain formal and stylistic features common to the *apologia* in general, and Newman's in particular. (183)

Newman's own spiritual autobiography is a detailed account of his soul and temper from his evangelical youth to his conversion to Roman Catholicism in 1845. What is remarkable about his narration is how he characterizes the subtle manifestation of God in everything he did or saw, a sort of epiphany that reveals itself by means of ordinary activities. This is precisely why, besides the style and formal features mentioned by Gordon, Newman is a starting point in the comprehension and analysis of *De Profundis*, particularly regarding its place among mystical literature.

On *De Profundis* as a Mystical Work

Mystical literature is a genre difficult to define because of the blurred boundaries it has. One tends to believe that its roots spread right out of the mystical religious experiences of persons with an extraordinary spirituality—such as Julian of Norwich, St. Teresa of Ávila or St. John of the Cross. Narrowing down what we mean by "mystical literature" is almost an impossible task, however we can allude to at least two key elements that converge in its creation: the emergence from a non-normative experience and the failure to be able to fully express it.

The essential aspect of mystical experiences concerns the way a person communicates with God in an extraordinary but not exclusively supernatural way. According to a Catholic perspective, mystical experiences follow human nature, allowing one to speak or act in a particular way. Such a disposition is often related to ascetic practices like self-denial or self-mortification that, in the case of Wilde, were present (albeit enforced rather than chosen) during his period in jail. It is evident in *De Profundis* that Wilde embraced them in the most spiritual way: at the peak of his humiliation, Wilde agreed with Christian mystics that by denying himself he would be able to find his purpose and true nature. Such intentionality resignifies whatever pain or crisis is faced: "What is not assumed is not redeemed," in the words of St. Ireneaus, emphasizing how Christ had to incarnate into human nature in order to save humanity (14). That same principle operates in the realm of mysticism: one needs to accept any kind of experience in order to take it to another level: "The only thing for me was to accept everything. Since then . . . I have been happier" (*DP* 926), stated Wilde. The same idea appears *Philippians* 2.7: when describing the humiliation of Christ, Paul coined the term κένωσις (from κενόω, "to empty") in order to express his self-emptying, the greatest form of humiliation but also the perfect way to prepare him for sacrifice. For its part, the final verses of Wilde's poem *The Ballad of Reading Gaol* also imply a sort of kenotic rupture:

And every human heart that breaks,
In prison-cell or yard,
Is as that broken box that gave
Its treasure to the Lord,
And filled the unclean leper's house
With the scent of costliest nard.

Ah! Happy they whose hearts can break
And peace of pardon win!
How else may man make straight his plan
And cleanse his soul from Sin?
How else but through a broken heart
May Lord Christ enter in? (*CW* 859)

As it is evident in *De Profundis*, what initially is a personal reproach to Alfred Douglas, his former lover to whom the prison letter is addressed, takes the shape of a Christian reflection on the nature and convenience of sorrow as an effective process towards redemption. Wilde's letter is the path of a repenting soul in search of his salvation by the realization of Beauty hidden under earthly corruption. For Christ, for instance, "Sorrow and suffering were modes through which he could realize his conception of the Beautiful" (Wilde *CW* 927). He "regarded sin and suffering as being in themselves beautiful, holy things, and modes of perfection. It sounds like a very dangerous idea. It is so. All great ideas are dangerous. That it was Christ's creed admits of no doubt. That it is the true creed I don't doubt myself" (Wilde *CW* 933). Arguing that Oscar Wilde underwent a "mystical experience" while he was in jail does not require a supernatural contact with any divine entity. Rather, I suggest that he developed a "mystical" sense in which everything he felt during his period in prison allowed him to experience what any mystical author tries to express in words and fails at: the mercy of God.

The ineffable, the failure in expressing mystical experiences, is a commonly repeated claim by authors such as Wilde himself: "I cannot put my sufferings into any form they took, I need hardly say" (*CW* 936). However, he realized that it was by means of a certain creative power, that of the artist, that Christ unveiled the Kingdom of Heaven and, in doing so, He did not speak plainly but by way of parables: that is to say, poetry. As a matter of fact, Wilde seems to have been aware of discussions about the *ipsissima verba Domini* ("the exact words of the Lord"), a theological controversy about which words Jesus said, given the fact that the Gospels are composed of several texts written by more authors than had been considered prior to the nineteenth century. Some theologians argue that at least two words were beyond any doubt spoken by Jesus: "*Abba*" *(Father)* and "Kingdom" (Jeremias). Every time Jesus alluded to the latter, he used parables; so the singular bridge between humanity and the understanding of the Kingdom of Heaven is poetry, figurative language. Let us briefly consider the imaginative narration, hyperboles and metaphors found in the speeches of Christ: "The Kingdom of Heaven is like a net that was thrown into the sea and caught fish of every kind" (Matthew 13.47). "The Kingdom of Heaven is as if someone would scatter seed on the ground and would asleep and rise night and day, and the seed would sprout and grow, he does not know how" (Mark 4.26–27). "It is like a mustard seed, which, when sown upon the ground is the smallest of all the seeds on earth; yet when it is sown it grows up and becomes the greatest of all shrubs" (Luke 4.31). "I am the true vine, you are the branches. Those who abide in me and I in them bear much fruit" (John 15.5).

Christ finds his kingdom in everything and everyone just like the poet finds poetry wherever it is. Christ "compares it to little things, to a tiny seed, to a handful of leaven, to a pearl. That is because one only realizes one's soul by getting rid of all alien passions, all acquired culture, and all external possessions be they good or evil" (Wilde *CW* 925). Moreover, it is typical in mystical experiences (and literature) for the author to identify in some stages with Christ, who did not possess anything. In Catholic tradition, for instance, certain mystics developed stigmata or suffered religious "ecstasy": in the first case, St. Francis of Assisi and St. Rita of Cascia; in the second, St. Theresa of Ávila. By conceiving of Christ as an artist, Wilde took his figure as the prototype: "I see a far more intimate and immediate connection between the true life of Christ and the true life of the artist" (*CW* 922–23); he compared his denunciation of hypocritical Victorian culture with how Christ "mocked at the 'withered sepulchres' of respectability" (*CW* 932).

There is no mysticism without asceticism. In the case of Wilde, ascetic practices came along with prison and hard labor. The development of his asceticism becomes obvious as *De Profundis* progresses, from resistance to acceptance of the whole picture of Beauty, that which implies pain and regret. Wilde was well aware of it: "While for the first year of my imprisonment I did nothing else, and can remember doing nothing else, but wring my hands in impotent despair, and say 'What an ending! What an appalling ending!' now I try to say to myself. . . 'What a beginning! What a wonderful beginning'" (*CW* 934–35). He understood that an artist cannot consider himself one without the school of sorrow, as he closed his letter:

> How far I am away from the true temper of soul, this letter in its changing, uncertain moods, its scorn and bitterness, its aspirations and its failure to realize those aspirations, shows you quite clearly. But do not forget in what a terrible school I am sitting at my task. And incomplete, imperfect, as I am, yet from me you may have still much to gain. You came to me to learn the Pleasure of Life and the Pleasure of Art. Perhaps I am chosen to teach you something much more wonderful, the meaning of Sorrow, and its beauty. (Wilde *CW* 957)

In Wilde's last years, aestheticism turned to mysticism as artistic experience became a mystical. "Wherever there is a romantic movement in Art, there somehow, and under some form, is Christ, or the soul of Christ" (Wilde *CW* 928). A similar idea was held by medieval thinkers as the basis of a particular Christian theology. For them, beauty as well as truth and goodness were intrinsically united to the point of being almost undistinguishable. Nevertheless, this identification does not imply a sort of aesthetic pantheism: "To the artist, expression is the only mode under which he can conceive life at all. To him what is dumb is dead. But to Christ it was not so. With a width and wonder of imagination, that fills one almost with awe, he took the entire world of the inarticulate, the voiceless world of pain, as his kingdom, and made of himself its eternal mouthpiece" (Wilde *CW* 927).

There are as many mystical experiences as ways through which God manifests himself. In the Old Testament we find him burning in a bush as well as in a pillar of cloud; in the New Testament Christ said he was inside those who were the least of this world. Mysticism is expressed through the lenses of personality and background. For instance, Pierre Teilhard de Chardin[4], a Jesuit French priest, used paleontology to create a new school of mysticism based on his belief in what he called the cosmic nature of Christ. He took elements of the natural sciences in order to build a whole new conception of humanity's relationship with God and to somehow express the divine revelations he found inside the material world. Likewise, Wilde developed a mysticism of suffering, the unveiling of a divine presence inside sorrow and pain that showed itself as a part of that Beauty he had been seeking his entire life. "The sympathy of the artistic temperament is necessarily with what has found expression" (Wilde *CW* 927), he stated. From his literary corpus, *De Profundis* is the culmination of his art in the sense that negative emotions were the last ones he put into words, even as this reading does not suggest that Wilde denied or put his previous work aside. As Patrick O'Malley suggests,

> Wilde himself insists, in *De Profundis*, that the letter constitutes neither a radical break from his past nor the teleological culmination of a life increasingly dedicated to Christ through suffering. Yes, he argues that "Suffering–curious as it may sound to you—is the means by which we exist, because is the only means by which we become conscious of existing" (884), but he doesn't here suggest that suffering changes the existence; on the contrary, because it is the most intense of aesthetic experiences, it is the very condition of all existence. (174)

Culmination is not rejection; rather, it is the summit of all the elements that converge within the mind of a true artist. In that sense, once again Wilde expresses his identification with Christ, whose last words, *"Consummatum est,"* emerged in a situation of suffering and despair, *de profundis,* from the depths of that human nature, he assumed for redeeming. The tragic connection between sin and mercy, sexual desire and asceticism, far from forming a flawed approach to divinity, allowed Wilde to shape a more detailed portrait of Him who, at the end of the author's life, called him to share that poetic Kingdom that Wilde lived through beauty and pain.

Notes

1. Richard Ellmann suggests it did, and several authors such as Joseph Pierce follow this position, but there is no evidence for it—neither in Wilde's nor in Newman's letters.

2. See Frank M. Turner, *John Henry Newman: The Challenge to Evangelical Religion,* New York: Yale U P, 2002; John Cornwell, *Newman's Unquiet Grave,* London: Continuum, 2010; Dominic Janes, *Visions of Queer Martyrdom: From John Henry Newman to Derek Jarman,* London: The U of Chicago P, 2015.

3. See W.S.F. Pickering, *Anglo-Catholicism: A Study in Religious Ambiguity,* New York: SPCK, 1989.

4. For a panoramic view on Teilhard's mystical work, see *The Divine Milieu, Hymn of the Universe,* and *The Heart of the Matter.*

Works Cited

Adams, James Eli. *Dandies and Desert Saints: Styles of Victorian Manhood.* New York: Cornell U P, 1995.

Augustine, St. *Confessions.* New York: Oxford U P, 2008.

Cornwell, John. *Newman's Unquiet Grave: The Reluctant Saint.* London: Continuum, 2010.

Faber, Geoffrey. *Oxford Apostles. A Character Study of the Oxford Movement.* London: Faber and Faber, 1974.

Gordon, Jan B. "Wilde and Newman: The Confessional Mode", *Renascence,* vol. 22, no. 4, 1970, pp. 183–91, www.pdcnet.org/renascence/content/renascence_1970_0022_0004_0183_0191.

Hilliard, David. "Unenglish and Unmanly: Anglo-Catholicism and Homosexuality," *Victorian Studies,* vol. 25, no. 2, 1982, pp. 181–210, www.jstor.org/stable/3827110?seq=1#page_scan_tab_contents.

Irenaeus of Lyon. *Five Books of Saint Irenaeus Against Heresies*. Translated by John Keble. Oxford: James Parker & Co., 1872.

Janes, Dominic. *Visions of Queer Martyrdom: From John Henry Newman to Derek Jarman*. Illinois: U of Chicago P, 2015.

Kosofsky Sedgwick, Eve. *Epistemology of the Closet*. Los Angeles: U of California P, 1990.

O'Malley, Patrick. "Religion." *Palgrave Advances: Oscar Wilde Studies*, edited by Frederick S. Roden. New York: Palgrave Macmillan, 2004, pp. 167–88.

Pickering, W.S.F. *Anglo-Catholicism. A Study in Religious Ambiguity*. New York: Routledge, 1989.

Roden, Frederick S. *Same-Sex Desire in Victorian Religious Culture*. New York: Palgrave Macmillan, 2002.

Turner, Frank M. *John Henry Newman: The Challenge to Evangelical Religion*. New Haven: Yale U P, 2002.

Waugh, Evelyn. *Brideshead Revisited*. London: Chapman & Hall, 1945.

Wilde, Oscar. *The Complete Letters*. Editors. Merlin Holland and Rupert Hart-Davis. New York: Henry Holt, 2000.

_____. *The Complete Works*. Ed. J. B. Foreman. London: Collins, 1966.

Transcending the Trauma: Theatrical Interventions in the Wilde Trials_____

Todd Barry

> Carson: Did you ever kiss him?
> Wilde: Oh, no, never in my life; he was a peculiarly plain boy.
> Carson: He was what?
> —*Regina v. John Douglas*, 4 April 1895

Introduction

In *The Juridical Unconscious: Trials and Traumas in the Twentieth Century* (2002), Shoshana Felman claims "that trauma—individual as well as social—is the basic underlying reality of the law" (172). How does this claim inform our reading of the Oscar Wilde trials? Can it inform our reading of Wilde's own literature and other literary production related to the trials? More specifically, how can dramatic literature and theatrical performance allow us a space to contemplate, resolve, or transcend legal trauma?

I read the Wilde trials as an example of what Felman terms a trauma trial: a riveting spectacle when seemingly irresolvable cultural conflicts are played out in a courtroom. These particular trauma trials expose the inextricable links between law and theatre. The cultural import of the Wilde trials can only fully be understood by examining their inherently theatrical elements; legal analysis does not adequately capture the dynamic social drama at work. Reading the trials against two dramatic works, Wilde's own *The Importance of Being Earnest* (1895) and Moisés Kaufman's recent play about the trials, *Gross Indecency* (1998), help us better understand the nature of the trauma inflicted on Wilde and the gay men in his historical wake. Theatre—whether it is discerned on a stage or in a courtroom—allows for a healing transcendence of legal trauma. The transcripts and performative rituals of the actual trials, Wilde's dramatic masterpiece *Earnest,* and Kaufman's contemporary play, which attempts to make sense of what happened, speak to one another in ways that can help us more fully understand the cultural significance and legacies of the trials.

Because theatre provides law with so much of its power and intelligibility, the Wilde trials are illuminated through the lens of a seemingly distinct text like *The Importance of Being Earnest,* or by witnessing dramatizations of speeches and moments from the trials in a production like *Gross Indecency. Earnest* playfully suggests that all identity is performative, in stark contrast to the legal conviction of Wilde that equated the emerging gay identity with sexual criminality. Wilde's play reveals the inevitably reductive fictions of identity that were produced in part as a response to legal discourse.

Gross Indecency has the hindsight of history and can more directly evaluate the past. Kaufman's play attempts to heal the repetition of trauma that the Wilde trials enacted within the history of early modern sodomy trials; it does this by sympathetically refiguring Wilde as a modern gay martyr sacrificed at the beginning of a political struggle for recognition and equality. These two dramatic texts provide theatres of aesthetic and political justice amidst and against legal traumas.

A Brief Overview of the Trials

Many people do not know that Wilde himself instigated the legal machinery that began moving toward his own imprisonment. He brought a criminal libel charge against the Marquess of Queensberry, father of Wilde's lover Lord Alfred Douglas. There had been animosity between Wilde and Queensberry for some time because the latter was incensed that Wilde and Bosie (Lord Alfred's nickname) publicly displayed an appearance of sexual intimacy. Queensberry had intended to disrupt the opening night of *The Importance of Being Earnest* on February 14, 1895, in fact, but was stopped because Wilde cancelled his ticket and notified the police (Foldy 4). The libel materialized in the form of a card that Queensberry left at Wilde's club The Albemarle on February 18, 1895. Queensberry wrote, "For Oscar Wilde, posing as a somdomite" [sic]. This libelous statement did not accuse Wilde of actually committing sodomy, but rather "posing" as the kind of person who might engage in such activity.

The common law defense for a libel is the justification of truth; the only way that Queensberry could avoid criminal penalty was to establish for a jury that, in fact, the evidence showed that Wilde *was* posing as a sodomite—not that the act of sodomy was actually occurring, which would have been more difficult to prove, but merely that there was the appearance of such activity in Wilde's behavior. During the libel trial, Queensberry was represented by Edward Carson, who first used Wilde's literature, including his novel *The Picture of Dorian Gray* (1891), as evidence of such immoral proclivities, and then introduced actual male witnesses who would deliver oral evidence of having sexual relationships with Wilde. These witnesses proved to be the turning point for Wilde's fortunes. The young men, referred to as "rent boys," had engaged in sex with Wilde for money or presents, and were prepared to give live testimony in the courtroom to not only acquit Queensberry of libelous wrongdoing, but provide the Crown with enough substantial evidence to bring a new criminal prosecution against Wilde for violating the law against "gross indecency" between men. The men had apparently been promised immunity in exchange for their testimony (Foldy 16).

In order to prevent the embarrassment of the rent boys' testimony, Wilde withdrew the charge of libel, but it was too late. Justice Collins ruled that the defense had proven its justification for publishing the written accusation against Wilde. That legal victory for Queensberry put Wilde in the defensive posture because it provided *prima facie* evidence that he had broken the law prohibiting "gross indecency" between men. The Criminal Law Amendment Act of 1885 prohibited "any male person" engaging in or soliciting "in public or in private . . . any act of gross indecency with another male person." Wilde and Alfred Taylor, the head of the brothel that Wilde frequented, were put into prison to await trial and were charged with twenty-five counts of violating the Criminal Law Amendment Act.

Wilde's trials had moments of compelling theatricality, whether it was Carson's riveting cross-examination of Wilde, Wilde's famous speech from the dock, or the dramatic sentencing by the judge. Wilde's first criminal trial featured testimony from the young men, who admitted in open court that they had engaged in homosexual activity with Wilde. The testimony was at times graphic and salacious, and it all pointed toward Wilde's legal guilt. However, due to some legal confusion regarding Wilde's joint trial with Taylor, as well as the inadmissibility of some of the evidence from the libel trial, there was a hung jury and Wilde was re-tried separately from Taylor. The second criminal trial involved much the same testimony from the same witnesses; this time it resulted in Wilde's conviction, and he was sentenced to two years imprisonment.

Contesting the Emerging Gay Identity: "Earnestness" on Trial

The Importance of Being Earnest opened on February 14, 1895, a month before Wilde brought his libel action against Queensberry. The play continued to run until Wilde's disgrace first forced his name from the front of the theatre, and then finally resulted in the play being cancelled altogether (Ellmann 458). In the same city, two dramas played out that involved the crisis and anxieties surrounding the production of a new identity; in fact, the crisis was over the nature and possibility of any kind of substantial identity, but specifically a gay male identity.

In his book *The Wilde Century* (1994), Alan Sinfield was the first scholar to argue that the Wilde trials crystallized the cultural image of the modern gay man:

> the trials helped to produce a major shift in perceptions of the scope of same-sex passions. At that point, the entire, vaguely disconcerting nexus of effeminacy, leisure, idleness, immorality, luxury, insouciance, decadence and aestheticism, which Wilde was perceived, variously, as instantiating, was transformed into a brilliantly precise image. . . . The principle twentieth-century stereotype entered our cultures: not just the homosexual, as the lawyers and medics would have it, but the queer. (3)

I agree with Sinfield and would like to deepen his argument by examining the complicated interplay between law and literature that continues to construct modern gay identity. According to Felman, a culturally resonant trauma trial, a "trial of the century," is marked by "its attempt to define legally something that is not reducible to legal concepts" (59). Felman argues that law, especially that within significant trials, attempts *"to throw a bridge over the abyss"* while "the purpose of the literary text is, on the contrary, to show or to expose again the severance and the schism, to reveal once more the opening, the hollowness of the abyss, *to wrench apart what was precisely covered over, closed or covered up by the legal trial"* (95, emphasis in original).

The intense cultural anxiety surrounding the emergence of the modern gay male identity can be mapped onto Felman's metaphor of a seemingly irresolvable conflict, an "abyss." While the abyss of gay identity was criminally categorized and punished in the Wilde trials courtroom, nearby, within the proscenium arch at The St. James Theatre, the same abyss was being comedically exploited and widened in *The Importance of Being Earnest*. The play exuberantly contended that *all* identities are reductive fictions. In this sense, the play presciently captures queer theorist Judith Butler's critical insight made almost a century later, that *"gender is a kind of imitation for which there is no original"* (21). Wilde's play is supposedly centered on the nature of identity, yet it consistently refuses to name names and articulate essences and realities. What could be more important than discovering one's own story, the secret to one's personality and destiny? Jack/Ernest politely asks, "I hate to seem inquisitive, but would you kindly inform me who I am?" (Wilde 53). Yet even at the end when Jack's identity as Ernest is revealed, things still retain the air of affectation.

The Importance of Being Earnest utilizes rhetorical strategies that are anathema to legal discourse: irony, punning, and paradox. The play ironically prevents the self from achieving semantic or physical stability by deconstructing it through language. In turn, language is figured as the vehicle for transcending the reductive categorizations of identity. In the play, ironic language and performance prohibit the physical body from holding precedence over language's meaning, because the play contends that meaning must be unstable when it arises from language. *Earnest* counteracts the stabilizing trajectory of the trials' discourse by exploding the very notion of a fixed identity to be discovered. In this sense, *Earnest* is a queer play while the trials' discourse generated a stigmatized gay identity.

The role of tone is crucial in understanding the relationship between Wilde's trials and his theatrical masterpiece. Irony suffuses *Earnest*, and even at the end when irony seems to collapse as a strategy, we are to understand that the collapse itself is ironic. The play's final line, "I've now realized for the first time in my life the vital Importance of Being Earnest," is so effective because it is simultaneously true and ironic (Wilde 54). It is true in terms of the pun of Earnest/Ernest because Jack realizes that is his name; it is ironic because the discourse of the play has been so successfully and comedically ironic throughout, and Jack only found his true identity by donning another one and being deceptive, thereby showing Wilde's and the play's commitment to frivolity and irony as the prized mode of discourse. There is nothing authentic about any of the dialogue or characters in the play, and the final scene mocks the very idea of heteronormative couplings and romantic love. The three couplings at the play's end, with everyone shouting "At last!" as they embrace, ironize heterosexual romance not to reveal homosexual identity, but to ironize gender itself as a performative process. The end of *Earnest* positions Jack as having located a stable identity, but ironically undercuts this identity because he was only successful at becoming earnest/Ernest by practicing deception throughout the play. All of the characters have located their identities through Wilde's parodic positioning of those identities as hollow affectations. Jack discovers his identity by the play's end, but the audience knows he has found nothing more than the pleasures of irony, paradox, and the pose.

Within the context of the trials, however, the legal system's demand for sincerity, or earnestness, was the method by which the truth of Wilde's innocence or guilt would be found. The trials worked to crystallize an aspect of Wilde's identity by legally stabilizing his theretofore aesthetic and ironic discourse. Mr. Gill concluded his opening speech for the prosecution in the second trial: "I ask you gentlemen, to give this case, painful as it must necessarily be, your most *earnest* and careful consideration" (Hyde 191, emphasis added).

Of course, the Wildean epigram revels in irony, puns, and paradox: it is a playful interrogation of earnestness and authenticity. Wilde tried to employ paradox and irony as rhetorical strategies in his first trial, but Edward Carson used the literal discourse required of law in order to make Wilde's more literary discourse unsuccessful. Carson began by cross-examining Wilde about his epigrams, in particular the "Phrases and Philosophies for the Use of the Young." Carson wanted the epigrams to be used as evidence for Wilde's immorality:

> Carson: Listen, sir. Here is one of your "Phrases and Philosophies for the Use of the Young": "Wickedness is a myth invented by good people to account for the curious attractiveness of others." (*Laughter.*)
> Wilde: Yes.
> Carson: Do you think that is true?
> Wilde: I rarely think that anything I write is true. (*Laughter.*)
> (Holland 74)

At another moment, Wilde disclosed an important aspect of his philosophy:

> Carson: Listen to this: "Pleasure is the only thing one should live for, nothing ages like happiness." Do you think pleasure is the only thing that one should live for?
> Wilde: I think self-realisation—realisation of one's self—is the primal aim of life. I think that to realise one's self through pleasure is finer than to realise one's self through pain. That is the pagan ideal of man realizing himself by happiness as opposed to the later and perhaps grander idea of man realising himself by suffering.
> (Holland 75)

Within the context of the trial, Wilde's "essential" self was realized only through the legal discourse of sexual crime. This realization of self is comedically ironized in *Earnest*, which is perhaps Wilde's artistic expression of "the pagan ideal of man realizing himself by happiness."

Although Wilde had enjoyed some of his trademark witticisms early on in the cross-examination, the tone of the trial pivoted, and Wilde's fortunes soured, when Wilde was asked about his possibly homosexual relationship with Walter Grainger (Holland xli). In the dialogue below, notice how Carson relentlessly uncovers the truth lying within Wilde's supposed irony. This excerpt is taken from Holland's version of the trial transcript. The cross-examination is presented in the form of a theatrical dialogue in Holland's text:

> Carson: Did you ever kiss him?
> Wilde: Oh no, never in my life, he was a peculiarly plain boy.
> Carson: He was what?
> Wilde: I said I thought him unfortunately—his appearance was so very unfortunate—very ugly—I mean—I pitied him for it.
> Carson: Very ugly?
> Wilde: Yes.
> Carson: Do you say that in support of your statement that you never kissed him? (Holland 207–08)

Wilde unsuccessfully attempted to utilize irony at this point, but the strategy failed because he was, in fact, being serious: he was not attracted to Grainger and was employing a truthful homosexual logic, unsuccessfully masked in a heterosexual irony, which in turn conflicted with the heterosexist logic of the criminal law. Wilde is also unsuccessful here because there actually is a physical truth underneath his logic, and it is not based on pure imagination, nonsense, and nothingness. Wilde finally appeared to put down his façade in the cross-examination: "Pardon me, you sting me, insult me and try to unnerve me in every way. At times one says things flippantly when one should speak more seriously, I admit that—I cannot help it. That is what you are doing to me" (Holland 209).

Wilde's trials required a desiring criminal subject who would fit neatly within the language of the law. Wilde committed acts that fell within the criminal law's reach, and, therefore, his actions resulted in the neat correlation between legal language and embodied desire: the criminal, the homosexual, the modern gay subject could be classified and punished. *The Importance of Being Earnest* uncovers the abyss that the Wilde trials tried to bridge. That is, the play revels in that (always failed) attempt to accurately locate an identity in language in general, and through the lenses of gender and sexuality in particular. *Earnest* comedically illuminates Wilde's ultimately queer philosophical stance that there is no essential self, gay or otherwise. In actuality, by the end of the trials, Wilde was reduced to silence and his identity was reduced and revealed to be that of a sexual criminal. The traumas of the trials lie in the conflicts inherent in the cultural process of recognizing a necessarily fictive identity—the gay subject—in order to accommodate a growing body of self-conscious men and their political aims. These traumas could not be fully understood without the blending of legal and theatrical discourses.

    Earnest comedically inverts the trauma that would attend Wilde at his trial; the play allows a space to more fully contemplate and re-visit past wounds. When the play is read and performed in the historical wake of the trials, it serves to raise the specter of the abyss and the philosophical ideas at the heart of the trials, but it does so without any attendant trauma. That is what makes it such a perfect comedy: it reaches sublimity without the need of suffering. Nevertheless, the play's ultimate sublimity is only achieved by looking through its artistic lens, from the safety of a theater, into the abyss exposed by the Wilde trials themselves. The play transcends the trials' traumas, but first makes us contemplate them once again. As for identity, *Earnest*'s queer vision of the instability of identity categories allows us to better understand the modern gay identity forged in the Wilde trials. We come to view the ascendant identity of the "gay man" with suspicion, as a necessary fiction resulting from law's limited discourse.

Gross Indecency: Theatrical Healing of Legal Trauma

Over the course of the twentieth century, the emerging gay subject would follow a trajectory in legal and theatrical representation, generally evolving from criminal to heroic martyr. This transformation was gradual, but it occurred through law and theatre working together to create, for gay lives, what sociologist Jeffrey

Alexander terms a "new master narrative" of a traumatized group (12).

Moisés Kaufman presents Wilde as a heroic gay martyr in *Gross Indecency* (1997) as a means of revising cultural understanding of the trials. This begins with the play's title, which obviously refers to the gross indecency statute that ensnared Wilde, but also doubles as a condemnation of the grossly indecent homophobic culture that would prosecute such a man. The play is a theatrical presentation of excerpts from the actual trial transcripts and press accounts. The Wilde trials deserve the title "trial of the century" because they worked "to repeat and to awaken, to *reopen* a traumatic history of trials" (Felman 63), hearkening back, in my view, to the early modern sodomy trials. Similarly, *Gross Indecency* theatrically "reopens" the Wilde trials, but the play works to heal the trauma of the collective gay identity that was formed in the trials. It does this by revising the terms of social justice and using the traumatic repetition as a catharsis for the audience to experience. The audience gets to experience and witness the Wilde trials as an unjust tragedy, and through experiencing the catharsis of the performance, the play works as a collective ritual of healing and transformation.

Jeffrey Alexander's sociological approach to cultural trauma is helpful for my purposes in this chapter. Alexander constructs a theory of trauma based on the processes by which a group establishes its identity in response to perceived trauma. This theory can be used to illuminate the cultural significance of the Wilde trials in interesting ways, especially when we see the trials as part of a larger history of cultural trauma extending back to early modern sodomy trials.

According to Alexander, the processes through which cultural identities are formed require efforts of imagination and representation (9–10). Trauma is only recognized, internalized, and evaluated, Alexander claims, through cultural representations of that emerging group identity. That group is often depicted as being persecuted in an unjust way, or as being inherently similar to other members of the society so as to prevent the dehumanization that justifies discrimination. Trauma is thus created, Alexander suggests, through various discourses of art, law, science, and government working cumulatively to make sense of a group's treatment at the hands of a larger society. These representations create a "new master narrative" that makes sense of the group's place in the larger society, and perhaps prompts political compensation for injuries. Creating a "new master narrative" of trauma involves storytelling: "this storytelling is . . . a complex and multivalent symbolic process that is contingent, highly contested, and sometimes highly polarizing" (Alexander 12). The Wilde trials were undoubtedly a "highly contested" form of "storytelling" for those spectators of the trials and readers of their press coverage. Was Wilde the symbol of an emerging threat to conceptualizations of gender and sexuality, or was he the victim of unjust persecution?

Through Kaufman's play, the Wilde trial is repeated in contemporary theatres for a new jury, the theatrical spectators/ witnesses. The legal result is represented in the theatre as it came down in 1895, but Kaufman's theatre of traumatic re-witnessing actually serves to first examine, and then attempts to *close up* the wound of trauma inflicted on past victims of the injustice. In this respect, *Gross Indecency* departs from Felman's description of literature's function. Felman claims that literature works to open up the traumatic wound in order to expose the persistent abyss of trauma, an abyss that law cannot adequately bridge. Kaufman's theatre tries to open the abyss and then seal it in order to achieve some closure and an opportunity for new histories to be made.

A major dramatic moment in Wilde's trials was his famous speech from the dock during the second trial, in which he earnestly defended "the love that dare not speak its name," in reference to Lord Alfred Douglas's poem "Two Loves." Kaufman successfully dramatizes the moment in his contemporary play *Gross Indecency* by using the language from Hyde's account of the trials.

> Gill: What is the "Love that dare not speak its name"?
> Wilde: The "Love that dare not speak its name" in this century is such a great affection of an elder for a younger man as there was between David and Jonathan, such as Plato made the very basis of his philosophy, and such as you find in the sonnets of Michelangelo and Shakespeare. It is that deep, spiritual affection that is as pure as

it is perfect. It dictates and pervades great works of art like those of Shakespeare and Michelangelo, and those two letters of mine, such as they are. It is in this century misunderstood, so much misunderstood that it may be described as the "Love that dare not speak its name," and on account of it I am placed where I am now. It is beautiful, it is fine, it is the noblest form of affection. There is nothing unnatural about it. It is intellectual, and it repeatedly exists between an elder and a younger man when the elder man has intellect and the younger man has all the joy, hope, and glamour of life before him. That it should be so the world does not understand. The world mocks at it and sometimes puts one in the pillory for it. (*Loud applause, mingled with some hisses.*) (Kaufman 110–11)

Kaufman basically takes the speech verbatim from Hyde's "official" legal account (see Hyde 201). However, as Leslie Moran has shown, the textual authenticity of Wilde's speech is uncertain because of the many different versions of the trial. Moran systematically compares the textual discrepancies among the versions given in Millard's *Oscar Wilde: Three Times Tried* (1912) and Montgomery Hyde's account of the trials. These discrepancies raise the issue of the ethics of transcription and to what extent different editors added material (Moran 245).

Lucy McDiarmid's scholarship uncovers equally provocative questions about the literary allusions of Wilde's speech in the dock. McDiarmid claims the speech originally appeared in *The Picture of Dorian Grey* (1890) five years earlier, when Dorian thinks about the kind of love that Basil has for him:

The love that he bore him—for it was really love—had nothing in it that was not noble and intellectual. It was not that mere physical admiration of beauty that is born of the senses, and that dies when the senses tire. It was such love as Michael Angelo had known, and Montaigne, and Winckelmann, and Shakespeare himself. Yes, Basil could have saved him. (qtd. in McDiarmid 455)

Given the uncertainty, Wilde's speech in the dock does not function as purely legal discourse. His own testimony was literary in nature, considering that he was quoting from his own novel.

Similarly, Kaufman utilizes legal testimony in a theatrical context in order to solidify what Alexander terms the "master narrative" of gay male identity shaped by the trauma that gay men historically endured. When Wilde delivered some version of his famous speech from the dock during the second trial (exactly what he said will never be known), the speech became a dynamic site for the master narrative of gay male identity. Havelock Ellis wrote in *Studies in the Psychology of Sex*: "No doubt the celebrity of Oscar Wilde and the universal publicity given to the facts of the case may have brought conviction of their perversion to many inverts who were only vaguely conscious of their abnormality and, paradoxically though it may seem, have imparted greater courage to others" (qtd. in Kaplan 264).

When Wilde came forth at the end of the second trial to answer for the previous testimony, his sincere speech trying to justify and give revisionary witness to the "love that dare not speak its name" was received in varying ways. Hyde writes that after he finished the speech, there was "loud applause, mingled with some hisses" (236). It is impossible to know what really occurred at that point in the trial, but the loud applause gives one pause to consider the positive potentialities of re-enacting and dramatizing historical trauma: the value of re-visionary martyrdom. In asking the contemporary audience to shift their sympathy and perspective toward those who gave "loud applause" after Wilde's speech, Kaufman in effect privileges the perspective of that minority for whom the witnesses sparked a certain self-recognition or consciousness. In the play's epilogue, the narrator tells us, "By the year 1920, Oscar Wilde was, after Shakespeare, the most widely read English author in Europe" (130). The audience is meant to re-evaluate Wilde's trials as unjust persecution, and instead sympathize with him as worthy of great admiration. Kaufman attempts to solidify the master narrative of the gay martyr and the trajectory of modern gay rights.

In legal discourse, the climax of a trial is the verdict. In Kaufman's play, however, Wilde's speech from the dock is the emotional climax: the moment when the dramatic suspense is at its height, when the final possibilities of the narrative are still open; the moment before the law is handed down as either a liberatory exculpation or an inexorable sentence of condemnation. *Gross Indecency* repeats the trauma of the Wilde trials, which in turn repeated the traumatic sodomy trials before them. However, the play is performed as a cathartic repetition meant to heal the wounds inflicted by the Criminal Law Amendment Act of 1885, and by extension, the wounds from all laws that criminalized and stigmatized male-male sexual intimacy throughout the twentieth century.

Works Cited

Alexander, Jeffrey C. "Toward a Theory of Cultural Trauma." *Cultural Trauma and Collective Identity*, edited by Jeffrey Alexander et al. Berkeley: U of California P, 2004, pp. 1–30.

Butler, Judith. "Imitation and Gender Insubordination." *Inside/Out: Lesbian Theories, Gay Theories*, edited by Diana Fuss. New York: Routledge, 1991, pp. 13–31.

Cocks, H. G. *Nameless Offences: Homosexual Desire in the 19th Century.* London: I.B. Tauris & Co, 2003.

Cohen, Ed. *Talk on the Wilde Side: Toward a Genealogy of a Discourse on Male Sexualities*. New York: Routledge, 1993.

Ellmann, Richard. *Oscar Wilde*. New York: Vintage, 1988.

Felman, Shoshana. *The Juridical Unconscious: Trials and Traumas in the Twentieth Century*. Cambridge: Harvard U P, 2002.

Foldy, Michael. *The Trials of Oscar Wilde: Deviance, Morality, and Late-Victorian Society*. New Haven: Yale U P, 1997.

Holland, Merlin. *The Real Trial of Oscar Wilde*. London: Fourth Estate, 2003.

Hyde, H. Montgomery. *The Trials of Oscar Wilde*. Mineola: Dover, 1962.

Kaplan, Morris. *Sodom on the Thames: Sex, Love, and Scandal in Wilde Times*. Ithaca: Cornell U P, 2005.

Kaufman, Moisés. *Gross Indecency: The Three Trials of Oscar Wilde*. New York: Vintage, 1998.

McDiarmid, Lucy. "Wilde's Speech from the Dock." *Textual Practice*, vol.15, no. 3, 2001, pp. 447–66.

Moran, Leslie J. "Transcripts and Truth: Writing the Trials of Oscar Wilde." *Oscar Wilde and Modern Culture*, edited by Joseph Bristow. Athens: Ohio U P, 2008, pp. 234–58.

Sinfield, Alan. *The Wilde Century: Effeminacy, Oscar Wilde and the Queer Moment*. New York: Columbia U P, 1994.

Wilde, Oscar. *The Importance of Being Earnest*. 1899. New York: Dover, 1990.

Picture This: Oscar Wilde's Mobile and Migratory "The Happy Prince"

Margaret D. Stetz

Arguments have gone on for decades over whether Oscar Wilde was a writer of fairy tales meant for children or of allegorical stories intended instead for all audiences, including adults. Some critics, such as Michelle Ruggaber, have tried to draw a distinction, claiming that his first volume of stories—*The Happy Prince and Other Tales*, published in 1888 by the London firm of David Nutt— was meant for younger readers, but that Wilde designed his second, *A House of Pomegranates* (1891), to appeal specifically to mature ones (141–42). Today, however, when issues of mobility and of migration are more relevant than ever, as are questions of social justice and equality, "The Happy Prince," the title story from Wilde's 1888 collection, has much to say about these subjects to everyone, regardless of their age, and its wide circulation through adaptations for multiple audiences merely underlines this point.

Throughout "The Happy Prince," Wilde poses problems for his characters regarding both mobility and migration. "The Happy Prince" turns on the mobility of one protagonist, a bird, and the immobility of another, a statue affixed to a "tall column" (Wilde "Happy" 13) high above an urban scene, even as their devotion binds them increasingly to one another. As the narrative proceeds and winter arrives, the statue repeatedly prevents the bird from migrating to Egypt with its fellows—delaying it with demands to perform acts of charity on behalf of the poor in the city that lies below—until the bird, too, is stilled by death. At that point, both his remains (the bird is gendered throughout as male) and the statue's broken heart are transported to Paradise by an angel. Love and self-sacrifice prove the keys to spiritual transmigration, lifting the souls of these two figures from earth and carrying them to a higher realm.

But Wilde's story itself has also been mobile and migratory, especially since the latter part of the twentieth century. It has moved into different genres and markets—from a 1974 Canadian animated film (written and directed by Michael Mills) for young audiences; to a live-action 2018 British cinematic drama about Wilde and his homoerotic relationships made for adult viewers; to an elaborate 2018 letter-press edition illustrated by Sandow Birk for the Arion Press and targeted at collectors of fine printing; as well as—perhaps most interestingly—into a series of picture books aimed squarely at children. With each new version, it has taken on different coloration (often quite literally, in terms of the tonal palette of the visuals) and acquired varied and contrasting significance, depending on the context surrounding it. In this way, it has been not only mobile but, as in the Italian sense of the word *mobile*, changeable and unstable.

Among the most recent examples of the story's extraordinary mobility is its unexpected use in a 2018 British biopic about Oscar Wilde's post-imprisonment years, *The Happy Prince*, written and directed by Rupert Everett, who also stars as Wilde. There the narrative of the statue and the swallow that Wilde created in 1888 appears in fragments throughout, from the beginning to the end of the film, forming a frame that holds together the action. First, the audience hears it as a bedtime story being spoken in English by a prosperous, successful Oscar Wilde to his two little sons in the early 1890s. Later, it is a tale told in French by a now disgraced and impoverished Wilde, following his release from prison in 1897 and exile abroad—an offering to a young Parisian boy who is living on the streets, as partial payment for "renting" (that is, for having sex with) the child's adolescent older brother. Finally, it recurs as an imaginary recitation that Wilde, who is dying in a hotel in Paris and hallucinating, makes to Queen Victoria and the British Royal family. For Rupert Everett, the tale of "The Happy Prince" is an allegory—a premonitory account of Wilde's destruction by those who once placed him atop a tall column and worshiped him, but also a tribute to the loyalty of Robert "Robbie" Ross, the one-time lover who remained with Wilde when others (especially Lord Alfred "Bosie" Douglas) flew away.

Everett's use of the story is almost an inversion of how it had functioned in an earlier British biopic, *The Trials of Oscar Wilde* (a.k.a. *The Green Carnation* in its U. S. release), written and directed by Ken Hughes. In Hughes's 1960 film, the placement of the scene in which Wilde recites lines from "The Happy Prince" to his young sons at bedtime—a scene sandwiched between two that involve Wilde's obsession with Lord Alfred Douglas—suggests that the filmmaker wishes the audience to connect the figure of the beautiful statue, "gilded all over with thin leaves of fine gold" and with "two bright sapphires" for eyes (Wilde "Happy" 1888 13), with "Bosie," the aristocratic golden boy, rather than with Wilde himself. At the same time, the pronouncement on the soundtrack about "suffering" as being "more marvellous than anything" (Wilde "Happy" 1888 18), taken from Wilde's own prose, seems meant here to reflect Wilde's sorrowful awareness of the misery that loving the unreliable Bosie will entail.

Clearly, Ken Hughes and Rupert Everett alike, in their roles as both screenwriters and directors, felt that Wilde's story, though nominally directed at children, was instead a text with resonance and complexities that could only be appreciated by adults. But is it necessary to draw such lines, and do they make sense in any case? Or can those boundaries be blurred in the process of creating, for instance, picture book versions of "The Happy Prince" that are ostensibly for young audiences, but that contain other dimensions added by the artists who supply the illustrations?

In considering these questions, we might take as a starting-point the assumptions articulated by Imogen Russell Williams, a British children's book critic. In a 2017 review-essay titled "Buzz-saw of the Imagination: The Sophisticated Concepts Communicated Via Illustration," Williams endorses the premise that "Sophisticated, demanding concepts may . . . be communicated via illustration," even to "readers unable or unwilling as yet to parse the complex language required" (27). Certainly, a number of highly challenging and controversial concepts underlie Wilde's "The Happy Prince." Some of them are communicated overtly through Wilde's prose, but many of them are unspoken, particularly those involving gender, sexuality, and homoerotic romance. The ways in which illustrators have addressed these—or retreated from depicting them—in various editions and adaptations is a topic worth exploring, as is the issue of the frames and formats in which these images appear.

Examining versions of "The Happy Prince" published between 1999 and the present—a period in which picture books for young readers based on this story have proliferated—means in most cases looking not at illustrated editions of Wilde's own text, but at adaptations of it that involve compression, changes in language and phrasing, and in some cases major rewriting and simplification (presumably to make the material better suited to contemporary publishers' notions of what a work for children should be like). Can illustrations still hint at complexity and at "sophisticated" ideas, even when the rewritten prose avoids them? In considering each new "The Happy Prince" in picture-book form, we also come up against the issue of the ways in which these adaptations do or do not present Oscar Wilde himself as a historical figure—where they decide to make the author visible, as well as what they choose to say or, in most cases, *not* to say about him in biographical notes.

The problem of how to "read" the illustrations for "The Happy Prince" is nothing new. It begins in 1888 with the frontispiece that the Arts-and-Crafts movement designer, Walter Crane (1845–1915), produced for the first edition of *The Happy Prince and Other Tales*. Crane's image allows us to see at the outset the two protagonists whom readers will encounter in the title story: a statue, covered in gold and jewels, representing a dead Prince, who in life was secluded in his palace, but who now overlooks a whole city; and a talking swallow, who has stopped briefly in mid-migration on his way to warmer climes before the winter frost comes. To review briefly what follows in the narrative—as the bird rests near the statue's feet, tears fall from the statue's eyes. In a series of short exchanges, the statue tells the swallow about the poverty and suffering that he observes throughout the city and, each time that he describes a specific case, he orders the swallow to remove some part of his lavish ornaments (the ruby from his sword hilt, then each jeweled eye, and finally all the gold leaf with which he is cloaked) and to distribute it to the needy. As this process continues over time, the weather grows colder. Finally, the statue, sightless and stripped of all decoration, bids farewell to the bird, saying, "'I am glad that you are going to Egypt at last . . . but you must kiss me on the lips, for I love you'" (Wilde "Happy" 1888 18). But the swallow will not and cannot leave him. As the third-person voice of the narrator tells us, "And he kissed the Happy Prince on the lips, and fell down dead at his feet," at which point the statue's lead heart breaks in two (Wilde "Happy" 1888 18).

Soon, the Mayor and Town Councillors come upon what they call the now "'shabby'" Prince and the corpse of a bird and, horrified by the fact that the statue is, in their words, "'no longer beautiful,'" have it removed and melted down (Wilde "Happy" 1888 19). But the heart will not melt, so it is thrown on a dust heap alongside the swallow's body. At this point, God enters—literally as a *deus ex machina*—asking for "the two most precious things in the city" to be brought to Him, and an angel obligingly fetches the discarded heart and corpse (Wilde "Happy" 1888 19). The story ends with God's final pronouncement: the bird and the Prince will be in His "garden of Paradise . . . for evermore," respectively to sing and to praise Him (Wilde "Happy" 1888, 19).

What Walter Crane's illustration—the only one that he supplied for this first story in the volume—creates for "The Happy Prince" is a distant historical time frame. So, too, the two headpieces and one tailpiece that another artist, George Percy Jacomb-Hood (1857–1929), drew for it appear to indicate some vaguely antique time. In the story itself, Oscar Wilde never specifies any particular decade or even century for the setting. The narrator gives no hint as to how long ago the Prince was alive, or when the action with the swallow is occurring. There is, however, one interesting clue: the presence in this tale of a "match-girl"—a poor child on the streets, selling matches (Wilde "Happy" 1888 17). Self-igniting matches were not invented until 1805, and the selling of matches by street vendors was an occupation impossible before the nineteenth century. In other words, this seemingly timeless moral fable is, in fact, time-bound, and it refers to social ills either of the present in 1888 or of the recent past—all of which might connect the unnamed city, moreover, with London. Indeed, in *Oscar Wilde's Fairy Tales: Origins and Contexts*,

Anne Markey has speculated that Wilde's golden statue was inspired by the "gaudy magnificence" of the gilt-covered bronze statue of the late Prince Albert, Queen Victoria's consort, which was fashioned by John Henry Foley and Thomas Brock in 1876 (and completed by George Gilbert Scott in 1878) as the centerpiece of the Albert Memorial (99).

Walter Crane's Prince, however, is clad in medieval armor and is standing high above a distinctly medieval city, not a modern urban scene—a decision on the artist's part that aestheticizes the narrative, but that also blunts its social criticism (Figure 1). At the same time, however, Crane does something else both subtle and significant: he makes the Prince an androgynous figure who looks, if anything, like Joan of Arc. Here, we might see hints of the possibility that Imogen Russell Williams has introduced: that the illustrations of works for children—and the first edition of *The Happy Prince and Other Tales* was certainly marketed to children, along with adults, as Ian Small has asserted (xvii)—can convey "sophisticated . . . concepts" even to those who might not be able to grasp those yet through words.

Figure 1

In this case, the "sophisticated" idea in question has to do with matters of gender and sexuality. According to Amanda Hollander, "Given that the relationship between the Swallow and the Prince combines male homoeroticism with a bond cemented through a strong sense of shared social justice, the story . . . makes a profound argument in favor of an ethical aesthetics grounded in and augmented by homosexual love" (135). John-Charles Duffy, in his 2001 essay "Gay-Related Themes in the Fairy Tales of Oscar Wilde," both qualifies and amplifies this perspective: "Since this love is shared between a swallow and a statue, it is patently non-sexual. Yet it is spiritually transforming, redeeming the Swallow"; Duffy, therefore, interprets the story as promoting an ideal of "devoted . . . male friendship" that replaces and surpasses heterosexual attachments (331).

Walter Crane's illustration for the frontispiece is right in line with such suggestions. While aestheticizing the landscape—turning a nineteenth-century city into an idealized medieval one, with no clouds of smoke obscuring or urban sprawl defacing it—Crane also aestheticizes and feminizes the statue of the Prince. His is a "beautiful" face and body and, moreover, he is young—although, in Wilde's tale, the age of the Prince that the statue represents goes completely unremarked, and there is no reason to think that he might be a mere youth. Crane's illustration gives us a "Happy Prince" that is potentially an object of desire, whether for the swallow alone or for the viewer, too. (And whether that desiring viewer is a child or an adult is for *us* to decide). Oscar Wilde—as well as the publisher, the firm of David Nutt—approved Crane's frontispiece and, in an 1888 letter to Florence Stoker, Wilde called Crane's work for the volume "pretty" (*Letters* 349). Clearly, no one was concerned as to whether this was or was not an appropriate image for young readers to be thinking about, as they began this story about a love that can magically transcend difference and that climaxes in a kind of *liebestod*—nor, evidently, was anyone troubled by the obvious phallic placement of the Prince's large, erect sword.

This late-nineteenth-century illustration proves daring and erotically charged in a way not usually associated by the general public today with Victorian book design. It sets a surprisingly high bar, therefore, for judging the images that have circulated more recently in turn-of-the-twenty-first-century versions of "The Happy Prince." Do these modern images demonstrate the same willingness to move into controversial territory? How do they handle the narrative's overt social criticism, along with its potential homoeroticism? What do they visualize or leave unrepresented?

A brief survey of a few of the adaptations of "The Happy Prince" that have appeared over the past twenty years presents interesting, and sometimes unexpected, answers to these questions. The earliest of these, from 1999, is a version of Wilde's story issued by an Italian publisher—Cideb, in Genoa, with illustrations by Gianni De Conno—but "retold" by Elizabeth Ann Moore in English. Fairy tales usually give their readers fairies. The front cover of this book, on the contrary, depicts an angel. It is holding the statue's cracked heart and the dead bird, and thus frames Oscar Wilde's work from the outset as a Christian tale with an emphasis on morality, rather than on more potentially subversive elements that are also found in the original. The volume's biographical component reinforces this conventional bent. Inside, a page titled "About the author" reproduces a photograph of Wilde at his most conservative, in his post-Aesthetic phase, when his hair was short and he wore sober suits instead of velvet jackets and silk stockings. There is a brief list of his literary accomplishments that makes no mention whatsoever of his personal life, let alone his prosecution for "gross indecency" with men.

In Gianni De Conno's illustrations, the depiction of the statue owes more to Cubism than to Art Nouveau, and the "Happy Prince" seems also somewhat depersonalized—an object, and certainly not an object that awakens desire. Yet, as in Walter Crane's 1888 illustration, he is again a figure from an earlier time, and there are no hints of a modern city surrounding him; thus, the targets of social criticism have been rendered remote. When Elizabeth Ann Moore's text arrives at the kiss between the statue of the Prince and the male bird, Wilde's own reference to lips has been excised. Here, the kiss occurs—where? On which part of the body? The narrative does not specify. The 1999 children's picture book strips Wilde's story of its erotic suggestiveness, along with its social relevance. As an introduction to Wilde at the start of the twenty-first century, this seems a disappointing way to usher in the new millennium.

Chronologically, the next example comes from 2005: a version in which the intentions of the editor—Merlin Holland, Oscar Wilde's grandson—appear to be at odds with the effects created by the illustrator, G. L. Brierley. Alone among recent editions of "The Happy Prince" for children, Merlin Holland's finds a way to deal explicitly, yet not sensationally, with the issue of homosexuality and with Oscar Wilde's own romantic and sexual orientation, through a lengthy and detailed biographical "Introduction." There, Holland writes of Wilde, "He fell in love with a young poet, Lord Alfred Douglas, the son of a nobleman, and after a disastrous court case (in those days love between men was a crime and an offence in England), he was sent to prison for two years" (7). What follows is Wilde's own text—slightly shortened and condensed, but with its language mostly unaltered.

As in Wilde's original, here the kiss between the statue and the bird happens on the lips. But the illustrator shows none of this; there is no image of romantic attachment or any visualized gesture of love between the bird and the statue, only the aftermath, with the swallow's corpse next to the heart. This statue, too, though spoken of as beautiful, seems curiously unattractive and remote. The historical period, moreover, is hard to pin down from visual cues; possibly, it is the nineteenth century, although there is nothing in the landscape to suggest a city of that era. Altogether, Brierley's illustrations create a feeling of estrangement from, rather than emotional (let alone erotic) engagement with, Wilde's story.

The year 2006 saw the release of an American children's book from Sleeping Bear Press in Michigan: "The Happy Prince" as "retold" by Elissa Grodin and illustrated by Laura Stutzman. This version is, in many ways, an outlier—wholly unlike others before and since. Not only do the illustrations set the action explicitly in the present day of 2006 and in an American city, in order to spur maximum reader identification and involvement (including outrage at social inequality and at the mistreatment of the poor by the well-to-do), but the book itself is part of a fundraising project to help the homeless, with some of the profits from sales going to a charitable non-profit organization. In the process, however, of making Wilde's tale serve a particular and somewhat limited vision of political reform, Grodin and her illustrator have conspired to strip "The Happy Prince" of its mystery and its religious elements. No God character speaks; no angel appears; the lead heart and the dead bird are honored instead by socially progressive humans, who place them inside a memorial to "Compassion" erected in a public park.

So, too, all hints of what came to be known during the prosecution of Oscar Wilde in 1895 as "the love that dare not speak its name"—i.e., male same-sex erotic love—have been expunged from this adaptation. In an illustration by Laura Stutzman, the Prince is represented as having been alive in a vaguely nineteenth-century setting (although he is, quite incongruously, wearing eighteenth-century knee breeches) and as clearly smitten with a young woman. Needless to say, no such scene of heterosexual infatuation occurs in Wilde's original. When it comes time, moreover, for the bird to kiss the Prince, the prose narrative informs us that he kisses him " gently . . . on the cheek"— not, as Wilde emphasized by using the phrase twice, on the lips (Wilde/Grodin 38).

Unlike this American publishing venture in support of a charity, Bill Bowler's 2008 adaptation of "The Happy Prince," with illustrations by Andrew Wicklund, is an Oxford University Press production. If this suggests to book buyers a version with high literary standards and, as they might assume, the use of Wilde's original language throughout, then they will have guessed wrong. When it comes time for the kiss between the statue and the swallow, it occurs not on the Prince's lips (though at least not on the "cheek" instead), but on the "mouth" (Wilde/Bowler 32), once again overriding Wilde's authorial decisions. Why? Is the mouth somehow a less sexually suggestive location? In any case, Andrew Wicklund provides no illustration of this moment, regardless of where the kiss occurs. In accord with this absence, the book's title-page offers a one-paragraph-long biography of Oscar Wilde that speaks of his having died at the age of forty-six in Paris, but gives no clue as to the reason for his exile to France and omits all other information, too, about his sexuality and his fate.

Somewhat unusually, Wicklund has, in his illustrations, set the tale firmly in Wilde's own time—that is, in the final years of the nineteenth century—where women ride bicycles, use sewing machines, and hold positions as journalists. But seemingly working against the text provided by Bill Bowler, Wicklund has also done something more subversive: he has created a Happy Prince statue that is, as in Walter Crane's 1888 vision of the character, physically attractive and androgynous, with flowing curls—perhaps even reminiscent of Lord Alfred Douglas. The mouth, moreover, on which the swallow will plant that (unillustrated) kiss is a reddened and sensual one. Thus, the homophobic silences and suppressions of this Oxford University Press edition are countered by the subtle eroticism of the illustrations, even without a visualized kiss.

Nathan Trewartha's illustrations for Compass Publishing's 2009 retelling by Ken Methold return young audiences to another vaguely nineteenth-century setting, in an unidentifiable city that looks more like a town, but clothe the Happy Prince's statue in garments that suggest a much earlier time. Once again, the circumstances of the kiss have been touched by censorship and a rather puritanical notion of what is acceptable in a book aimed at children. In Methold's text, there is no mention of either lips or mouth; all that readers learn is that the bird "kissed the Happy Prince and fell down dead at his feet" (Wilde/Methold 21). Nathan Trewartha's images of them together place the swallow and the statue in profile, both looking outward, rather than with the bird gazing at the Prince in an attitude that might indicate devotion. On the other hand, Nathan Trewartha captures, as few of these contemporary illustrators have, the pain and the social protest against injustice that is also inherent in Wilde's story, with an illustration of the poor match girl covering her face and weeping in despair. Here, the image breaks through the historical distance to visualize and evoke a powerful emotion and to assign its cause to a social ill in a way that resonates with young viewers.

Given that audience enthusiasm is a desirable effect (and one that sells books), it is surprising that, at a moment when graphic novels have become a highly popular genre, adaptations of Wilde's tale in the first decade of the twenty-first century have yet to take this form. Nonetheless, in 2012, the artist P. Craig Russell came closest to producing a graphic novel of "The Happy Prince" with his comic-strip-influenced illustrations. Many of the pages of this version for NBM Publishing (which does indeed specialize in graphic novels) are divided and laid out in multiple panels, and dialogue issues from speech balloons. The statue of the Happy Prince, moreover, has been glamorized and rendered desirable, as an androgynous figure with wavy hair and high cheekbones, looking not unlike the British actor Benedict Cumberbatch. In the imprecisely eighteenth-century setting that appears during his recollections of being alive, the Prince is drawn as both boyish of face and gracefully feminine of body. Perhaps the most interesting innovation, however, on the part of Russell as illustrator, is to anthropomorphize the face of the bird. Here, the swallow has recognizably human eyes, as well as changing expressions.

P. Craig Russell's adaptation does not hesitate to include the kiss on the lips from the original tale, but its most transgressive element comes purely from the imagination of the artist, rather than from Wilde's story. On the final page, the angel who rescues the heart and the swallow's corpse from oblivion is a delicate and suggestively androgynous nude figure that could have escaped from a Pre-Raphaelite painting by Simeon Solomon (1840–1905), who was prosecuted for same-sex relations with men years before Wilde was, or from a drawing by Charles Ricketts (1866–1931), the gay artist who worked with Oscar Wilde as a book designer and illustrator—most notably on Wilde's poem, *The Sphinx* (1894). Through this image, Russell introduces a note of both gender and sexual ambiguity more explicitly than Wilde did in prose in 1888.

Nicola Baxter's retelling of six stories by Oscar Wilde, including "The Happy Prince," for Anness Publishing's 2014 volume introduces young readers immediately to Wilde himself with a paragraph of information opposite the title-page. Once again, however, the absence of any mention of his romantic or sexual life with men, or reference to how British society punished him for it, begins to look like homophobia by omission. Baxter leaves intact some important moments in Wilde's text, particularly the kiss on the lips. Jenny Thorne's illustrations, however—which seem to place the story in the eighteenth century through visual references to tail-coats and powdered wigs—steer completely clear of that physical demonstration of love, thus distancing young audiences from it. In Thorne's images, the figure of the Happy Prince has, despite his longish hair, a noticeably bulked-up and even swaggering appearance. While this statue might earn the title of being handsome, its embodiment by Thorne does not seem in keeping with an object meant to be—as Wilde himself labeled it, using the more feminized term—"beautiful." In this 2014 version, the androgyny and ambiguity of Walter Crane's first illustration have been removed in favor of something not only more solid, but stolid.

Erasing same-sex erotic possibilities from the statue's relations with the swallow is also the hallmark of a 2015 Korean adaptation that was released simultaneously in the United States in an English-language version by Joy Crowley. In Crowley's text, the bird's attitude toward the Prince is merely one of reverence, with no potentially transgressive love expressed on either side: "Winter came and snow started falling. Being cold and tired, the swallow could not fly. It kissed the feet of the prince. 'Goodbye, my prince,' it said and then died" (Wilde/Crowley 27). Accompanying this is the artist Hye-ryeon Jang's illustration of the scene, which shows the bird lying dead in the street, but with no statue even visible. Here, too, the characters' relations appear to remain safely within non-romantic bounds, even after ascension to Heaven: "The angel came back with the swallow and the heart of the Happy Prince. They were both reborn as angels and remained friends forever" (Crowley 31). On the facing page is an image of the Happy Prince as a small, golden-haired, and seemingly pre-sexual child sitting on a crescent moon, looking at the swallow, who is perched atop the point of that moon and, therefore, not in close physical proximity.

In direct contrast, a picture book of "The Happy Prince" published in London by Thames & Hudson in 2017 contains illustrations that offer a joyful vision of same-sex relations that might have pleased even Wilde himself. The visual setting in this version, for which Maisie Paradise Shearring served as both adapter and artist, combines elements of the past with scenes clearly reflecting a modern urban world, so that viewers are at once brought closer to the action and allowed a certain distance. In the scenes of suffering, those who live in poverty include figures recognizable as people of color. Most striking, though, are the fantasy elements involving identity itself, with a seamless blending in visual terms of the human and non-human, the animate and the inanimate. Shearring's swallow has, at times, a human face and uses his wings as human arms, most strikingly when embracing and kissing the statue on the lips, even as the statue's lips pucker to kiss him in return, making this a scene of mutually-experienced emotions and actions.

Perhaps the most memorable invention on Shearring's part, however, is her depiction of a Paradise in which the Prince and the bird are given the form of two smiling youths, allowed to live together companionably and eternally in God's garden. They stroll together, clearly enjoying their close communion, with the hand of the slightly taller Prince resting on the swallow's back. As this image demonstrates unequivocally to the audience (whether that audience is composed of adults or children), God has no problem with such a relationship. Thus, this 2017 British picture book returns us to Imogen Russell Williams's idea of how illustrations might be used to communicate sophisticated notions wordlessly to a variety of audiences.

And yet, all is not rosy here either, for this is not the final image in the 2017 picture book. Although Shearring concludes by drawing a portrait of Oscar Wilde himself that portrays him in his aesthetic phase, with long hair and a decidedly feminized, gender-bending appearance, that view of the author is accompanied by a biographical summary of extreme reticence, with no mention of Wilde's relations with men. The only information about his life that readers receive is that he wrote "The Happy Prince" for "his two sons, Cyril and

Vyvyan[,]" and that he "died in Paris on November 30, 1900, at the age of 46" (Shearring 50). Such a refusal to acknowledge the facts of Wilde's own story undercuts the pleasant fantasy of the Happy Prince and the swallow as a couple strolling through Paradise.

Altogether, this survey of recent illustrated editions of "The Happy Prince" for young readers reveals that, when it comes to visually daring images and homoerotic content, the modern makers of books have much to learn from their late Victorian counterparts. To make this point, we have only to look at one of the artist G. P. Jacomb-Hood's two illustrated headpieces for the 1888 *The Happy Prince and Other Tales* volume published by David Nutt in Britain and by Roberts Brothers in the United States (Figure 2). In his edition of Wilde's short fiction for Oxford University Press, Ian Small has referred to this depiction of undressed young boys as an "illustration of children at play" (xxix), but that is not an accurate description. It is actually something less innocent—an image inspired by the scene in which the swallow mentions to the Prince that he dislikes boys because, a year ago, "'there were two rude boys, the miller's sons, who were always throwing stones at me'" (Wilde "Happy" 1888 15). Here, Jacomb-Hood shows the bird about to be subjected to their assault. More important, however, it is clear from this illustration that both the artist and the audience he addresses—most likely one meant to include adult male viewers—do *not* dislike boys, whatever they may be doing to the swallow, but instead find their bodies, at least, charming and beautiful. The draping of a cloak over one of the otherwise nude figures produces a visual allusion to classical sculpture and through it to the world of so-called "Greek love," which was the common late-nineteenth-century euphemism for male homosexuality.

Figure 2

Jacomb-Hood's illustration thus takes us further in terms of mobility, by moving into the controversial territory of what Oscar Wilde's contemporaries called "Uranian," or man-and-boy, love, through the relationship between the naked and nearly naked bodies of children depicted here (whose state of dress is never mentioned in Wilde's text) and an appreciative adult male spectator who may be consuming that image. To find anything comparable, we must go not to modern children's books, but to cinema. I conclude, therefore, where I began: with Rupert Everett's 2018 biopic visualizing the last days of Oscar Wilde, which re-imagines "The Happy Prince" as a story about Wilde himself, torn down from his pedestal and stripped of everything, but never of the company of adored and adoring youths.

In her study of Wilde's 1882 lecture tour across America, *Making Oscar Wilde* (2018), Michèle Mendelssohn has described Wilde's "remarkable rise" to prominence as "a fairy tale in which a young nobody becomes a somebody" (3), and his fall in 1895 as equally fairy-tale-like: "a Cinderella story in reverse," with an ending "swift and grim" (7). Yet Wilde's own version of "The

Happy Prince," along with those of the many artists who have been continuing to picture it, reminds us that death is never the end of the story. Whether or not, in these subsequent versions, the tale of "The Happy Prince" has been interpreted as one of homoerotic romance, and whether or not that message has been visualized for its audiences, the once immobile statue and the non-migrating bird always make their final move to Paradise *together.*

Works Cited

Duffy, John-Charles. "Gay-Related Themes in the Fairy Tales of Oscar Wilde," *Victorian Literature and Culture*, vol. 29, no. 2, 2001, pp. 327–49.

The Happy Prince. Screenwriter and Director Rupert Everett. Maze Pictures, 2018.

The Happy Prince. Directed by Michael Mills. Potterton Productions, 1974.

Holland, Merlin. "Introduction." *Stories for Young People: Oscar Wilde*, edited by Merlin Holland; illustrated by G. L. Brierley. New York: Sterling Publishing, 2005, pp. 4–7.

Hollander, Amanda. "Oscar Wilde, Evelyn Sharp, and the Politics of Dress and Decoration in the Fin-de-Siècle Fairy Tale." *Oscar Wilde and the Cultures of Childhood,* edited by Joseph Bristow. Cham, Switzerland: Palgrave Macmillan/Springer, 2017, pp. 119–43.

Markey, Anne. *Oscar Wilde's Fairy Tales: Origins and Contexts.* Dublin: Irish Academic P, 2011.

Mendelssohn, Michèle. *Making Oscar Wilde.* Oxford: Oxford U P, 2018.

Mills, Michael, adapt. *The Happy Prince.* By Oscar Wilde. Dir. Michael Mills. Potterton Productions, 1974.

Ruggaber, Michelle. "Wilde's *The Happy Prince* and *A House of Pomegranates*: Bedtime Stories for Grown-Ups." *English Literature in Transition, 1880–1920*, vol. 46, no. 2, 2003, pp. 141–53.Small, Ian. "Introduction." *The Complete Works of Oscar Wilde. Vol. VIII: The Short Fiction*, edited. Ian Small. Oxford: Oxford U P, 2017.

Wilde, Oscar. *The Fairy Tales of Oscar Wilde.* Introduction by Merlin Holland, illustrations by Sandow Birk. San Francisco: Arion P, 2018.

_____. *The Complete Letters of Oscar Wilde*, edited by Merlin Holland and Rupert Hart-Davis. New York: Henry Holt, 2000.

_____. *The Fairy Tales of Oscar Wilde: The Happy Prince*. Illustrated by P. Craig Russell. New York: NBM Publishing, 2012.

_____. "The Happy Prince." 1888. *The Complete Works of Oscar Wilde*, vol. VIII: *The Short Fiction*, edited by Ian Small. Oxford: Oxford U P, 2017, pp. 13–19.

_____. *The Happy Prince*. Retold by Ken Methold, illustrated by Nathan Trewartha. St. Petersburg, FL: Compass, 2009.

_____. *The Happy Prince*. Text adaptation by Bill Bowler, illustrated by Andrew Wicklund. Oxford: Oxford U P, 2008.

_____. *The Happy Prince. The Selfish Giant*. Retold by Elizabeth Ann Moore, illustrated by Gianni De Conno. Genoa: Cideb, 1999.

_____. *The Happy Prince. A Story by Oscar Wilde*. Retold by Joy Cowley, illustrated by Hye-ryeon Jang. Seoul: Yeowon Media/ Big & Small, 2015.

_____. *The Happy Prince: A Tale by Oscar Wilde*. Illustrated and adapted by Maisie Paradise Shearring. London: Thames & Hudson, 2017.

_____. *Oscar Wilde's The Happy Prince*. Retold by Elissa Grodin, illustrated by Laura Stutzman. Chelsea, MI: Sleeping Bear P, 2006.

_____. *The Selfish Giant and Other Classic Tales. Six Illustrated Stories by Oscar Wilde*. Retold by Nicola Baxter, illustrated by Jenny Thorne, London: Anness, 2014.

_____. *Stories for Young People: Oscar Wilde*, edited by Merlin Holland, illustrated by G. L. Brierley. New York: Sterling Publishing, 2005.

The Trials of Oscar Wilde. Screenwriter and Dir. Ken Hughes. United Artists, 1960.

Williams, Imogen Russell. "Buzz-saw of the Imagination: The Sophisticated Concepts Communicated Via Illustration." *TLS*, 17 Dec. 2017, pp. 27–28.

"A Strange Fascination": Oscar Wilde, the Dangers of Captivated Reading, and Twenty-First-Century Media Consumption _____

Amanda Farage

In *The Picture of Dorian Gray*, Oscar Wilde writes that "the effect of art, and chiefly the art of literature," was to reveal "the mysteries of life" to the viewer or reader, as this "dealt immediately with the passions and the intellect" (51). Many Victorians agreed with this sentiment and felt that one of the principal purposes of novels and other fictional works was to help develop the intellect and provide knowledge of life. Yet, as evidenced by lively periodical debates of the time, this idea of literature engaging "the passions and the intellect" was also perceived to have a dark side—one that encouraged the development of deviant desires and mental, moral, and physical degeneration in readers.[1] For a reader to become passionate about a fictional character meant an immersion in the text, and this immersion went hand in hand with a detachment from reality. To become absorbed in a novel or other fictional work to the extent that one could identify with and feel sympathy for a character meant that one risked losing touch with the reality of a world in which the character did not exist. A more objective or detached approach to literature thus proved to be a safer way of engaging with texts, but this did not stop the idea of captivated reading from becoming a divisive topic, with some Victorian commentators endorsing this form of textual interaction and others cautioning against its possible effects.

This debate about healthy reading habits persisted throughout the latter half of the nineteenth century, and it was in this climate that Oscar Wilde and his works arrived. Whether it was due to his own seemingly scandalous lifestyle, his provocative writing style, or the unconstrained reactions many readers had to his literature, Wilde became a locus of Victorian anxiety regarding unhealthy textual captivation. Indeed, absorptive encounters with various kinds of literature play key roles in two crucial narratives by Oscar Wilde published in the last decade of the nineteenth century—"The Portrait of Mr W. H." (1889) and *The Picture of Dorian Gray* (1890). Wilde provides fictional examples of captivated reading and its ensuing dangers in these two works that were sometimes deemed immersive themselves.

Just two years before "The Portrait of Mr W. H," the captivation in fictional worlds that could arise from unbridled passion for books and reading was examined in an 1887 *Blackwood's* article entitled "Literary Voluptuaries." The piece begins with the provocative declaration, "Perhaps the greatest pleasure in life is an ill-regulated passion for reading" (805). Alarm-bells should have sounded in good Victorians' minds from the very beginning of this short sentence. The fact that the author dares to announce that pleasure is derived from not just reading, or a passion for reading, but from an *ill-regulated* passion for this pastime would have been troublesome to those who felt a more objective engagement with literature was best.

The author, however, feels that this reading style is ideal as it creates "blissful oblivion or abstraction" in the mind of the reader ("Literary" 806), and he encourages readers to sample different books until they find one that they resonate with and whose fictional world beckons them so they can experience this oblivion. True bliss comes when, "abandoning self-will and self-control, he [the reader] has been charmed into the oblivion of absorbed attention . . . when the minutes are flying by unconsciously" ("Literary" 815). Again, the author emphasizes the lack of restraint necessary to enjoy reading. Readers need to cast off societal expectations of real life (self-control, moderated emotions, strong willpower) and immerse themselves fully in the literary worlds they encounter. Appropriate for the themes of free abandon and loss of control promoted by the author, he also compares the act of reading to loving someone, with skim reading considered "slight flirtations" with books and absorptive reading "actually falling in love" ("Literary" 805). Books and other texts are not just objects, but rather entities capable of forming reciprocal relationships with readers. Just as with human interactions, the author encourages readers to seek deep, meaningful, long-lasting engagements with texts and the worlds they contain rather than simply scanning the words on the page.

A strong counterpoint to the idolization of such captivated reading occurred throughout the century, and the bluntly titled newspaper article, "Excessive Reading" (1869), perhaps best captures this wariness. "Excessive" is the key term throughout the article, and it alludes to the divide between more objective engagement with literature and a more involved, immersive reading of literary works. While discussing the various inequities of modern Victorian society, the author suggests that "it would seem that the vice of excessive reading has done a good deal of harm" to English culture ("Excessive"). The author of this article sees hardly any good that can come from reading, or at least too much reading, due to the detrimental "effect of so much literature habitually swallowed on the mental and moral condition of men and women" ("Excessive"). The self-indulgence so lauded by the author of "Literary Voluptuaries" is here excoriated as we read that "indulgence in reading whatever takes our fancy is gradually ruinous to our intellectual tone" ("Excessive").

Absorptive reading introduces people "into a world that [they] like better than the real one," and when they give themselves over to this fantasy world, they are at the mercy of the views espoused by the author ("Excessive"). Such captivation can be deceptively dangerous, particularly since the "more charming [the author's] style and the more elevated his tone the more injurious will be our thoughtless acceptance of his opinions" ("Excessive"). It is not only fictional books or novels that create this effect in the reader (although they act as the gateway drug that establishes this pattern of reading). After these texts "drug the moral sense" of readers, more serious works, such as articles, essays, and treatises are consumed in a less critical manner ("Excessive"). In this way, literary voluptuaries or "incessant readers" develop "passive brains" that gradually degenerate and lead to an overall decomposition of readers' mental and moral capacities ("Excessive").

Given these polarizing Victorian attitudes, the way Wilde portrays captivated reading (and viewing) in his two works, as well as the effects these stories have on readers, is particularly startling. The contemporary response to Wilde's works, and *The Picture of Dorian Gray* in particular, intriguingly mirrors the narratives themselves. In an 1890 letter to Wilde, Robert Ross, his close personal friend and later executor of his literary works, wrote, "at the Savile Club . . . all I could hear was praise" regarding the novel, "though . . . it is said to be very dangerous" (qtd. in Bristow xliv). The supposedly dangerous element of reading Wilde's work arose from the fact that many "grateful readers" wrote that they found the story to be quite "absorbing and suggestive" (qtd. Bristow in xlviii). This immersive reading of a novel whose subject matter was often deemed unseemly caused many reviewers to publish caustic criticisms. In response to one such scathing review published in the *Scots Observer*, Wilde wrote that he heartily disagreed with the assertion that the novel should only "be read by the most depraved members of the criminal and illiterate classes" (qtd. in Bristow li). Wilde argued that his narrative does not make explicit "What Dorian's sins are," so whatever debauched ideas a reader conjures, he "has brought them" himself, not as a result of the reading (qtd. in Bristow xlviii).

Concerns about readers of *The Picture of Dorian Gray* were ironically imitative of the narrative itself insofar as one of the most famous instances of dangerous reading in late-Victorian literature is found in the very novel that provoked these fears. Wilde describes the "yellow book" given to Dorian Gray by Lord Henry as "the strangest book that he had ever read" and "a novel without a plot" (Dorian 103–04). If the color of the book is not enough to put us on our guard, its categorization as a novel—and a plotless one at that—should warn us that nothing good can come from reading it. Wilde confirms these suspicions as he provides greater detail about the book and Dorian's interaction with it. The narrator baldly states, "It was a poisonous book," one in which Dorian easily "became absorbed" (Wilde Dorian 104). This absorption allows "the sins of the world [to pass] in dumb show before him. Things that he had dimly dreamed of were suddenly made real to him. Things of which he had never dreamed were gradually revealed" (Wilde Dorian 104). The kind of reading Dorian practices encompasses many of the fears Victorians felt about captivated reading. The yellow book both gives form to Dorian's vague, morally degenerate ideas and infects his mind with new "sins" of which he had previously been unaware.

Eventually this reading "produced in the mind of the lad . . . a form of reverie, a malady of dreaming, that made him unconscious of the falling day and creeping shadows" (Wilde 104). Dorian soon becomes so obsessed, or in his words "fascinated," with the novel that he "could not free himself from the influence of the book" for many years (Wilde Dorian 104). His reading and re-reading of the novel becomes an addiction—he is literally "under the influence" of it, and this addiction poisons his mind, damages his morals, and would cause physical decay if the portrait did not manifest his deeds in place of his body. Dorian venerates the textual object as well as the narrative it contains, buying "no less than nine large-paper copies of the first edition" from Paris and binding them "in different colours, so that they might suit his various moods and the changing fancies of a nature over which he seemed, at times, to have almost entirely lost control" (Wilde Dorian 105). Soon the book has usurped his willpower, taking control of Dorian's mental faculties and detrimentally affecting him in every aspect of life.

He even begins to see the book and its main character as a prefigurement of his life, believing "the whole book seemed to him to contain the story of his own life, written before he had lived it," which indicates that Dorian begins to make dissolute decisions based on the fictional character's choices (Wilde Dorian 105). This blending of fiction and reality echoes the fears put forth by Victorian writers about susceptible minds being influenced by what they read to the extent that they would mimic characters and actions found in the fiction they consumed. Dorian's rapid descent comes not merely from the decadent material found in the novel, but from his type of engagement with the text. The feeling of blissful abandon on the part of the reader as evocatively described in "Literary Voluptuaries" is dramatized to disastrous effect in *Dorian Gray*. His absorption and engrossment with the fictional world created by the book leads to his downfall.

The Picture of Dorian Gray is not Wilde's only story about overwrought interactions with textual and art objects. A year prior to *Dorian Gray's* publication, his short story, "The Portrait of Mr W. H.," was first published in *Blackwood's Magazine*. Aside from their similar titles, the two works share considerations of art, its relation to life, and the manner in which readers and viewers engage with fiction. The plot of this story revolves around the obsession of several men trying to uncover the true identity of the mysterious "Fair Youth" dedicatee in some of Shakespeare's sonnets, which two of the men in the tale (Cyril and Erskine) believe to be Willie Hughes, or "W. H." Wilde, therefore, blends a real-world mystery with a fictional narrative and characters, creating a plot that blurs the lines between reality and fantasy, actuality and art.

Cyril commissions a fake portrait of Hughes, which Erskine believes to be authentic, but later learns is a fake. In support of its validity, Cyril commits suicide and leaves the portrait to Erskine. Despite knowing its true nature as a falsification, Erskine quickly becomes enthralled with the artwork and the mysterious story of Hughes. Upon his death from an illness, he leaves the "fatal picture" to the narrator with a letter declaring his belief in Hughes's identity, and a false implication that he, like Cyril, has committed suicide as the ultimate proof of his belief in the portrait and its story (Wilde "Portrait" 243). As evidenced by its continued existence despite the knowledge of its forgery, we read at the very beginning of the tale that this portrait holds "a strange fascination" for each of the men that they are unable to escape (Wilde "Portrait" 222).

Almost like a disease, Cyril's unhealthy fascination is transferred first to Erskine, and upon their deaths, to the narrator, who continues the obsession with the portrait that now hangs in his home. There are obvious general parallels between this short story and Wilde's subsequent novel, from the central role played by a painting to the deadly conclusions of several main characters. Yet, one of the more subtle connections between these two works is the consideration of the effects of captivated or entranced interactions with literary and art works on people—and in both cases, the effects range from deleterious to deadly.

Apprehensions about becoming enthralled by fantasy worlds and lost to reality were not unique to the Victorian era, although they did reach a fascinating meridian during the nineteenth century. Indeed, these sentiments belong to a long tradition of anxiety about the inability to separate reality from fiction that reaches back at least to *Don Quixote* in the early seventeenth century. We are now continuing to participate in this centuries' long tradition, with a distinct shift in the way we perceive fictional immersion occurring in our present moment, as the late twentieth and early twenty-first century have revealed new forms of media to draw our concern— from binge-worthy television shows to hyper-realistic video games. In the face of such nontextual media, reading (particularly fiction reading) has become a form of media engagement in which we encourage people to become immersed.

Due to the vast advances in various scientific fields since the nineteenth century, we can now view the act of reading from a new, scientific standpoint that Victorians would no doubt have envied; yet, our study of reading and its effects has become even more intense due to the desire to comprehend even the most minute aspects of the process. Researchers wonder: precisely how does reading operate on a neurological level? How do our brains react to what we read? Are they permanently changed or are the effects ephemeral? In other words, what might be the characteristics of Dorian's "malady of dreaming" or Cyril's "strange fascination"? Advances in the sciences have been matched with advances in medical technology that have enabled researchers to seek answers to these questions. In 1993, cognitive scientist Richard Gerrig postulated that the way people interact with the real world and the way they engage with fictional narratives are "subserved by the same cognitive mechanisms" so that fantasy and reality are perceived as the same on a neurological level (Mar et al. "Bookworms" 695). This hypothesis has been upheld by various studies and experiments in the ensuing decades that show "thoughts and emotions predicated on the fictional context" of a book or nontextual medium "have lasting real-world consequences" on the reader or viewer (Mar et al., "Bookworms" 695).

Psychology professor Rolf Zwaan furthered these ideas and suggested in 2004 that words themselves "automatically activate neural events similar to those that occur during the actual experience of events," a theory that was then corroborated by research studies (Mar et al. "Bookworms" 696). Such a relation not only exists between emotions associated with reading about real-world feelings, but actions as well. Neuroscientist Friedemann Pulvermüller and his team found in 2001 that reading "particular action words," such as "'to kick' or 'to talk'" activates "the motor cortex specific to those areas that represent the relevant part of the body typically used for that action" (Mar et al., "Bookworms" 697). When we read about a character's actions, we are participating in those same behaviors on some neurological level—the very scenario that many Victorians suspected and feared, and that Wilde dramatized in his works.

Some further research in this field has been done, although much more remains to be explored. In 2013, neuroscientists at Emory University began to analyze the physical effects reading has on the brain—not just during the act of reading, but the effects that linger for days after reading (Clark). Lead researcher and psychiatry professor Gregory Berns used functional magnetic resonance imaging to compare the brain function of twenty-one undergraduate students during the days when they all read from Robert Harris's 2003 fictional novel *Pompeii*, and the days when they did not. The researchers found that the morning after reading from *Pompeii*, there was "heightened connectivity in the left temporal cortex, an area of the brain associated with receptivity for language," even though the students were not reading anything at the time of the scan (Clark). Moreover, students also showed heightened activity in the "primary sensory motor region of the brain," which is "associated with making representations of sensation for the body" (Clark). Readers, even when not reading, still experienced the simulated neurological effects as if they actually underwent the actions and events depicted in the narrative. When Dorian felt that the yellow book "seemed to him to contain the story of his own life, written before he had lived it," he was perhaps experiencing this same sensation.

As Berns evocatively states, the "neural changes that we found associated with physical sensation and movement systems suggest that reading a novel can transport you into the body of the protagonist" (qtd. in Clark). The fact that the reactions of the Emory University students occurred during the mornings after the assigned readings and then for five days after the last reading, at which point the study concluded, alerts scientists to the possibility that reading fictional narratives has mental and biological effects that last far longer than previously thought. Berns and his team are not sure precisely how long these effects continue in readers, but he points out that since these neural changes are detectable "over a few days for a randomly assigned novel," there is a good possibility that "your favorite novels could certainly have a bigger and longer-lasting effect on the biology of your brain," since readers would have stronger feelings for narratives of their choice that contain characters with whom they closely associate (Clark). As Dorian Gray illustrated, literary works with which readers can form deep connections have the greatest impact on the reader's mental and emotional state.

Indeed, reading stories of our choosing and in which we are emotionally invested can contribute to a manner of information processing that "leads to potentially increasing and long-lasting persuasive effects" in the reader (van Laer et al. 800). Marketing and sociology researchers point out that readers who experience narratives in this manner are "engrossed in a story in a way" that is neither "inherently critical nor involves great scrutiny" (van Laer et al. 800). It is this lack of critical attention to the narrative that caused anxiety in many Victorians, who believed that one should always be actively engaged with literary material for the purpose of mental and moral development. When readers are not critically and somewhat detachedly interacting with literature, they are at risk of becoming too absorbed in the stories and characters, as with Dorian, or indeed, the readers of Wilde's novel who found it "absorbing and suggestive." This absorption could, of course, only have detrimental effects—effects that impacted readers' physical, mental, and emotional states.

Whereas Victorians often saw captivated reading as a gateway to real-world delinquency or death, contemporary studies show that, while the influence of reading is as great as Victorians imagined, it is not necessarily negative, and can indeed incite positive changes in readers. Not every portrait or literary mystery will create Cyrils and Erskines, just as not every yellow book will create Dorians. Cognitive psychologist Raymond Mar and his team have found that, while frequent fiction readers "are removed from actual social contact" during their reading, the act itself "may bolster or maintain social-processing skills" ("Bookworms" 695). Conversely, frequent readers of nonfiction literature experience the same isolation from social contact in the real world as fiction readers, but without the benefit of "simulation experience in a fictional one" (Mar et al., "Bookworms" 695). Therefore, fiction reading (especially absorptive fiction reading) actually has more real-world value than nonfiction reading.

When we are enthralled by a narrative, "we experience a simulated reality and feel real emotions in response to the conflicts and relationships of story characters" (Mar et al. "Exploring" 407–08). Our ability to immerse ourselves in a fictional world and its characters "may assist in projecting oneself into another's mind in order to infer their mental states" in the real world, thus helping with both empathy and socialization in a more general sense (Mar et al. "Exploring" 421). Unlike Dorian's dark descent into manipulative criminality, Mar and his colleagues have repeatedly found that frequent fiction readers appear to show greater "empathy and social understanding" than those who read nonfiction on a regular basis ("Exploring" 408).

While fiction reading is not nearly as controversial today as it was in Wilde's time, Mar's research combats contemporary negative stereotypes about bookworms and their supposed lack of social adjustment. Mar found that "reading narrative fiction was associated with more social support," while those reading nonfiction reported feeling "less social support and more stress" ("Exploring" 422). Why might fiction readers feel that they have more social support than nonfiction readers? One suggestion postulated by the psychologists is that fiction readers are "drawing support from the fictional characters they encounter" and thereby "engaging in a form of parasocial relationship" (Mar et al. "Exploring" 422). Along similar lines, Mar cites previous research that has indicated "favourite television characters can influence us in a manner similar to real peers, particularly if they are seen as 'real'" ("Exploring" 422). Based on these findings, it is probable that the author of "Literary Voluptuaries" is correct and novel readers experience an intense connection with literary characters that actually supplements their daily social lives.

The advantages reading provides are not limited to the emotional or psychological, for a recent study conducted by Yale University's School of Public Health has found that immersive reading actually prolongs the reader's lifespan by about two years. Research conducted over two decades shows that people who regularly read fiction books for as little as thirty minutes a day display a "20% reduction in mortality" than those who participate in other sedentary activities, such as watching television (Bavishi 47). Readers of periodicals and newspapers did not experience the extended longevity that book readers did, and the scientists theorize this is because books promote "'deep reading,' which is a slow, immersive process" that engages the brain in various cognitive activities (Bavishi 44).

In sharp contrast to the recent discoveries about captivated reading, when considering interactions with newer forms of media, we find familiar Victorian misgivings about the detrimental effects of excessive immersion in fantasy. Several studies have shown that watching entertainment television "is negatively associated with reading achievement," thus interfering with our ability to gain the benefits of reading (Saleem and Anderson 88). Given that UNESCO has claimed that "the biggest single indicator of whether a child is going to thrive at school and in work is whether or not they read for pleasure," such findings about the negative impact newer, nontextual media has on our interactions with older, print media is disturbing (Boyce qtd. in Paton).

Concerns have also arisen specifically about the depictions of violence in the absorptive worlds of film, television, and video games, and their relation to violent activity. A 2007 study about the developing technology for visual graphics in video games revealed that "newer, more graphically sophisticated video games produce higher levels of presence, involvement, and arousal than analogous, less sophisticated older games" (Sestir and Green 284). Similar issues regarding violence in movies surfaced after the 2012 movie theater shooting perpetrated by a man dressed as the Joker at a showing of *The Dark Knight Rises*. In response to these tragedies, Emanuel Tanay, a retired clinical and forensic psychiatrist, has claimed that "violence in the media has been increasing and reaching proportions that are dangerous . . . You turn on the television, and violence is there. You go to a movie, and violence is there. Reality is distorted. If you live in a fictional world, the fictional world becomes your reality" (qtd. in Kaplan).

Like Victorian commentators of reading before him, Tanay expresses the opinion that people who consume violent media will ultimately become violent themselves. Aggression in the fictional worlds of visual media can thus cause a lack of self-control and affective distance from the effects of violence in the real world. In this current climate of anxieties about media consumption, Wilde's depictions of the dangers of uncritical reading and viewing are particularly fitting.

Wilde insightfully writes that the yellow book revealed to Dorian "things of which he had never dreamed," much as parents and educators today worry about video games, television, or films giving people ideas of acts they might not conceive of on their own. When Wilde notes that Dorian feels a deep connection to the book's main character that influences his actions, he offers a perceptive description of the experience that many readers or viewers have when they feel that a character relates to them or represents them in some manner. As he states in "The Portrait of Mr W. H.", "all Art . . . [is] an attempt to realise one's own personality on some imaginative plane", whether artist or consumer (221). Depending upon the person and their mental and emotional state, such a realization can be a wonderful, parasocial moment, or it can possibly degenerate into dressing up as the Joker and emulating his mass murdering behavior.

The study of the complex variety of Victorian ideas and concerns about captivated reading, particularly as distilled in the works of Oscar Wilde, helps us to understand how they have been transposed to present-day anxieties about the ubiquity of new digital media and the technologies that can make any phone, tablet, or computer screen a portal to a vast visual legacy of fictional narratives. The simulated worlds accessible through such media have become fruitful fields for contemporary apprehensions about immersion that mirror what the Victorians expressed regarding absorptive encounters with literature and the dangers of ungoverned reading. Compared to today's ever multiplying nontextual media and various iterations of screens, reading and its effects on the brain have become a subject of no apprehension at all. It is fascinating to hear the vocabulary of absorption and immersion being used in the twenty-first century to describe the pleasures and benefits of reading, whereas in the nineteenth century, such language was deployed to caution against the dangers inherent in such captivation. The narratives of Oscar Wilde's *The Picture of Dorian Gray* and "The Portrait of Mr W. H." thus provide us with a fresh context for twenty-first century perspectives on books and reading, as well as our own anxieties about various other forms of nontextual media.

Note

1. See works such as Wilkie Collins' "The Unknown Public" (1858), Thomas Wright's "Concerning the Unknown Public" (1883), Joseph Ackland's "Elementary Education and the Decay of Literature" (1894), and Arnold Haultain's "How to Read" (1896).

Works Cited

Bavishi, Avni, Martin D. Slade, and Becca R. Levy. "A Chapter a Day: Association of Book Reading with Longevity." *Social Science & Medicine*, vol. 164, no. 1, 2016, pp. 44–48.Bristow, Joseph, editor. *The Complete Works of Oscar Wilde: Volume 3: The Picture of Dorian Gray: The 1890 and 1891 Texts*. New York: Oxford U P, 2005.

Clark, Carol. "A Novel Look at How Stories May Change the Brain." *Emory University eScience Commons*, 17 Dec. 2013, esciencecommons. blogspot.com/2013/12/a-novel-look-at-how-stories-may-change. html.

"Excessive Reading." *Pall Mall Gazette*, no. 1356, 1869.

Kaplan, Arline. "Violence in the Media: What Effects on Behavior?" *Psychiatric Times*, vol. 29, no. 10, 5 Oct. 2012, www.psychiatrictimes. com/child-adolescent-psychiatry/violence-media-what-effects-behavior.

"Literary Voluptuaries." *Blackwood's Edinburgh Magazine*, vol. 142, 1887, pp. 805–17.

Mar, Raymond A., et al. "Bookworms Versus Nerds: Exposure to Fiction Versus Non-fiction, Divergent Associations with Social Ability, and the Simulation of Fictional Social Worlds." *Journal of Research in Personality*, vol. 40, no. 5, 2006, pp. 694–712.

_____. "Exploring the Link Between Reading Fiction and Empathy: Ruling Out Individual Differences and Examining Outcomes." *Communications*, vol. 34, 2009, pp. 407–28.

Paton, Graeme. "Children with Short Attention Spans 'Failing to Read Books.'" *The Telegraph*, 20 June 2012. www.telegraph.co.uk/ education/educationnews/9342391/Children-with- short-attention-spans-failing-to-read-books.html.

Saleem, Muniba, and Craig A. Anderson. "The Good, the Bad and the Ugly of Electronic Media." *Using Social Science to Reduce Violent Offending*, edited by Joel A. Dvoskin, et al. New York: Oxford U P, 2012, pp. 83–101.

Sestir, Marc, and Melanie C. Green. "You Are Who You Watch: Identification and Transportation Effects on Temporary Self-concept." *Social Influence*, vol. 5, no. 4, 2008, pp. 272–288.

Van Laer, Tom, et al. "The Extended Transportation-Imagery Model: A Meta-Analysis of the Antecedents and Consequences of Consumers' Narrative Transportation." *Journal of Consumer Research*, vol. 40, no. 5, 2014, pp. 797–817.

Wilde, Oscar. *The Picture of Dorian Gray*. New York: W. W. Norton, 2007.

_____. "The Portrait of Mr W. H.". *The Collected Works of Oscar Wilde*. New York: Wordsworth Editions, 1997, pp. 219–43.

RESOURCES

Chronology of Oscar Wilde's Life

Kimberly J. Stern

1854	Born on October 16 in Dublin.
1864	Joins his brother, William ("Willie") Wilde, at Portora Royal School, Enniskillen.
1871	Matriculates at Trinity College, Dublin.
1874	Matriculates at Magdalen College, Oxford.
1878	Wins Newdigate prize for *Ravenna* and earns a rare double-first in Greats, thus, completing his Oxford experience.
1879	Writes "The Rise of Historical Criticism" for the Chancellor's English Essay Prize at Oxford; no prize is awarded that year, and the essay remains unpublished until 1908.
1880	Wilde writes *Vera; or, The Nihilists.*
1881	Publishes his first volume, *Poems.*
1882	Gives a lecture tour of North America.
1883	Produces his first play, *Vera; or, The Nihilists*, at New York's Union Square Theatre. The play is unsuccessful and closes after only one week. Wilde also writes *The Duchess of Padua,* which will not be produced until 1891.
1884	Marries Constance Lloyd.
1885	Eldest son Cyril is born.

1886	Younger son Vyvyan is born.
1887	Becomes editor of *Woman's World* and publishes "The Canterville Ghost" in *The Court and Society Review.*
1888	Publishes *The Happy Prince and Other Tales.*
1889	Publishes "The Portrait of Mr W. H." in *Blackwood's Magazine.* "The Decay of Lying" appears in *The Nineteenth Century.*
1890	Publishes *The Picture of Dorian Gray* in *Lippincott's Magazine.* An early version of "The Critic as Artist" appears in *The Nineteenth Century* under the title "The True Function and Value of Criticism."
1891	Publishes *A House of Pomegranates*, *Lord Arthur Savile's Crime and Other Stories*, and *Intentions* (a collection of critical essays that includes "The Critic as Artist," "The Decay of Lying," "Pen, Pencil and Poison," and "The Truth of Masks"). Wilde also publishes in book form a revised and expanded version of *The Picture of Dorian Gray*. *The Duchess of Padua* is produced at the Broadway Theatre in New York but closes after only three weeks. Wilde meets and falls in love with Lord Alfred ("Bosie") Douglas.
1892	*Lady Windermere's Fan* is written and performed at the St. James's Theatre, London. Wilde writes *Salomé* in French, but it is banned from the English stage on the grounds that it represents a Biblical subject.
1893	*A Woman of No Importance* is performed at London's Haymarket Theatre. Wilde writes his poem "The Sphinx" and publishes *Salomé* in French.

1894	Publishes the first English edition of *Salomé* with illustrations by Aubrey Beardsley.
1895	*An Ideal Husband* is produced at the Haymarket Theatre, and *The Importance of Being Earnest* is performed simultaneously at the St. James's Theatre, London. John Douglas, the Marquess of Queensberry, leaves a note for Wilde at the Albemarle Club: "For Oscar Wilde posing somdomite [sic]." Wilde brings a libel suit against Marquess of Queensberry. After the failure of the libel suit, he is charged with acts of "gross indecency" and sentenced to two years of hard labor.
1896	Lady Wilde dies while Wilde is incarcerated at Reading Gaol.
1897	Writes the document that will later be titled *De Profundis*. Wilde completes his prison term this year and moves to the Continent. He reunites briefly with Douglas in Naples and writes *The Ballad of Reading Gaol*.
1898	Constance dies of complications following surgery. She was likely suffering from multiple sclerosis, which was not widely recognized at the time.
1900	Wilde dies in the Hotel D'Alsace in Paris, attended by friends Robert Ross and Reginald Turner.
1905	Robert Ross publishes a portion of *De Profundis* and assigns it this now famous title.
1909	Wilde's remains are transported from a humble cemetery at Bagneux to Père Lachaise Cemetery in Paris.

1950	The ashes of Robert Ross, who died in 1918, are deposited into Wilde's tomb.
1962	The complete text of *De Profundis* is published. An early edition of the *Letters* is published.
2000	A "complete" letters of Oscar Wilde is published by his grandson Merlin Holland.

Selected Works by Oscar Wilde

Rebecca Nesvet, with James Duffy

Timeline: World Premieres of Completed Dramatic Works

1883, New York: *Vera, or, the Nihilists*

1892, London: *Lady Windermere's Fan*

1893, London: *A Woman of No Importance*

1893, London: *Salomé* cancelled by official theatre censorship before premiere

1894, Paris: *Salomé*

1895, London: *An Ideal Husband*

1895, London: *The Importance of Being Earnest*

Collected Works and Letters: Scholarly Editions of Record

Bristow, Joseph, et al, editors. *The Complete Works of Oscar Wilde.* 10 vols. Oxford: Oxford U P, 2000–2019

Hart-Davis, Rupert, and Merlin Holland, editors. *The Complete Letters of Oscar Wilde.* New York: Holt, 2000

Individual and Selected Works: First Published Editions

Ravenna, Recited in the Theatre, Oxford. Oxford: Thomas Shrimpton and Son, 1878

Poems. London: David Bogue, 1881

Vera, or, The Nihilists: A Drama in Prologue and Four Acts. London: Ranken, 1880

Impressions of America, edited by Stuart Mason (Robert Baldwin Ross). Sunderland: Keystone, 1906

The Harlot's House. London: Mathurin, 1885

Essays and Lectures, edited by "the author's literary executor" (Robert Baldwin Ross) London: Methuen, 1908

The Happy Prince and Other Tales. London: David Nutt, 1888

A House of Pomegranates. London: McIlvaine, 1891

The Picture of Dorian Gray. London: Ward, Lock, and Co., 1891

Lady Windermere's Fan. London: John Lane, 1893

Salomé, Drame en Une Acte. Translated by Lord Alfred Douglas. Illustrated by Aubrey Beardsley. Paris: Librairie de l'Art Independent, 1893

Salomé, a Tragedy in One Act. Translated by Lord Alfred Douglas. Illustrated by Aubrey Beardsley. London: Elkin Matthews and John Lane, 1894

A Woman of No Importance. London: John Lane, 1894

The Ballad of Reading Gaol, by C33. London: Leonard Smithers, 1898

The Importance of Being Earnest. London: Leonard Smithers, 1899

An Ideal Husband. London: Leonard Smithers, 1899

De Profundis. London: Methuen, 1905

Salomé, A Florentine Tragedy, Vera. London: The Edinburgh Society, Clements Inn, 1908[1]

Individual and Selected Works: Modern Scholarly Editions

Frankel, Nicholas, editor. *The Uncensored Picture of Dorian Gray.* Harvard: Harvard UP, 2012

Gladden, Samuel Lyndon, editor. *The Importance of Being Earnest.* Peterborough, Ontario: Broadview, 2009

Gagnier, Regenia, and Dennis Denisoff, editors. *The Harlot's House.* Central Online Victorian Educator (COVE) Editions, 2018. editions.covecollective.org/edition/harlots-house/editorial-introduction-harlots-house

Page, Norman, editor. *The Picture of Dorian Gray.* Peterborough, Ontario: Broadview, 1998

Raby, Peter, editor. *The Importance of Being Earnest and Other Plays.* Oxford: Oxford U P, 2008

Stern, Kimberly J., editor. *Salomé.* Peterborough, Ontario: Broadview, 2017

Tóibín, Colm, editor. *De Profundis and Other Prison Writings.* London: Penguin, 2013

Bibliography

Mason, Stuart. *A Bibliography of Oscar Wilde, (with a Note by Robert Ross)*. London: T. Werner Laurie, 1914

Apocrypha

Wilde, Oscar. *Teleny, or, the Reverse of the Medal*. New York: Mondial, 2006

Anon. *Des Grieux: The Prelude to "Teleny."* Library of Alexandria, 2015

Note

1. The first publication of *A Florentine Tragedy* "was in a Russian translation by Michael Lykiardopulos, which appeared in *Viessy,* Moscow, vol, IV, no. 1, Jan. 1907, pp. 17–38 (Mason, Bibliography, p. 464).

Select Bibliographies

Rebecca Nesvet, with James Duffy

Biographies of Oscar Wilde

Belford, Barbara. *Oscar Wilde: A Certain Genius*. London: Bloomsbury, 2000.

Coakley, Davis. *Oscar Wilde: The Importance of Being Irish*. Dublin: Town House, 1994.

Ellmann, Richard. *Oscar Wilde*. New York: Alfred A. Knopf, 1988.

Frankel, Nicholas. *Oscar Wilde: The Unrepentant Years*. Cambridge, MA: Harvard UP, 2017.

Holland, Merlin. *The Wilde Album*. New York: Henry Holt and Company, 1997.

Knox, Melissa. *Oscar Wilde: A Long and Lovely Suicide*. Yale U P, 1994.

McKenna, Neil. *The Secret Life of Oscar Wilde: An Intimate Biography*. New York: Basic Books, 2009.

Sherard, Robert. *The Life of Oscar Wilde*. London: Mitchell Kennerly, 1906.

Stern, Kimberly J. *Oscar Wilde: A Literary Life*. New York: Palgrave Macmillan, 2019.

Sturgis, Matthew. *Oscar: A Life*. London: Head of Zeus, 2018.

Biographies of Wilde's Family, Friends, and Love

Fitzsimmons, Eleanor. *Wilde's Women: How Oscar Wilde Was Shaped by the Women He Knew*. London: Duckworth, 2015.

Fryer, Jonathan. *Robbie Ross: Oscar Wilde's Devoted Friend*. London: da Capo, 2001.

Holland, Vyvyan. *Son of Oscar Wilde*. New York: E. P. Dutton, 1954.

Melville, Joy. *Mother of Oscar: The Life of Jane Francesca Wilde*. London: John Murray, 1994.

Murray, Douglas. *Bosie: A Life of Lord Alfred Douglas*. New York: Hyperion, 2000.

O'Sullivan, Emer. *The Fall of the House of Wilde: Oscar Wilde and His Family*. London: Bloomsbury, 2016.

Tóibín, Colm. *Mad, Bad, Dangerous to Know: The Fathers of Wilde, Yeats, and Joyce.* New York: Scribner, 2018.

Critical Monographs, Anthologies, and Articles
General Criticism

Powell, Kerry, and Peter Raby, editors. *Oscar Wilde in Context.* Cambridge: Cambridge UP, 2003.

Raby, Peter, editor *The Cambridge Companion to Oscar Wilde.* Cambridge: Cambridge UP, 1997.

Robbins, Ruth. *Oscar Wilde.* London: Continuum, 2011.

Roden, Frederick, editor. *Palgrave Advances in Oscar Wilde Studies.* New York: Palgrave, 2004.

Sammells, Neil. *Wilde Style: The Plays and Prose of Oscar Wilde.* New York: Longman, 2000.

Schenkar, Joan. *Truly Wilde: The Unsettling Story of Dolly Wilde, Oscar's Unusual Niece.* London: Virago, 2000.

Sloan, John. *Authors in Context: Oscar Wilde.* Oxford: Oxford World's Classics, 2003.

Wilde in His Era

Behrendt, Patricia Flanagan. *Oscar Wilde: Eros and Aesthetics.* New York: St. Martin's, 1991.

Blanchard, Mary Warner. *Oscar Wilde's America: Counterculture in the Gilded Age.* New Haven: Yale UP, 1998.

Bristow, Joseph, editor. *Wilde Writings: Contextual Conditions.* Toronto: U of Toronto P, 2003.

Brown, Julia Prewitt. *Cosmopolitan Criticism: Oscar Wilde's Philosophy of Art.* Charlottesville: U P of Virginia, 1997.

Dever, Carolyn, and Martin Taylor, editors. *Reading Wilde: Querying Spaces.* New York: Fales Library, New York U, 1995.

Eltis, Sos. *Revising Wilde: Society and Subversion in the Plays of Oscar Wilde.* Oxford: Clarendon, 1996.

Gagnier, Regenia. *Idylls of the Marketplace: Oscar Wilde and the Victorian Public.* Stanford U P, 1986.

Killeen, Jarlath. *The Faiths of Oscar Wilde: Catholicism, Folklore, and Ireland.* New York: Macmillan, 2005.

Kohl, Norbert. Oscar Wilde: *The Works of a Conformist Rebel.* Cambridge: Cambridge U P, 2011.

Mahaffey, Vicki. *States of Desire: Wilde, Yeats, Joyce, and the Irish Experiment.* New York: Oxford U P, 1998.

McCormack, Jerusha. *Wilde the Irishman.* New Haven: Yale U P, 1998.

Mendelssohn, Michèle. *Making Oscar Wilde.* Oxford: Oxford U P, 2018.

Morris, Roy. *Declaring His Genius: Oscar Wilde in North America.* Cambridge, MA: Harvard U P, 2013.

Nunokawa, Jeff. *Tame Passions of Wilde: The Styles of Manageable Desire.* Princeton: Princeton U P, 2003.

Powell, Kerry. *Oscar Wilde and the Theater of the 1890s.* Cambridge: Cambridge UP, 1990.

Ross, Iain. *Oscar Wilde and Ancient Greece.* Cambridge: Cambridge U P, 2012.

Wright, Thomas. *Oscar's Books: A Journey through the Library of Oscar Wilde.* London: Vintage, 2009.

Wilde's Trials

Bristow, Joseph. "The Blackmailer and the Sodomite: Oscar Wilde on Trial." *Feminist Theory,* vol. 17, no. 1, 2016, pp. 41–62.

Foldy, Michael S. *The Trials of Oscar Wilde: Deviance, Morality, and Late-Victorian Society.* New Haven: Yale U P, 1997.

Holland, Merlin, editor. *Irish Peacock and Scarlet Marquess: The Real Trial of Oscar Wilde.* London: Fourth Estate, 2003.

Hyde, H. Montgomery. *The Three Trials of Oscar Wilde.* New York: U Books, 1956.

Hyde, H. Montgomery. *The Trials of Oscar Wilde.* 1948. London: Dover, 1973.

Wilde's Legacies

Bartlett, Neil. *Who Was that Man? A Present for Mr. Oscar Wilde.* London: Serpent's Tail, 1998.

Bentley, Toni. *Sisters of Salome.* New Haven: Yale U P. 2002.

Böker, Uwe, Richard Corballis, and Julie Hibbard, editors. *The Importance of Reinventing Oscar: Versions of Wilde During the Last 100 Years.* Amsterdam: Rodopi, 2002.

Bristow, Joseph, editor. *Oscar Wilde and Modern Culture: The Making of a Legend.* Columbus: U of Ohio P, 2008.

Hoare, Philip. *Oscar Wilde's Last Stand: Decadence, Conspiracy, and the First World War.* London: Duckworth, 1997.

Markovich, Heather. *The Art of the Pose: Oscar Wilde and Performance Art.* New York: Peter Lang, 2010.

NíChuilleaníin, Eiléan, editor. *The Wilde Legacy.* Dublin: Four Courts, 2003.

Pine, Richard. *The Thief of Reason: Oscar Wilde and Modern Ireland.* New York: St. Martin's, 1995.

Salamensky, S. I. *The Modern Art of Influence and the Spectacle of Oscar Wilde.* New York: Palgrave, 2012.

Sinfield, Alan. *The Wilde Century: Effeminacy, Oscar Wilde, and the Queer Moment.* London: Bloomsbury, 1994.

Smith, Philip E., editor. *Approaches to Teaching the Works of Oscar Wilde.* New York: MLA, 2008.

Biographical Drama

Eagleton, Terry. *Saint Oscar and Other Plays.* Oxford: Blackwell, 1997.

Hare, David. *The Judas Kiss: A Play.* New York: Samuel French, 1999.

Kaufman, Moisés. *Gross Indecency: The Three Trials of Oscar Wilde.* New York: Dramatists Play Service, 1999.

Stoppard, Tom. *The Invention of Love.* New York: Grove, 1998.

About the Editor

Dr. Frederick S. Roden is Professor of English at the University of Connecticut, where he is Stamford Campus Coordinator for English and Judaic Studies. The author of *Same-Sex Desire in Victorian Religious Culture* (Palgrave, 2002) and *Recovering Jewishness: Modern Identities Reclaimed* (Praeger, 2016), he is also the editor of *Palgrave Advances: Oscar Wilde Studies* (Palgrave, 2004) and *Jewish/Christian/Queer: Crossroads and Identities* (Ashgate, 2016), and the co-editor of *Catholic Figures, Queer Narratives* (Palgrave, 2006) as well as an edition/translation of Marc-André Raffalovich's 1896 *Uranism and Unisexuality* (Palgrave, 2016). In addition to a commentary on the medieval theologian Julian of Norwich published as *Love's Trinity* (Liturgical Press, 2009), Roden is the author of many articles, reviews, and lectures on religion and culture, LGBTQ studies, and the Victorian period.

Contributors

Anne Anderson, Ph.D., FSA is Honorary Associate Professor at the University of Exeter. With a first degree in archaeology and a PhD in English, Anne was a senior lecturer in Art and Design History at Southampton Solent University for 14 years. During 2009–2010, Anne worked on *Closer to Home,* the reopening exhibition at Leighton House Museum, Kensington. Her book on *The Perseus Series* was published in conjunction with the *Edward Burne-Jones* exhibition, Tate Britain (2018). She writes for the *The Wildean: A Journal of Oscar Wilde Studies*. Her most recent publication on Wilde is "Private Views William Powell Frith, Harry Furniss and Oscar Wilde" for *William Powell Frith, The People's Painter* (2019). She has held several prestigious fellowships including Fellow of the Huntington Library, CA (2008 and 2018) and Fellow of the Henry Francis DuPont Winterthur Library and Museum (2009/10). Currently a tutor for the V&A Learning Academy, Anne specializes in Aestheticism and the Arts and Crafts movement. Her career as an international speaker has taken her all over the world.

Todd Barry, J.D., PhD is an Assistant Professor of English at Three Rivers Community College in Norwich, CT, where he teaches Introduction to Literature, Composition, and Drama. Todd earned his law degree and doctorate from the University of Connecticut. His dissertation, *From Wilde to Obergefell: Gay Legal Theatre, 1895–2015*, examines the close relationship between law and LGBTQ drama since the Wilde trials. In 2018, Todd was the System Award Winner of the Faculty Scholarly Excellence Award for the Connecticut Community Colleges based on the work in his dissertation. At Three Rivers, Todd advises the student drama club, coordinates the Honors Program, and Co-Chairs the Educational Technology Committee.

Sharon Bickle is a lecturer in English Literature at the University of Southern Queensland. Her research interests are in Late-Victorian women's writing with particular interest in the collaborative partnership of "Michael Field." She is co-editor of *The Latchkey: A Journal of New Woman Studies.*

Colin Cavendish-Jones's principal research interests are European Nihilism; the Victorian religious unsettlement; the Romantic, Aesthetic and Modernist movements; the reception of Classical literature; and connections between literature and philosophy, particularly in the nineteenth century. He has written on a variety of nineteenth and early twentieth-century writers, including Pater, Wilde, Trollope, Hardy, Chesterton, and Proust as well as on the reception of Shakespeare in Asia and America. Dr. Cavendish-Jones studied Classics at Magdalen College, Oxford, and subsequently practiced as an international lawyer in London, Dubai, and the United States. After working as a teacher, lecturer, journalist, and theatre director in numerous countries throughout Europe, Asia, and the Americas, he returned to academia and completed a PhD at the University of St. Andrews on Art as a counterforce to Nihilism in the works of Oscar Wilde.

James Duffy is completing his BA in English at University of Connecticut, where he has also studied Psychological Sciences. An accomplished actor, improv leader, and sportsman, he will be pursuing a Master's in Social Work for mental health counseling.

Nikolai Endres received his PhD in Comparative Literature from the University of North Carolina-Chapel Hill in 2000. As Professor of World Literature at Western Kentucky University, he teaches Great Books, British literature, classics, mythology, critical theory, film, and gay and lesbian studies. He has published on Plato, Ovid, Petronius, Gustave Flaubert, Richard Wagner, Walter Pater, Oscar Wilde, E. M. Forster, André Gide, F. Scott Fitzgerald, Mary Renault, Gore Vidal, and others. He just completed a first book on the late American novelist Patricia Nell Warren, author of the famous gay novel *The Front Runner*. His next project is an investigation of the Romosexuality of E.M. Forster's *Maurice*.

Amanda Farage received her PhD from Washington University in St. Louis in May 2017. Her dissertation, "Fatal Books: Dangerous Reading in Victorian England, 1850–1900," considers the ways in which nineteenth-century anxieties about captivated reading, mechanical reading, and the proliferation of print material in the latter half of the century can be traced to twenty-first century trepidations about the ubiquity of textual and nontextual media and their consumption. She held a one-year position as Assistant Professor of English at the United States Air Force Academy from 2017 to 2018 and is now working on archival research for a book manuscript based upon her dissertation themes.

Eleanor Fitzsimons has an MA in Gender Studies from University College Dublin. She is a researcher and writer who specializes in historical and current feminist issues. Her work has been published in a range of newspapers and journals including *The Sunday Times, The Guardian, History Today,* and *The Irish Times,* and she is a regular radio and television contributor. Her first book, *Wilde's Women: How Oscar Wilde Was Shaped by the Women He Knew,* was published by The Overlook Press in 2015. Her next book, *The Life and Loves of E. Nesbit,* is due from Abrams in October 2019. She is an honorary patron of the Oscar Wilde Society and a member of the editorial board of society journal, *The Wildean.*

Chris Foss is Professor of English at the University of Mary Washington, where he specializes in nineteenth-century British literature, with a secondary emphasis on disability studies. He served as the lead editor for *Disability in Comic Books and Graphic Narratives,* published by Palgrave's Literary Disability series in 2016 and is currently working on a new book project entitled *The Importance of Being Different: Intersectional Disability and Emotional Response in Oscar Wilde's Fairy Tales.*

Oswaldo Gallo-Serratos holds an MPhil and is a professor of Philosophy at Universidad Iberoamericana. His passion for studying Cardinal Newman's epistemology has led him to the study of his Victorian contemporaries, such as Gerard Manley Hopkins and Oscar Wilde. In addition to lecturing, he has published some articles and reviews both in Mexico and the United States on epistemology, Newman's theology, and Victorian culture.

Marie Heneghan has recently completed her doctoral thesis at the University of Southern Queensland, entitled "Re-Forming Faith: Idolatry and the Victorian Novel." This includes a chapter on Oscar Wilde's *Salomé* and *The Picture of Dorian Gray.*

Benjamin Hudson is Assistant Professor at Rollins College, where his research and teaching focus on nineteenth-century British literature; his secondary interests are in aestheticism, sexuality studies, and the intellectual history of amateurism. His current manuscript *Exquisite Amateurs* explores dilettantism as a crucial intellectual ideal at the *fin de siècle*. His research has appeared recently in *Victorian Poetry* and *The Eighteenth Century: Theory and Interpretation*.

Melissa Knox's recent work on Oscar Wilde has appeared in *Philosophy and Oscar Wilde* (Palgrave, 2017) and *Oscar Wilde's Society Plays* (Palgrave, 2015). Her most recent book is *Divorcing Mom: A Memoir of Psychoanalysis* (Cynren, 2019). She has written extensively on Wilde and other nineteenth-century writers. Her narrative nonfiction has appeared in *Eclectica, Empty Mirror, Lunch Ticket, Drunk Monkeys, Concho River Review,* and other magazines. She teaches American literature and culture in Germany and writes a blog, *The Critical Mom.*

Annette M. Magid, PhD, affiliated with SUNY Erie Community College, Buffalo, NY, has published *Quintessential Wilde: His Worldly Place, His Penetrating Philosophy and His Influential Aestheticism, 2017; Apocalyptic Projections: A Study of Past Predictions, Current Trends and Future Intimations as Related to Film and Literature, 2015; Wilde's Wiles: Studies of the Influence on Oscar Wilde and His Enduring Influences in the Twenty-First Century, 2013; You Are What You Eat: Literary Probes into the Palate, 2008;* and a volume of poetry, *Tunnel of Stone, 2002.* Her areas of expertise include American/ British Utopian literature and film, poetry, theater, science-fiction literature and film, as well as children's literature. In addition, she has published articles in a variety of utopian journals and monographs. Her book on the *Speculations of War: Conflicts Viewed through the Lens of Science Fiction, Fantasy and Utopia* will be published in 2019.

Rebecca Nesvet is an Associate Professor of English at the University of Wisconsin, Green Bay. Nesvet has published research on romantic and Victorian literature in journals including *Nineteenth Century Studies, Victorian Network, Notes and Queries, Scholarly Editing: The Journal of the Association for Documentary Editing, The Keats-Shelley Journal,* and

Essays in Romanticism. Edited collections to which Nesvet has recently contributed include *Women's Literary Networks and Romanticism: "A Tribe of Authoresses"* (Liverpool University Press 2018), *Teaching Victorian Literature in the Twenty-First Century* (Macmillan 2017), and *Jean-Jacques Rousseau and British Romanticism* (Bloomsbury 2017).

Ruth Robbins is Professor of English Literature and Director of Research for Cultural Studies at Leeds Beckett University, United Kingdom. She is the author of *Literary Feminisms* (2000); *Pater to Forster, 1873–1924* (2003); *Subjectivity* (2005); with Andrew Maunder and Emma Liggins, of *The British Short Story, An Introduction* (2010); and of *Oscar Wilde* (2011). She also edited the collection of nineteenth-century medical advice books for and about women, *Medical Advice for Women, 1830–1915*.

Julie-Ann Robson teaches literature and drama at the University of Western Sydney. She has published on Irish and Australian drama, the Gothic, and on Oscar Wilde. She has a keen interest in Wilde's aesthetic writings, particularly the relationship between his critical and literary writings. She is also a founding member of the National Alliance for Public Universities in Australia.

Kimberly J. Stern is Assistant Professor of English at the University of North Carolina at Chapel Hill, where she specializes in Victorian literature and culture. She has published an edition of Oscar Wilde's *Salomé* (Broadview Press, 2015) and is the author of *The Social Life of Criticism: Gender, Critical Writing, and the Politics of Belonging* (University of Michigan Press, 2016) and *Oscar Wilde: A Literary Life* (Palgrave Macmillan, 2019).

Margaret D. Stetz is the Mae and Robert Carter Professor of Women's Studies and Professor of Humanities at the University of Delaware, Maryland. She has published more than 120 essays on topics such as Victorian feminism, the politics of animated films, British modernist literature, Oscar Wilde and women writers, and neo-Victorian dress. Her books include monographs (*British Women's Comic Fiction, 1890–1990*), catalogues of exhibitions on print culture that she has curated (*Gender* *and the London Theatre, 1880–1920*; and *Facing the Late Victorians*), and co-edited essay collections (*Michael Field and Their World*; and *Legacies of the Comfort Women of WWII*). She serves on numerous editorial boards of scholarly journals and presses and, in 2015, she was named by the magazine *Diverse: Issues in Higher Education* to its list of the 25 top women in U. S. higher education.

Anne Varty is Professor of Victorian Literature at Royal Holloway University of London, where she has taught in both the Department of Drama and the Department of English. She has published widely on Victorian theatre, and Wilde in particular, including *A Preface to Oscar Wilde* (1998), an edition of Wilde's *Plays* (2002) for Wordsworth Classics, and the "Oscar Wilde" entry for Oxford Bibliographies Online (2017). She is Co-Director of Royal Holloway TeacherHub>English, a resource for Secondary School Teachers and Students of English Literature.

Index

Ellis, Havelock 226
Ellmann, Richard 35, 42, 76, 153, 212
Eltis, Sos 46
Eminent Domain 76, 80
empiricism 41
English Catholicism 202
"English Renaissance of Art, The" 16, 149, 159
Epistemology of the Closet 43, 52, 213
Erlynne, Mrs. 93, 104, 106, 108, 109, 110, 115, 116, 117, 118, 120, 122
Essays and Criticisms by Thomas Griffiths Wainewright 175
establishment 5, 79, 114, 119, 144
ethics ix, xvi, xvii, xxi, xxiii, xxiv, 30, 31, 34, 90, 122, 151, 157, 225
Eucharist, the xxxvii
Evans, Edith 62
Everett, Rupert 37, 66, 67, 230, 231, 245, 246
exceptionalism xxv
excessive reading 250
exposition 112, 113, 115, 116, 117, 119, 120, 121, 123

Fairfax, Gwendolen 94
fairy tales 26, 63, 64, 229
fan culture 164
fantasy 197, 243, 244, 250, 253, 254, 258
farce 121, 125, 138
Fawcett, Millicent xxxi
Felman, Shoshanac 214
feminism 46
Field, Kate 84

fin-de-siècle 46, 174
Fineman, Joel 162
Fish, Arthur 88
Flower, Wickham 21
Foley, John Henry 234
forgery 39, 160, 161, 162, 163, 166, 168, 169, 171, 253
Forster, John 179
Foucault, Paul-Michel 54
Frankel, Nicholas xxii, xxxviii, xxxix, 52, 66, 160
Franklin, Maud 21
Frankl, Viktor xv, xxvi
French Revolution 133
Frith, William Powell 4
Froude, J.A. 178
Fuller, Margaret 84

Gagnier, Regenia 47, 189
Gatiss, Mark 198
Gautier, Théophile 149, 158
Gaveston, Piers 57
gay x, xi, xiv, xviii, xxi, xxii, xxiii, 42, 43, 44, 46, 53, 54, 57, 58, 62, 63, 67, 82, 102, 103, 111, 196, 198, 201, 204, 214, 215, 217, 218, 219, 221, 222, 223, 226, 241
gay identity 215, 217, 218, 219, 222, 223
Gay Rights Movement 34
gay studies xviii
gender x, xii, 42, 45, 46, 50, 54, 88, 121, 122, 191, 218, 219, 222, 224, 231, 236, 241, 243
General Course in Linguistics 136
Gerrig, Richard 254
Gilbert and Sullivan 9, 71, 72, 76, 77, 149, 150

Gilbert, William S. 188
Gilded Age 79, 80
Gill, Thomas Patrick 187
Gissing, George 101
gluttony 62
Godwin, E.W. 19, 149, 155, 159
Goffman, Erving 129
Goldfarb, Sheldon 191
good and evil xvii, 29, 109
Goodbye to Berlin 196
Gordon, Jan B. 206
Goring, Lord 27, 29, 30, 31, 121,
    122, 123
Gothic art 78
Graham, Cecil 102
Grainger, Walter 221
Gray, Dorian xi, xvii, xxii, xxvi,
    xxviii, xxxiv, 26, 27, 37, 38,
    43, 45, 47, 48, 52, 53, 55,
    56, 58, 60, 67, 91, 92, 104,
    110, 126, 142, 143, 148,
    150, 159, 164, 165, 170,
    172, 174, 180, 183, 184,
    185, 186, 187, 190, 191,
    193, 195, 200, 203, 216,
    248, 249, 251, 252, 253,
    256, 260, 261
Gray, John xxiii, xxvii, xxix, 203
Greek pederasty 56
Greeley, Horace 84
green 5, 11, 73, 168, 173, 174,
    175, 176, 177, 179, 180,
    182, 185
Green Carnation, The 176, 231
Green, Jesse 63
Grodin, Elissa 238, 247
*Gross Indecency: The Three Trials
    of Oscar Wilde* 227
Grosvenor, Archibald 9

Grosvenor Gallery 3, 173
Guy, Josephine M. xxxix, 175

Hadley, James 11
Haggard, Henry Rider 101
Hallward, Basil 43, 164, 184
Hanson, Ellis 49
Hanson, Eric 58, 67
*Happy Prince and Other Tales,
    The* 91, 229, 232, 234, 244
Happy Prince, The (movie) 37,
    66, 246
Hardy, Thomas 101
"Harlot's House, The" 45
Harper's Weekly 21, 88, 95
Harris, Frank 32
Harris, Robert 255
Harry, Lord 165
Hart-Davis, Rupert 22, 36, 96,
    111, 159, 186, 206, 213, 247
Haweis, Mary Eliza 79
Haweis, Mrs. 17
Hawthorne, Julian 92
Hayes, Tanner 58, 67
Hazlitt, W. Carew 175
Headlam, Stewart xxxvi
Hegel, Friedrich xxxi
Herbert, William 162
heterosexual irony 221
heterosexuality 40, 53, 58, 102,
    170, 219, 221, 236, 239
Hichens, Robert 176
Higgins, Professor 27, 34
Hints on Household Taste 17
Hogarth, William 98
Hollander, Amanda 236
Holland, Merlin xxxviii, xxxix,
    18, 36, 44, 52, 96, 111, 124,